T0310542

TRADE AND COMMERCE

CARLETON LIBRARY SERIES

The Carleton Library Series publishes books about Canadian economics, geography, history, politics, public policy, society and culture, and related topics, in the form of leading new scholarship and reprints of classics in these fields. The series is funded by Carleton University, published by McGill-Queen's University Press, and is under the guidance of the Carleton Library Series Editorial Board, which consists of faculty members of Carleton University. Suggestions and proposals for manuscripts and new editions of classic works are welcome and may be directed to the Carleton Library Series Editorial Board c/o the Library, Carleton University, Ottawa KIS 5B6, at cls@carleton.ca, or on the web at www.carleton.ca/cls.

TRADE AND COMMERCE

Canada's Economic Constitution

Malcolm Lavoie

Carleton Library Series 261

McGill-Queen's University Press
Montreal & Kingston • London • Chicago

© McGill-Queen's University Press 2023

ISBN 978-0-2280-1646-5 (cloth)
ISBN 978-0-2280-1647-2 (ePDF)
ISBN 978-0-2280-1648-9 (ePUB)

Legal deposit first quarter 2023
Bibliothèque nationale du Québec

Printed in Canada on acid-free paper that is 100% ancient forest free
(100% post-consumer recycled), processed chlorine free

This book has been published with the help of a grant from the Canadian Federation
for the Humanities and Social Sciences, through the Awards to Scholarly Publications
Program, using funds provided by the Social Sciences and Humanities Research
Council of Canada.

Funded by the   Financé par le
Government   gouvernement
of Canada   du Canada   Canada Council   Conseil des arts
                                                        for the Arts   du Canada

We acknowledge the support of the Canada Council for the Arts.

Nous remercions le Conseil des arts du Canada de son soutien.

Library and Archives Canada Cataloguing in Publication

Title: Trade and commerce : Canada's economic constitution / Malcolm Lavoie.

Names: Lavoie, Malcolm, author.

Series: Carleton library series ; 261.

Description: Series statement: Carleton library series ; 261 | Includes bibliographical
references and index.

Identifiers: Canadiana (print) 20220419779 | Canadiana (ebook) 2022041984I |
ISBN 9780228016465 (cloth) | ISBN 9780228016472 (ePDF) | ISBN 9780228016489 (ePUB)

Subjects: LCSH: Trade regulation – Canada – Provinces. | LCSH: Non-tariff trade
barriers – Canada – Provinces. | LCSH: Canada – Commerce. | LCSH: Canada.
Constitution Act, 1867. | LCSH: Canada – Economic conditions. | CSH: Interprovincial
commerce – Canada.

Classification: LCC HF3226.5 .L38 2023 | DDC 381/.50971 – dc23

This book was designed and typeset by Peggy & Co. Design in 10.5/13 Sabon.

For Frances and Mary

Contents

Preface

I began work on this book during the spring of 2020 – a time of great difficulty and uncertainty for many. That I was able to spend so much of my time during the pandemic working on a project I was passionate about has been an enormous privilege. I owe that privilege partly to my employer, the University of Alberta, where I have been a faculty member since 2015. I am grateful to my colleagues at the University of Alberta Faculty of Law, both for giving me the opportunity to join this esteemed institution, and for the many insights I have gained in discussions over the years.

The central argument in this book is that there is a coherent and morally compelling economic vision underlying the Canadian Constitution. While I only recently sat down to write this book, I have been thinking about these ideas for some time. My previous work on property law, Indigenous rights, the trade and commerce power, and constitutional protections for free trade all provided some grounding for this work. That said, the key arguments in this book are new. My hope is that they will contribute to a deeper understanding of the foundations of the Canadian constitutional order, though I leave it to readers to assess that for themselves.

In addition to my role as a full-time faculty member at the University of Alberta Faculty of Law, I also maintain a limited legal practice. I must disclose that in that capacity, I have represented clients in cases involving issues addressed in this book. Specifically, I have acted for First Nations governments on self-government issues and on issues relating to the duty to consult. I have also advised a provincial government on federalism issues, and represented interveners pro bono in the Supreme Court of Canada in cases dealing with barriers to interprovincial trade and the doctrine of de facto expropriation. I am currently associate counsel with Miller Thomson LLP, a national law firm that represents clients on a wide range of matters. The ideas expressed in this book are mine alone and do not represent the position of the firm or its clients.

Thank-you to everyone who helped me with this book project. Eric Adams, Richard Albert, Jessica Fleming, Grant Huscroft, Andrew Irvine, Gerard Kennedy, Rainer Knopff, Andrew Leach, Blair Major, Mark Mancini, Dwight Newman, Steven Penney, Emmanuelle Richez, Roger Shiner, Geoffrey Sigalet, Leonid Sirota, Kimberly Wasylenchuk, Moin Yahya, and two anonymous reviewers provided valuable feedback on drafts of the manuscript. Elisa Carbonaro, Talia Ferreira, Sarah Hanson, Samuel Teunissen, and Connor Vaandering provided excellent research assistance throughout the drafting and editing process. Lisa Aitken, Jonathan Crago, Jacqueline Mason, and the staff at McGill-Queen's University Press provided valuable editorial support. On a more personal note, my mother, Cecilia Lavoie, and our children's nanny, Lina Te, provided childcare that allowed me to spend more of my time on this book.

Finally, thank-you to my wife, Moira Lavoie, for many hours spent discussing the ideas in this book, as well as for giving me the time to work on it. When I began writing the book at the start of the pandemic, we had one daughter under the age of two and another on the way. As I write these lines, we have two thriving young girls, Frances and Mary, one nearly four and the other nearly two. *Res ipsa loquitur*, as they say – the thing speaks for itself. There is simply no way I could have completed this project without Moira's hard work, dedication, and commitment to our family.

TRADE AND COMMERCE

1

The Economic Vision
of the Constitution

Canada's Constitution reflects a vision of economic relations. The Constitution presupposes an economic system based on property rights and markets and, at the same time, establishes policies and structures for how that system is to function. That the Constitution assumes a market-based economy is relatively easy to see. For instance, the provincial power to make laws about "Property and Civil Rights" and the federal power over "Trade and Commerce" are only really intelligible in reference to a market economy of some kind. Yet the Constitution also contains a forward-looking vision for how economic relations are to be structured, providing for economic diversity grounded in property rights and locally regulated markets, while at the same time creating a platform for national markets with secure channels for interprovincial trade. The Constitution cannot be fully understood – or correctly interpreted – without an appreciation for the economic vision that lies behind it. This book is about the understanding of the economy that underpins the Constitution, and how it can be best understood in the twenty-first century.

Canada's Economic Constitution

The need for a renewed understanding of the economic vision behind the Constitution has become apparent in recent years as policymakers have grappled with the fractured state of the Canadian economy.[1] The issue of barriers to trade between provinces appears to be an intractable political problem, with provincial governments each seeking to maintain protectionist policies in industries from construction to viticulture, while at the same time professing a commitment to the general idea of free trade.[2] Recent international trade treaties have raised the prospect that barriers to trade with some foreign countries could actually be lower than those that exist within Canada's own borders.[3] At the same time, vigorous policy disagreements over natural resource development among provincial and Indigenous governments have threatened to shut down the flow of trade in a number of sectors.[4] Commentators have asked whether this state of affairs is really consistent with the Constitution, which was hailed at the time of Confederation as bringing about a common economic citizenship that would transcend provincial boundaries.[5]

The unusual case of *R. v. Comeau* emerged as a focal point for public discussion on these ideas, revealing divergent views on the relationship between the economy and the Constitution.[6] The facts of the case were disarmingly simple: on an overcast Saturday in October 2012, a retired steelworker named Gérard Comeau tried to bring beer from Quebec (where prices were lower) back to his home in New Brunswick. By all accounts, the beer was for his own personal consumption. The police pulled Comeau over, confiscated the beer, and wrote him a ticket charging him with possession of out-of-province liquor.[7] Comeau fought the ticket in court, with assistance from a public interest law firm, arguing that the law he was charged under was unconstitutional. His argument was based on the long-neglected section 121 of the Constitution Act, 1867 (formerly known as the British North America Act, 1867), which requires that goods be "admitted free" from one province to another.[8]

In a surprising decision that departed from established precedent, a judge of the New Brunswick Provincial Court agreed with Comeau's submissions, holding that the provincial law, which banned the possession of all but modest quantities of out-of-province liquor, was not consistent with section 121.[9] In coming to his decision, the trial judge quoted extensively from the debates leading up to Confederation in 1867.[10] According to the trial judge, the framers intended that Confederation would bring about a free trade zone within the new dominion, a fact that should inform the interpretation of provisions like section 121.

The *Comeau* trial decision received sustained national attention, stimulating public discussion about the persistent (and sometimes outright absurd) barriers to trade within Canada's borders. Canadians heard about truckers having to change tires at provincial borders in response to provincial standards that required certain tires in one province while prohibiting those same tires in another.[11] They also heard about rules that mandated different sizes for milk containers from one province to the next, requiring the duplication of production processes in order to sell in different markets.[12] The *Comeau* case was the subject of dozens of newspaper op-eds on internal trade, alongside numerous policy papers, academic articles, and parliamentary reports.[13]

The general thrust of this discussion was that something was wrong with the state of interprovincial trade in Canada, and that perhaps a renewed understanding of the Constitution could help solve the problem. While federal and provincial governments responded to pressure on this issue by pointing to ongoing negotiations on a new internal free trade agreement, similar efforts had yielded disappointing results in the past.[14] Indeed, when the new Canadian Free Trade Agreement (CFTA) between the federal government and the provinces was released in 2017, it was found to contain hundreds of pages of exceptions that provinces had carved out from the general principle of free trade.[15]

The *Comeau* case seemed to resonate with the public, perhaps in part because of its simple and relatable set of facts. Indeed, the degree of popular engagement with the Constitution that was spurred by the *Comeau* trial decision may help explain the unusual path it took to the Supreme Court. Despite the fact that the New Brunswick Court of Appeal denied leave to appeal, the Supreme Court of Canada granted leave.[16] This meant that the case would leapfrog from a provincial court, at the bottom of the judicial hierarchy, all the way to the Supreme Court at the apex (a feat that may actually be unprecedented in the history of the Supreme Court).[17] There were other signs of how significant the case might be. The Supreme Court set aside two full days to hear the case, a rare distinction more typically reserved for references from the federal Cabinet on signature policy initiatives, not roadside tickets issued to budget-conscious beer shoppers.[18] Nearly all provinces and territories intervened in the appeal, along with the federal government and dozens of interest groups. The stage appeared to be set for a definitive statement on the relationship between the Constitution and interprovincial trade, one that many hoped would help bring to fruition the integrated national economy that had motivated the framers at Confederation.[19]

Yet, when Comeau's lawyers reached the Supreme Court, they came up against a wall of jurisprudential resistance to the idea that section 121 should be understood as a robust tool against local protectionism. In a particularly interesting exchange during the hearing, Justice Malcolm Rowe made a claim that seemed to encapsulate the approach the Court would eventually take: "Now, you've said to us that essentially [section] 121 is an anti-protectionist measure. You know ... [the] Constitution Act, 1867 wasn't a document that set out policies; it set out frameworks and competences. Why should we read section 121 as incorporating a policy?"[20] In other words, the Constitution is neutral on questions of economic policy. The idea seems to be that the structural provisions of the Constitution, which are found primarily in the Constitution Act, 1867, provide for flexible and open-ended grants of policymaking authority to Parliament and provincial legislatures, without any orientation toward one set of policies over another.

This view seems to have guided the Court's ultimate decision in the case. The Court cautioned that "the federalism principle does not impose a particular vision of the economy that courts must apply."[21] And indeed, the substance of the decision reflected a more far-reaching view, according to which the structural provisions of the Constitution have little to say about economic policy. In upholding the New Brunswick law that Comeau was charged under, the Court set out a test for section 121 that was based on a particularly permissive version of the analysis of whether a law affecting interprovincial trade is within provincial jurisdiction in the first place.[22] The Court's approach is thus fully aligned with a flexible vision of federalism, according to which regulatory measures are to be upheld as long as they have some rational connection to a matter within the jurisdiction of the enacting legislature.[23] Flexible federalism, which really only emerged in the past few decades, serves to facilitate economic regulation from both orders of government, even when the link to a government's jurisdiction is tenuous.[24] It aims to get the Constitution out of the way of policymaking, implicitly reflecting the view that the Constitution has little to say about economic issues.

While widely held, the view that the Constitution is neutral on questions of economic policy is wrong both as a historical matter and as a matter of legal interpretation, with implications that extend far beyond the proper approach to section 121. I will argue in this book that the Constitution affirmatively endorses an economic order in which decision-making is decentralized in important ways, through property rights as well as provincial jurisdiction over matters such as private law. At the same time, the Constitution aims to secure the preconditions for an integrated national economy, including protections for interprovincial trade and uniform national laws on issues that transcend local borders or require national coordination. These policy commitments can be linked to a diverse set of normative grounds, including not just the economic growth that an economy structured along these lines promises to deliver, but also the political goal of reconciling national unity with regional diversity, and the enhanced national security that a vibrant and integrated national economy can provide.

This economic vision underlying the Constitution would have been familiar to the framers in 1867. Indeed, as others have argued, reconciling national economic citizenship with local decision-making was a central objective of Confederation, reflected not just in the text of the Constitution but also in speeches, debates, and print sources of the era.[25] What is not as well-appreciated is that the basic economic vision of the Constitution remains relevant today, and continues to resonate with a broad spectrum of the public.[26] Gérard Comeau's legal ordeal captured the attention of Canadians in no small part because it seemed to call into question their assumptions about what it means to be part of the same country as those living in other provinces.

The continuing relevance of the Constitution's economic frame-work, so many years after the original enactment of the Constitution Act, 1867, is striking. It reflects the fact that the Constitution is grounded in certain basic assumptions about political economy that transcend the particular historical context of Confederation. While much has changed since 1867, the Constitution presents solutions to enduring challenges that come with governing an economy in a large and diverse country. These structural challenges and the associated solutions remain relevant today. Two ideas are particularly important. Firstly, in order to be effective, economic decision-making in a large and complex country needs to be decentralized, in order to account for knowledge of local circumstances as well as diverse local values and priorities.[27] Secondly, economic integration in such a country requires mechanisms to solve collective action problems.* These tend to arise when local governments prioritize local interests or fail to coordinate their activities in ways that impose costs on outsiders and harm the national interest.[28]

The first key idea is that effective economic decision-making requires decentralization. This decentralization takes two distinct forms, both crucial to Canadian constitutional identity. Firstly, the Canadian Constitution is premised on systems of property and contract, which devolve important forms of economic decision-making authority to individuals, families, and firms. These forms of private authority are constitutional both in the broad sense of being constitutive of our systems of political and economic governance, and in the narrower sense of being reflected in Canada's constitutional texts.[29] I will argue that a commitment to secure property rights is among the foundational

---

* The term "collective action problem" refers to situations in which multiple parties face individual incentives that lead them to act in ways that are contrary to the interests of the group as a whole. Collective action problems can take many forms – for instance, a communal microwave in the workplace is often the site of a collective action problem. The workers as a whole would be better off if everyone took the time to clean up any messes in the microwave, but each individual worker may be tempted not to clean up a mess and free ride on the cleaning efforts of others. I argue that provinces imposing trade barriers are a bit like workers who do not clean up the mess they make in the microwave. Their decision-making does not fully account for the costs they impose on others. (My thanks to Eran Kaplinsky for the microwave example.)

commitments of our Constitution, albeit one reflected primarily in the way executive, legislative, and judicial authority is structured, rather than in a constitutionally entrenched right to property.

The other form of decentralization is found in the wide-ranging jurisdiction of provincial legislatures and, increasingly, Indigenous governments, including powers to regulate, limit, and redefine the economic rights of private parties. I will argue that the Constitution is committed to local autonomy and the principle of subsidiarity, according to which authority is presumptively held at the local level unless centralization is necessary for effective governance.[30] This commitment is reflected in provincial legislatures' exclusive jurisdiction over most economic matters, including property and civil rights, as well as the growing jurisdiction of Indigenous governments over an analogous range of subjects. Together, two separate layers of decentralization – property rights and local governance autonomy – help to manage the complexity inherent in a large national economy and society.

The second key idea to understanding the economic vision of the Constitution is that federalism sets up collective action problems that require an institutional response. While local governments are empowered to enact a range of economic policies in pursuit of local interests and values, they cannot reliably be counted upon to consider the effects of their policies on the national market and on other parts of the country.[31] A federal system of government creates a persistent structural challenge, in which local governments are tempted to privilege local interests in ways that may interfere with the national economy. This can take many forms, including not just overt acts of protectionism, but also regulations that have a disproportionate effect on parties in other jurisdictions. At the same time, effective policymaking in certain areas, such as currency and the census, requires national coordination. On these issues, local governments may fail to coordinate to the necessary degree. Our Constitution, like the constitutions in other federations around the world, was built to address these collective action problems through features that protect national markets and promote economic integration.[32]

The question of reconciling local authority with national economic interests is therefore not just a matter of economic policy best left to elected politicians. It is also an enduring structural challenge that goes to the heart of our constitutional order. I will argue that the Constitution is committed to economic integration and free trade. This commitment is reflected in mechanisms of both positive integration and negative integration. Positive integration refers to positive acts that lower barriers to trade, such as the enactment of harmonized laws in a given area, while negative integration refers to restrictions against trade barriers.[33] The Constitution's commitment to positive economic integration is reflected primarily in Parliament's jurisdiction over a range of economic subjects that transcend local interests. The commitment to negative integration is seen in both the denial of provincial jurisdiction over matters of national concern that is implicit in the exclusive nature of federal jurisdiction, as well as in stand-alone provisions, such as section 121, that limit permissible trade barriers.

To sum up, the economic vision of the Constitution includes commitments to secure property rights, local autonomy and subsidiarity, economic integration, and free trade. These commitments create a tension between decentralization and integration, which the Constitution must resolve. I will argue that it does so in impressively thoughtful ways. The Constitution privileges centralized authority in areas, such as currency and interprovincial trade, where this is necessary to maintain an integrated national economy, while at the same time providing for largely decentralized economic decision-making through property, markets, and the extensive jurisdiction of local governments.

The classical economic justification for property, markets, and free trade was familiar to the framers and remains relevant today.[34] Yet, the economic vision of the Constitution rests on broader normative grounding than economic efficiency alone. The decentralized economic decision-making provided for by the Constitution creates space for normative pluralism within a larger national state. This pluralism exists both on a micro scale, when property owners make economic decisions based on their own distinctive knowledge, values, and priorities, as well as on a macro scale, at the level of provincial, territorial, or Indigenous governments. This pluralism coexists with a wider national identity and an integrated national economy. Economic integration helps provide a basis for common citizenship, and creates a platform for national cooperation on issues of common concern. It also provides greater security and stability than would be possible for smaller jurisdictions that have a greater dependency on international trade. In an age of global disruption, as international supply chains appear less reliable than in the recent past, a renewed appreciation for the significance of these strategic benefits of an integrated national economy may be emerging.[35]

Overview of the Argument

There are four principal claims that I advance in this book. First, I argue that the Constitution reflects a coherent vision of economic relations based on commitments to secure property rights, local autonomy and subsidiarity, economic integration, and free trade. Chapters 2 through 6 present the argument that the text of the Constitution, as read in its original historical and legal context, does indeed reflect these commitments. In making this argument, I rely principally on the text, though I also draw on sources that shed light on the broader context of its enactment, as well as statements by contemporaries regarding its accepted meaning and purposes.

Chapter 2 argues that the Constitution is committed to secure property rights, a commitment manifested in limits on the powers of the executive branch of the state vis-à-vis the legislative and judicial branches, in doctrines that require clear legislative authorization for certain types of interference with property rights, and in procedural requirements for legislation that structure decision-making in ways that protect property rights. The commitment to secure property rights is reconciled with the autonomy of local governments and the economic jurisdiction of Parliament by the ultimate authority of these legislative bodies to infringe property rights, subject to interpretive, procedural, and structural safeguards enforced by the courts.

Chapter 3 argues that the Constitution is committed to local governance autonomy and the principle of subsidiarity. This commitment is reflected primarily in the broad and exclusive jurisdiction afforded to the provinces on most economic subjects, in particular, the property and civil rights power. The principle of subsidiarity mediates between the Constitution's commitment to local autonomy and the economic jurisdiction of Parliament, providing for federal jurisdiction on economic questions only in areas in which centralization is reasonably necessary for effective policymaking.

Chapters 4 and 5 deal with positive integration, arguing that Parliament's economic powers fall into a limited number of categories that transcend local interests. These include interjurisdictional economic relations, the infrastructure of exchange, national fiscal policy, non-rivalrous national goods (e.g., intellectual property), and economic activity with direct extraprovincial effects (e.g., fisheries). Centralization is justified in these areas either because decisions in one locality have important effects on parties in other localities, or because national policy coordination is a paramount consideration.

Chapter 6 addresses negative integration, arguing that restrictions against barriers to trade come from two principal sources: (1) the exclusive nature of federal economic powers, including the power over interprovincial trade, which indirectly prevents provincial legislatures from enacting measures directed at areas important to economic integration; and (2) stand-alone provisions such as section 121 and the mobility rights guaranteed by section 6 of the Canadian Charter of Rights and Freedoms (the Charter), which restrict barriers to trade.

A key theme that emerges in this section of the book concerns the nature of the relationship between the structural provisions of the Constitution and their underlying objectives. The Constitution tends to pursue economic objectives in an indirect manner, structuring governance authority in ways that are favourable to particular objectives without directly mandating outcomes. For instance, with respect to property rights, the Constitution limits the authority of the executive to infringe property rights in the absence of a clear statutory authorization. It also structures the legislative process, for instance with respect to taxation, in a manner that makes infringements of property rights less likely unless they are justified. There is no constitutionally entrenched right to property, and the legislature remains the ultimate arbiter of property rights and the public interest, even as policymaking is structured by the Constitution in ways that tend to favour secure property rights.

Similarly, the constitutional commitments to local autonomy and subsidiarity, economic integration, and free trade are also promoted indirectly, through the exclusive nature of the jurisdiction accorded to Parliament and provincial legislatures under sections 91 and 92 of the Constitution Act, 1867.* The division of powers is important not just for the powers it grants to one order of government, but also for the powers it implicitly *denies* to the other. Jurisdictional exclusivity reinforces local governance autonomy, by preventing local control from being undermined over time by expansive conceptions of federal jurisdiction. At the same time, Parliament's exclusive economic powers allow it to coordinate policy on matters of national concern without interference from provincial laws prioritizing local interests. Finally, jurisdictional exclusivity is a particularly important source of negative economic integration under the Constitution. By denying provinces jurisdiction over matters such as interprovincial trade and

---

* The division of powers between the federal Parliament and provincial legislatures is set out in sections 91 to 95 of the Constitution Act, 1867. Sections 91 and 92 provide for most of the federal and provincial powers. As I emphasize throughout the book, the powers in these two sections are exclusive. That means that subjects falling under federal jurisdiction are excluded from the ambit of provincial jurisdiction, and vice versa. For instance, the federal power over interprovincial trade is exclusive, meaning that provinces do not have the power to legislate in relation to interprovincial trade. Similarly, the provincial power over property and civil rights is exclusive, meaning the federal Parliament does not have the power to legislate in relation to property and civil rights (unless the matter falls under a more specific federal power in this area, like bills of exchange). The term "jurisdictional exclusivity" is used in this book to connote the exclusive nature of federal and provincial jurisdiction under the Constitution.

indirect taxation, the Constitution provides a check against barriers to trade enacted in the pursuit of local objectives, including outright protectionism, that fail to account for the national interest.

Complete jurisdictional exclusivity – what is pejoratively referred to as the "watertight compartments" approach to the division of powers – is impractical and fails to give full, purposive effect to the heads of power under the Constitution. Nevertheless, exclusivity is an important feature of the Constitution, reflected in both the text and its underlying purposes. I argue that jurisdictional overlap should be limited to cases where such overlap is necessary to give full effect to the relevant heads of power. For instance, a law enacted by one order of government should only be allowed to regulate matters under the jurisdiction of the other order of government in any significant way where that is reasonably necessary to achieve an objective within the enacting legislature's jurisdiction. We might helpfully distinguish this approach from an absolute conception of exclusivity by saying it is based on the idea of "water-resistant," rather than "watertight" compartments.[36]

The second main argument I advance in this book is that the economic vision of the Constitution remains a part of Canada's living constitutional order and that its principal commitments remain relevant today. In chapter 7, I track key developments in the economic Constitution since 1867, including those stemming from judicial interpretation, the political practice of the Constitution, and constitutional amendment. I argue that despite significant changes, the Canadian constitutional order has been marked by a remarkable fidelity to the economic vision of the Constitution, at least until quite recently.

In chapter 8, I address the underlying justifications for the economic Constitution, and in particular, the continuity and change in these justifications over time. The range of accepted justifications for the decentralizing features of the Constitution has expanded over time. Property rights, which in the eyes of the framers were seen to be justified primarily in terms of Lockean natural rights and utilitarian maximization, are today seen to be justified on broader and more pluralistic grounds. Similarly, the justifications for local governance autonomy have expanded with the growing appreciation in the late twentieth century of the importance of knowledge linked to local context and the increased respect for diverse values and priorities of local communities. In particular, the emerging recognition of Indigenous self-determination has provided new understandings of the importance of community-based decision-making. In contrast with the evolving justifications for the decentralizing features of the Constitution, the accepted justifications for the Constitution's commitment to economic integration and free trade have remained remarkably consistent over time. These arguments are rooted in basic principles of political economy, and seek to provide the preconditions not only for economic growth and prosperity, but also peace and security.

The third and fourth main arguments in the book are closely connected, and are set out in chapters 9 and 10. I argue first that legal discourse in this country, as reflected principally in recent jurisprudence of the Supreme Court, has begun to lose touch with the economic vision of the Constitution. I then go on to show what a renewed understanding of the economic vision of the Constitution would look like in the context of contemporary issues and debates.

Chapter 9 deals first with the decentralizing features of the Constitution. I argue that courts' lack of appreciation for the constitutional commitment to secure property rights has manifested itself in the erosion of protections available through the doctrine of de facto expropriation, as well as in the narrow reading of procedural requirements for taxation measures. Renewal in this area would require courts to give meaningful effect to the protections for property under the Constitution, while at the same time recognizing the ultimate authority of legislatures to redefine and expropriate property where they clearly authorize that outcome.

The commitment to local governance autonomy and subsidiarity has also been diminished in recent years, primarily by the growing acceptance of a flexible conception of federalism that allows for federal intrusions into areas of provincial jurisdiction. This trend threatens to undermine local autonomy, making provincial jurisdiction subject to supervening federal authority under the doctrine of paramountcy. I argue that the economic vision of the Constitution demands a renewed commitment to the principle of jurisdictional exclusivity, which protects a sphere of local autonomy. Principles favouring local decision-making should also continue to be extended to recognize the place of Indigenous peoples more fully in Canada's constitutional order. The Constitution provides a compelling model for how to reconcile the local autonomy of Indigenous peoples with national unity. Secure Indigenous property rights in natural resources and presumptive Indigenous governance jurisdiction over matters of local concern are two important mechanisms for achieving this result, and ensuring that the Constitution's commitments can be more fully recognized with respect to Indigenous peoples.

Finally, chapter 10 addresses the current trends relating to economic integration and free trade, as well as the potential for renewal in this area. With respect to positive integration, some federal powers have been unduly limited by the courts, including the interprovincial and international trade and commerce power. At the same time, there has been a political unwillingness by Parliament to use the powers available. Renewal in this area would require courts to give meaningful effect to federal powers, including the trade and commerce power, allowing legislation in this area to have secondary effects on intraprovincial transactions where that is reasonably necessary to achieve a federal purpose. At the same time, Parliament could take positive steps to lower trade barriers in a range of industries, from trucking to liquor sales, while acting within its enumerated powers.

I conclude with a discussion of negative integration, including the disappointing result in the *Comeau* case. The Constitution's commitment to negative integration has been threatened most significantly in recent years by the trend toward flexible federalism. This approach has allowed for provincially enacted trade barriers in areas of federal jurisdiction, based on relatively tenuous links to provincial objectives. The fact that the Supreme Court's approach to interpreting section 121 mirrored this flexible approach to the division of powers was regrettable, but perhaps understandable given the broader trends in federalism jurisprudence. Constitutional renewal in this area would require courts to reaffirm their commitment to jurisdictional exclusivity, limiting provincial trade barriers to those reasonably necessary to achieving valid, non-protectionist provincial objectives.[37] This approach should be informed, and reinforced, by the unambiguous commitment to free trade contained in section 121. A renewed commitment to negative integration could also lead to a reinvigorated doctrine of interjurisdictional immunity (IJI), which protects the core of heads of federal power from provincial interference. Finally, courts should be prepared to recognize more fully the economic purposes of section 6 of the Charter, which protects mobility rights, despite past decisions that have downplayed those purposes.[38]

Textual Purpose and Constitutional Interpretation

Throughout this book, I make claims that depend on the relationship between the text of the Constitution and its underlying purposes. I seek first to infer the economic purposes of the Constitution from its text, as understood in its original historical and legal context. I then argue that those purposes – what I call the economic vision of the Constitution – remain relevant today and can be adapted to address present concerns. Finally, I use those purposes as a guide to constitutional interpretation. In my view, the economic vision of the Constitution provides a theory that both fits the text of the Constitution and helps to justify it.[39] It is on that basis that I argue that the theory is an appropriate guide to legal interpretation.[40]

In Canada, all constitutional interpretation – indeed, all interpretation of statutes – is supposed to be purposive and contextual in nature.[41] This means that the text is to be read in a manner that takes into account the objectives of the enactment and the context surrounding its passage, which can inform its meaning. If a hypothetical law requires that there be "no vehicles in the park," to use a famous example from legal theory, one might consider the objectives served by banning "vehicles" in determining what constitutes a "vehicle" for the purposes of the rule.[42] The perceived problems with the park at the time of the enactment and the commonly understood meaning of the term "vehicle" at the time and place of the law's passing are also potentially relevant to the meaning. A bicycle, which might constitute a "vehicle" under some ordinary understandings of the term, might not be held to constitute a "vehicle" if the purposes of the enactment – reducing noise, for example – are not served by banning bicycles. Similarly, when confronted with a constitutional provision that protects freedom of religion, or that requires free interprovincial trade in goods, the purpose of the provision matters to its interpretation.[43]

Yet it does not follow from a commitment to purposive interpretation that courts are bound by the subjective intentions of individual legislators who participate in enacting a law.[44] One of the core postulates of the rule of law is that society ought to be governed by laws set out in advance and made available for all to see, rather than by the preferences of the powerful.[45] It does not matter what the principal framers of the Constitution, including John A. Macdonald, wanted per se. A society under the rule of law is not governed directly by the wishes of even its most powerful leaders. The many public statements of Macdonald and other "fathers of Confederation" are only properly relevant to constitutional interpretation to the extent that they can shed light on the linguistic and historical context of the enactment, and what an informed contemporary would have taken the text's meaning and purpose to be.[46]

The problems associated with looking directly to the intentions of legislators are relatively well-documented. They include the rule-of-law problem described above, along with the problem of indeterminacy.[47] Different legislators may support an enactment for a range of different and often conflicting reasons. That was clearly true in the case of Confederation, which involved compromises among competing interests.

In interpreting legislation or the Constitution, there is seldom a single legislative "intent" to speak about as a literal, descriptive matter. Accordingly, focusing on the subjective intentions of legislators can often lead in multiple, inconsistent directions, rendering text less determinate rather than more.

These problems help explain the broad rejection in recent years of approaches to constitutional interpretation based on "original intent." This form of originalism has been discredited even in the United States, where other forms of originalist constitutional interpretation, notably "original public meaning" originalism, have become increasingly influential.[48] The latter form of originalism, which focuses on the meaning of the text as it would have been understood by a contemporary audience, is largely consistent with my arguments in this book, but is not a necessary premise to what follows. One can allow for gradual evolution, along the lines of the "living tree," while still taking the original meaning of the text as the necessary starting point.

The framers were, in fact, surprisingly univocal in their understanding of the four economic purposes I have identified, though they did differ somewhat on the question of how these purposes were best reconciled. In the analysis that follows, I will draw not just on the constitutional text but also on historical sources, including statements made by the framers of the Constitution Act, 1867. However, I do so in order to shed light on the purpose of the text as understood at the time, as well as on the linguistic and historical context out of which the text emerged, not out of a belief that constitutional meaning can or should be directly derived from the intentions of legislators.

Conclusion

More than anything else, this book aims to open a discussion. In recent decades especially, the interpretation of the structural provisions of the Constitution has been beset by a detached and mechanical approach, which contrasts markedly with the muscular purposivism brought to bear in Charter adjudication. One by-product of this approach to the structural Constitution has been a drift toward interpretations that, in my view, are fundamentally at odds with the purposes underlying the Constitution. While many of the arguments in this book may prove controversial and contestable, I hope at the very least to encourage a dialogue on the ideas that animate our constitutional order, and how they are best understood in the twenty-first century.

Property and the Constitution

Indirectness and Constitutional Purpose

A twenty-first century Canadian sitting down to read Canada's key constitutional documents is presented with a mix of the familiar and the arcane. Some elements likely seem intuitive and recognizable, while others are technical, esoteric, and even downright strange. The Canadian Charter of Rights and Freedoms falls mostly into the former category.[1] Its list of fundamental rights seems natural and relatable, in no small part due to the role the Charter has assumed as a cornerstone of a post-ethnic Canadian identity.[2] A particularly astute reader might notice the absence of property rights, a feature that makes the Charter almost unique among equivalent bills of rights around the world.[3] However, apart from that and a few other wrinkles, including language rights, it reads like a direct and transparent statement of the fundamental values of a modern liberal society.

By contrast, the Constitution Act, 1867 is not quite so easily comprehensible.[4] It is a technical document, drafted by lawyers for lawyers. A current-day reader of the act would be likely to grasp its significance in setting out the principal structures of the Canadian state – the monarch and vice-regal officers, the federal Parliament and provincial legislatures, the judiciary, and so on – but large aspects of the document are likely to strike a contemporary Canadian as odd or obscure. The division of powers between Parliament and provincial legislatures contains an almost humorous assortment of the general and specific. Parliament is responsible for "laws for the Peace, Order, and Good Government of Canada" and "Trade and Commerce," but also for "Beacons, Buoys, Lighthouses, and Sable Island."[5] Provincial legislatures are given jurisdiction over "Property and Civil Rights in the Province" at the same time as "Shop, Saloon, Tavern, Auctioneer, and other Licences."[6] In addition to possibly wondering which order of government would be responsible for licensing a saloon on Sable Island,[7] a reader might also ask what unifying theory could explain the array of powers allocated to Parliament, on the one hand, and provincial legislatures, on the other.

Other aspects of the Constitution Act, 1867 are also likely to raise questions. Under the heading dealing with the legislative power of Parliament, there are three sub-headings: "The Senate," "The House of Commons," and "Money Votes; Royal Assent."[8] The first two are easy to understand, but the third, which addresses in detail the process applicable to bills dealing with taxation and the appropriation of funds, might cause puzzlement. What is it about money votes that explains the presence of detailed and specific procedures in a constitution that otherwise deals with legislative power in more general terms?[9] One might also ask other questions. What does "direct taxation" mean, and why are provincial legislatures denied (by implication) the authority to levy "indirect" taxes?[10] How does one reconcile provincial authority over "property and civil rights" with the many federal heads of power that also relate to these matters?[11] And what is meant by a constitution "similar in principle to that of the United Kingdom," in the language of the Preamble?[12]

The relative obscurity of the Constitution Act, 1867 is partly a product of its older vintage. The passage of time inevitably makes it harder to understand the meaning of a text that was drafted in another historical context. The distinction between "direct" and "indirect" taxes, for instance, is based on the ideas of nineteenth-century political economists, and is no longer seen as a descriptively useful way to classify taxes.[13] Similarly, a reader might assume that references to amounts in "dollars" in the Constitution Act, 1867 were understood to be denominated in the Canadian dollar we know today. But the uniform Canadian dollar was not instituted until after Confederation. There were different "dollars" with different values in the pre-Confederation colonies, which makes the reference somewhat more ambiguous than a contemporary reader might presume.[14] The older historical context of the Constitution Act, 1867, and the fact that it is drafted in a more technical, lawyerly way than the Charter, go part of the way to explaining the greater difficulty in understanding its purposes. However, there is also more to it. The challenge in understanding the Constitution Act, 1867 stems in large part from the fact that it mostly achieves its purposes *indirectly*, by establishing governance structures, procedures, and institutions, rather than in the more direct manner of the protected rights in the Charter.

For instance, as discussed in later chapters, the Constitution Act, 1867 provides for free interprovincial trade in part through indirect means. By allocating exclusive jurisdiction over interprovincial trade to the federal Parliament, the Constitution denies this authority to provincial legislatures, which are more likely than the federal Parliament to establish discriminatory trade barriers favouring local interests.[15] Similarly, by denying provinces the power to levy "indirect" taxes, the Constitution ensures that provincial legislatures cannot impose tariffs on interprovincial or international imports or exports, a further manifestation of the commitment to free trade.[16] Of course, not all the purposes in the act are pursued solely through indirect means. With respect to free trade, the objectives are reinforced by a separate provision, section 121, which states, in just about the clearest possible terms, that trade in goods among the provinces is to be free.[17] But the overall orientation of the act is indirect, in the sense of establishing institutions with defined structures, procedures, and lines of authority, rather than directly mandating a desired state of affairs.

The indirectness of the core structural provisions of the Constitution in achieving their purposes helps explain the diminished understanding of these purposes in recent years by Canadian lawyers, judges, politicians, and members of the public. The Constitution Act, 1867, may be more subtle in communicating its purposes than the Charter, but those purposes are nevertheless readily ascertainable. As I will argue in this book, the Constitution reflects a vision of economic relations that is committed to: (1) secure property rights; (2) principles of subsidiarity and local autonomy, ensuring local governance aligned with local circumstances and values; (3) economic integration, including through federal jurisdiction over systemic and structural features of the economy; and (4) free internal trade. I begin in this chapter with the commitment to secure property rights, which is mainly achieved through indirect means.

Property Rights in the Constitution Act, 1867

One of the foundational commitments of the Constitution Act, 1867, consistently neglected in recent years, is to the security of property rights. The legal mechanisms for securing property rights are more subtle than one might find in a bill of rights providing direct protections for property. Yet the textual signals are nonetheless clear, and are reinforced by the legal and historical context of the act, along with the understanding shared by the framers that the new constitutional order would be committed to the security of property rights.

In order to properly understand how the Constitution Act, 1867 relates to property rights, it is important first to outline some of the key features of the British political and legal institutions that the framers expected to import as part of a constitution "similar in Principle to that of the United Kingdom," to use the language of the Preamble. One of the central narratives of English legal history up to the nineteenth century was the increasing restrictions that came to be placed on the Crown's authority to interfere with the property rights of subjects. This historical arc was closely linked to the broader development of the rule of law.[18] Over time, the Crown's prerogative powers (i.e., inherent powers, not requiring statutory authorization) were limited. The diminishment of the Crown's prerogative power over property rights began in earnest with the Magna Carta of 1215, which provided that: "No freemen shall be … disseised … except by the lawful judgment of his peers or by the law of the land."[19] In other words, the Crown, acting in its executive capacity, in the absence of a law passed by Parliament or a judgment of the courts, does not have a general prerogative power to take property rights in land.

Further major developments came in the seventeenth century, during the course of the intense struggles between Parliament and the Crown over the scope of royal authority. A line of judicial decisions indicates that the Crown's prerogative power to take property is specifically restricted to cases involving the "defence of the realm."[20] These cases begin with Lord Coke's report of *The King's Prerogative in Saltpetre* (1606), which upheld the authority of the Crown to take saltpetre, a necessary ingredient in gunpowder, but also held that other takings for non-defence-related purposes were not within the scope of the prerogative.[21] Later authorities reinforced the principle that the Crown's prerogative power to infringe property rights was limited to emergencies involving the defence of the realm.[22]

The seminal 1765 case of *Entick v. Carrington* further strengthened legal protections of property owners against the government.[23] The case held that where agents of the Crown enter onto the property of a subject without authorization from a statute or a recognized common law privilege, they commit actionable trespass according to the ordinary law of the land.[24] Except in the narrow applicable exceptions, including under the prerogative power relating to the defence of the realm, the Crown is obliged to respect the property rights of subjects unless specifically authorized by Parliament to infringe those rights.

The state of the Crown's prerogative power to take property in the nineteenth century was aptly summarized in an influential text by

Joseph Chitty.[25] Chitty wrote in 1820 that the king, in addition to having a prerogative right in gunpowder, "in case of necessity, may enter on the lands of his subjects to make fortifications."[26] However, even this limited prerogative power comes with a warning about its narrow scope. Immediately after outlining the prerogative powers relating to the defence of the realm, Chitty quotes Lord Erskine: "What is termed the war prerogative of the King is created by the perils and exigencies of war for the public safety, and by its perils and exigencies is therefore limited."[27] As Chitty's treatise makes clear, by the nineteenth century it was well-established that, in times of peace, the Crown had no prerogative power to take property without parliamentary authorization.

Over this time period, courts also developed principles of statutory interpretation based on the idea that Parliament is presumptively committed to secure property rights. Parliament is presumed not to authorize interference with vested property rights, and not to authorize the taking of property without compensation.[28] Clear statutory language is required in order to overcome these presumptions.[29] This was as far as courts could go in protecting property rights in a manner consistent with the prevailing commitment to parliamentary supremacy.[30] While courts could not directly contradict Parliament under the prevailing constitutional theory of nineteenth-century Britain, the expectation was that Parliament would serve as an effective guardian of property rights and that a presumption to this effect was therefore consistent with parliamentary intent.

Parallel developments occurred with respect to the fiscal powers of the Crown that could affect the property interests of subjects. Decades of conflict over the scope of royal authority were ultimately resolved in Parliament's favour with the Glorious Revolution of 1688 and the resulting English Bill of Rights, 1689.[31] Among the provisions of the Bill of Rights is a clause prohibiting the Crown from levying taxes or appropriating funds without parliamentary approval.[32] While this strengthened the power of Parliament vis-à-vis the Crown, it was also in keeping with ideological commitments which took the protection of property rights to be a central purpose of government, and which viewed Parliament as the body that could be most reliably counted upon to protect property rights.

John Locke, the political philosopher, was a contemporary of the Glorious Revolution, and his life was intertwined with the politics of the era.[33] His most significant work, the *Two Treatises of Government*, was written before 1688 but only published after the Glorious Revolution.[34] The *Two Treatises* became a leading justification for natural rights to property and the duty of governments to uphold and protect those rights.[35] For Locke, the purpose of government is to protect individuals' natural rights, especially rights to property.[36] In Locke's conception, the best way to set up institutions in keeping with these rights is to require that the consent of the people be given through their legislature for state actions that affect their property rights.[37] For Locke, then, the role of protecting property rights falls primarily to the legislature, with the principal threat to those rights coming from the Crown.

Locke's theory was thus closely aligned with the post-Glorious-Revolution British institutions which greatly restricted the Crown's prerogative powers to infringe property rights, and which required legislation passed by Parliament for expropriation, taxation, and the appropriation of funds. The people were required to give their consent, through their representatives in Parliament, before property rights could be infringed. Locke's work significantly influenced legal and political thought in the eighteenth and nineteenth centuries, including most famously the drafters of the Declaration of Independence and the US Constitution.[38] Yet his work was also important to British legal thought. For example, the decision in *Entick v. Carrington*, discussed above, clearly draws on Locke's account of natural rights in stating that "[th]e great end, for which men entered into society, was to secure their property."[39]

It had become well-established by the nineteenth century, then, that Parliament's approval was required for the taking of property, the levying of taxes, or the appropriation of funds. The most widely accepted justifications for this state of affairs were Lockean, based on the natural rights of citizens to their property, which governments are obliged to uphold.[40] These ideas, including the Lockean justification for them, were among the commitments which were shared by the framers of the Constitution Act, 1867 and which were generally not controversial among them. As Janet Ajzenstat has persuasively argued, the framers, rather than being simple, practical men uninterested in theoretical ideas, were in fact deeply influenced by Lockean political ideas.[41] According to her, "most or all believed that security for the individual – the right to life, liberty, and property, to use Locke's phrase – is Parliament's original and primary purpose."[42]

The legislative debates about Confederation in the British North American colonies are replete with references to Lockean ideas of popular sovereignty and secure property rights.[43] The statements by the framers repeatedly measure the quality of institutions according to their ability to secure the Lockean ideals of life, liberty and property.[44] Charles Tupper's 1866 statement in the Nova Scotia House of Assembly, is typical: "It is necessary that our institutions should be placed on a stable basis, if we are to have that security for life and property, and personal liberty, which is so desirable in every country."[45] He later continued: "We all know that the feeling of loyalty to one's country, the pride in its institutions, lies to the fact that [its] institutions are able to afford protection for life and property."[46] Judge John Black in the Red River colony, during the convention debating the terms of admission of the colony into Confederation, invoked Locke in his support for joining Confederation, stating: "The great object of all government is, undoubtedly, due protection of life and property."[47] Both supporters and opponents of Confederation looked to the security of property rights as a key criterion for evaluating institutions, with opponents raising hypothetical scenarios in which property rights might be threatened under the proposed regime, and supporters responding by pointing out the ways in which the Constitution served to protect those rights.[48]

References to the importance of property rights in the Confederation debates are often specifically linked to British legal traditions and institutions.[49] As Ajzenstat has observed, this tendency reflected the view that rights must be secured by law in order to be effective and that the British legal heritage described above was particularly well-suited to this task.[50] In addition to abstract Lockean theory, then, the framers were also drawing on the specific legal and institutional arrangements of the United Kingdom, including the common law constitutional principles outlined above, which restricted the authority of the executive to infringe property rights and which assigned the principal role of protecting those rights to the legislature. These principles inform the separation of powers, limiting executive power and requiring clear legislative language in order for the judiciary to permit certain infringements. Such principles are constitutional in the sense that they define the relationship among the citizenry and the executive, legislative, and judicial branches of the state, and they are part of what would have been understood as a constitution "similar in principle to that of the United Kingdom."

It should be noted at this point that among the residents of Lower Canada, expectations and attitudes regarding the protection of property rights would have also been informed by the civil law, and in particular the 1866 Civil Code of Lower Canada.[51] The 1866 Civil Code was the first codification of the civil law in Canada, coming into force on the eve of Confederation. Indeed, it was passed by the same legislature of the Province of Canada that passed the Quebec Resolutions in favour of Confederation.[52] The Civil Code included provisions that reflected

commitments analogous to those of the common law regarding the
importance of property rights and the relationship between property
owners and the state. Article 406 defined ownership as "the right of
enjoying and disposing of things in the most absolute manner, provided
that no use be made of them that is prohibited by law or by regulations."[53] Article 407 in turn required that "[n]o one can be compelled
to give up his property, except for public utility and in consideration
of a just indemnity previously paid."[54] Under the Civil Code, as under
the common law, property was secure against infringement by the
government, except where a law passed by the legislature had specifically
authorized the infringement.[55]

   With this context in mind, the commitments of the text of the
Constitution Act, 1867 to the security of property rights are easier to
see. The reference in the Preamble to a constitution "similar in principle to that of the United Kingdom" comprehended within it a great
deal.[56] Most famously, it is generally taken to include the principles
of responsible government.[57] However, the repeated references to the
need for institutions that secure property rights in the Confederation debates point to another aspect of British institutions which the
framers expected the Constitution to replicate, namely the common
law constitutional protections for property outlined above. A constitution "similar in principle to that of the United Kingdom" is one in
which the executive has limited powers, outside of an emergency, to
infringe the rights of individuals, including their rights to property.
The power to expropriate, tax, and spend belong to the legislature in
such a regime, and any executive action in this regard must be clearly
authorized by legislation.

   The provisions under the "Legislative Power" heading of the Constitution Act, 1867 provide further textual support for the commitment
of the Constitution to the protection of property rights under a system of
responsible government. As Ajzenstat has argued, these provisions are
intended to protect property rights, in keeping with Locke's vision of a
legislature that must consent in the name of the people to infringements
of those rights.[58]

   Firstly, the tripartite nature of the Parliament – consisting of the
monarch, the Senate, and the House of Commons – ensures that a range
of different constituencies must each give their consent to a measure
that affects citizens' rights, making it less likely that the infringement
of those rights will occur unless justified.[59] The seemingly technical
provisions under the sub-heading "Money Votes; Royal Assent" are
equally significant. Section 53, requiring that "Bills for appropriating

any Part of the Public Revenue, or for imposing any Tax or Impost shall originate in the House of Commons," reflects the Lockean idea that the consent of the people is necessary for such measures.[60] Section 54, which requires that taxation and spending measures must be recommended by the cabinet, reduces the potential for earmarking by individual legislators motivated by local interests, which could have the cumulative effect of increasing spending and therefore taxation.[61] Such earmarking was apparently a problem in the pre-Confederation legislature of the Province of Canada, one that was effectively solved by section 54.[62] Instead, taxation and spending measures must now be initiated by a cabinet concerned with the views of the electorate as a whole, rather than individual legislators focused on more narrowly local interests. These money vote provisions are made equally applicable to provincial legislatures through section 90.[63]

The combined effect of these provisions is to create institutional constraints that make it less likely that taxation and spending measures that affect property interests will be enacted unless they are justified. They restrict the potential sources of money bills to a singular one: the cabinet, introducing a bill in the lower, elected chamber of Parliament. At the same time, they recognize multiple constituent parts of the Parliament with the power to veto such measures. The regime is what one would expect in a Lockean constitutional system, in which it is anticipated that the legislature will occupy the principal role as the guardian of property rights. At the same time, these provisions reinforce responsible government, by requiring the government to maintain the support of the elected assembly on fiscal matters.[64]

Other aspects of the Constitution reflect the commitment to property rights. The nature of the Senate itself, consisting of members with security of tenure who meet a minimum property-holding qualification,[65] seems to reflect the expectation that part of its role would be to represent the interests of property owners in tempering the potentially populist measures passed in the lower house. And indeed, speeches in the Confederation debates specifically identify this as one of the roles for the Senate.[66] The legislative councils of Quebec, Nova Scotia, and New Brunswick, all since abolished, would have been expected to fulfill much the same role as the Senate at the federal level. The power of the governor general and lieutenant governors to disallow or reserve legislation also deserve mention as potential constraints on the power of legislative majorities to infringe property rights.[67] Indeed, these powers were touted as safeguards to that effect in the Confederation debates.[68]

The Senate and legislative councils, of course, did not ultimately provide a meaningful constraint on fiscal policies in the lower houses, and the disallowance and reservation powers were used sparingly before falling into disuse. Nevertheless, these features of the Constitution do still tell us something about the underlying normative commitments that animate the text. Safeguards for property rights are part of the Constitution, even if some features no longer fulfill their original purpose.

Finally, it is worth noting that the most significant source of jurisdiction that the Constitution Act, 1867 allocates to provincial legislatures, the power over "Property and Civil Rights in the Province," is defined in relation to the institution of property rights. This means of defining provincial jurisdiction indicates a shared understanding that property rights would be an enduring feature of Canadian legal and economic life, albeit one clearly subject to the ultimate authority of provincial legislatures.

Conclusion

It is important not to overstate the level of protections for property in the Constitution. The text of the Constitution does not restrict the power of legislatures or Parliament to authorize expropriation through clear statutory language. Indeed, expropriation powers were used on linear projects like canals and railways throughout the nineteenth century in both Britain and Canada.[69] A.V. Dicey, for instance, specifically cites the importance of Parliament's expropriation powers in relation to railways in his seminal 1885 work, *Introduction to the Study of the Law of the Constitution*.[70] The use of expropriation can often be necessary for linear projects such as railways, canals, pipelines, and transmission lines to succeed, since these projects require a single, contiguous corridor. In the absence of an expropriation power, such projects could be held up by a single landowner, even if the benefits of the project greatly outweigh the costs.[71] Since canals and railways were among the key engines of economic growth at the time of Confederation, the use of expropriation powers was undoubtedly something that contemporary observers would have expected, and there is nothing in the text of the Constitution that would preclude expropriation if clearly authorized in legislation.

That said, expropriation must be the exception, rather than the norm, in any stable and secure property system.[72] The commitment of the Constitution to the security of property rights is clear from the text, context, and shared understanding of the Constitution at the time of its enactment. Rather than a direct constitutional entrenchment of property rights, the mechanisms adopted by the Constitution were the indirect protections that had developed in the British institutions of the time. These included common law constitutional protections that restricted the power of the executive to infringe property rights, while at the same time requiring clear language in legislation authorizing property rights infringements. Such common law constitutional protections, adopted as part of a constitution similar in principle to that of the United Kingdom, were combined with the carefully structured procedures for Parliament and provincial legislatures provided for in the text. It is these legislative bodies that were expected to take on the principal role of protectors of property rights.

The legislature in such a regime has the ultimate power to limit property rights, reconciling private interests with the common good.[73] Yet by requiring clear legislative language authorizing an infringement of property rights, courts promote the legislature's deliberative function in assessing whether the infringement is justified. By requiring that certain property-infringing measures must be implemented clearly and directly, rather than implicitly and possibly inadvertently, the courts make it more likely that legislators will take up their role in actively considering whether the infringement is justified.

Writing in 1983, Gérard La Forest emphasized the constitutional significance of the commitments to secure property rights that are part of Canada's legal heritage:

> So far as legislative action is concerned, the courts are vigilant in reminding Parliament and the legislatures of the basic political understandings underlying our parliamentary democracy. The English Revolution was not intended to replace a personal despot by a legislative despot. The authors of our system of parliamentary democracy were actuated by a philosophy of individual freedom, a philosophy that continues to inform our fundamental political institutions. The courts through a series of presumptions designed "as protection against interference by the state with the liberty or property of the subject" interpret statutes so as to ensure that individual freedom or private rights of property are not arbitrarily restricted or abridged. In doing this the courts exercise what is in essence a constitutional function. They are working along with the legislative branch to ensure the preservation of our fundamental political values. The legislature

can, of course, by clear language overturn the court's ruling, but by insisting on such clarity the courts help to promote second thought and public debate, a debate that all recognize as an essential safeguard in a parliamentary democracy.[74]

The current-day salience of the constitutional commitment to property rights will be explored in later chapters. For the time being, it is sufficient to acknowledge that despite the indirectness of the mechanisms adopted, the Constitution is premised upon, and committed to, secure property rights.

Local Autonomy and Subsidiarity

Local Autonomy and the Canadian Constitution

On the first of April, 1999, the territory of Nunavut was established. As the clock struck midnight, fireworks filled the sky over Iqaluit, the new capital, as a crowd looked on.[1] The day was filled with celebrations. The many visiting dignitaries were invited to a community feast, where caribou, musk ox, and raw seal were served.[2] The performances that day included both Inuit folk dancing and a heavy metal concert.[3] The creation of Nunavut was more than just a mere redrawing of the map. It meant self-government for the Inuit people. In the crowd that day, there would have been elders who had experienced significant abuses of the centralized power of the federal government, including forced relocations to the far north designed to serve the strategic interests of southern Canadians.[4] The creation of Nunavut promised a new chapter in Canada's relationship with the Inuit. The new territory faced significant challenges, including high rates of unemployment, crime, and substance abuse, and the establishment of a new territory would not immediately solve those problems.[5] But it did mean local control, a key element of good governance that had been largely missing from the Inuit experience within Canada up to that point. And that was an achievement clearly worth celebrating.

Nunavut was carved out of the eastern portion of the Northwest Territories, pursuant to a term in the Nunavut Land Claims Agreement.[6] That agreement sought to settle outstanding land claims by the Inuit of Nunavut to their traditional territory, reinforcing Canadian claims to sovereignty in the Arctic, while recognizing the Inuit as partners in Con-federation with control over their own lands and territory. The terms of the agreement reflect a commitment to decentralized decision-making and local control. This commitment was manifested partly through the recognition of collective ownership by Inuit communities of much of the land and natural resources in the new territory.[7] However, the creation of the new territory of Nunavut, with its own legislature and governance structures, was equally important to the local autonomy of Inuit people. Roughly 85 per cent of the population of the new territory was Inuit (by design), and it has since functioned as a de facto Inuit government.[8]

Nunavut has the most extensive jurisdiction of any Indigenous-controlled government in Canada or the US (with the possible exception of American Samoa).[9] The section in the Nunavut Act setting out the jurisdiction of the new territory was based on the existing precedents of the other territories, which were in turn based on the jurisdiction accorded to provincial legislatures under the Constitution Act, 1867.[10] The linchpin of Nunavut's self-government powers is its far-reaching jurisdiction over "property and civil rights," a legal term of art that had already been part of Canada's constitutional order for more than two centuries at the time of Nunavut's creation.[11] As discussed below, local control over property and civil rights was initially a means of recognizing the distinctiveness of French-Canadian society following the British conquest of New France. After Confederation, the property and civil rights power was crucial to the local autonomy of provincial legislatures. This power has been one of the principal sources of decentralization in Canada's constitutional order, and an indispensable element in the Constitution's commitment to local autonomy. In 1999, that constitutional commitment was extended to include a people that had previously been subject to oppressive oversight and control by the federal government. It is no exaggeration to say that with the creation of Nunavut, Canada's Constitution came to embody its own underlying ideals more fully.

The example of Nunavut helps illustrate the need for significant decentralization of governance in a large and diverse country like Canada. The distinctive history, culture, languages, and geography of Nunavut all underscore the importance of local decision-making. At the same time, the Nunavut Act shows the adaptability of the governance structures provided for under Canada's Constitution. Those structures were initially devised with a handful of British North American colonies in mind. Yet the underlying principles have since been successfully extended to provide for local self-government by a number of other societies that were beyond the contemplation of the framers, including Nunavut.

This chapter deals with the Constitution's commitment to local governance autonomy. This is a separate and distinctive layer of decentralization, beyond the commitment to secure property rights described in the previous chapter. In this chapter, I argue that the Constitution is committed to local autonomy, as well as to the principle of subsidiarity on economic questions. Though the specific term "subsidiarity" only came to prominence in constitutional thought in the twentieth century, the underlying idea is a simple one[12] – subsidiarity just means that centralized authorities should have a subsidiary function, performing tasks that cannot effectively be performed at a more local level.[13] In other words, instances of centralized authority should be justified in functional terms, on the basis that local decision-makers would not be able to effectively address a given subject.

Even if the framers themselves would not have used the term "subsidiarity," the text of the Constitution they enacted reflects a commitment to this idea, at least on economic questions. There are two key aspects to this claim. First, the Constitution provides for presumptively decentralized decision-making on economic questions. Second, the Constitution provides for centralization on subjects that transcend local concern and cannot effectively be addressed at the local level.

While there were famously disagreements among the framers over exactly how decentralized the federation should be, the text of the Constitution provides for presumptive provincial authority over "property and civil rights," which is properly understood to encompass the full spectrum of private law. Private law governs legal relations, including economic relations, among private parties.[14] As I argue below, the "property and civil rights" power is a broad grant of jurisdiction which, when taken together with other provincial powers, amounts to presumptive authority to govern economic subjects. However, the Constitution also establishes a number of more specific federal economic powers. These federal powers are consistent with the principle of subsidiarity because, as I will argue in later chapters, they relate to subjects that, for various reasons, cannot be effectively addressed by the provinces.

Property and Civil Rights

The core provincial economic power is found in section 92(13) of the Constitution Act, 1867, which confers jurisdiction over "Property and Civil Rights in the Province."[15] On its face, the power may not seem particularly significant. In order to properly understand just how capacious "property and civil rights" would have been understood to be in 1867, one must appreciate the historical context surrounding that phrase. By the time of Confederation, "property and civil rights" was a well-established term of art in Canadian law, with an accepted meaning that encompassed the full range of topics connected to private law.[16]

The legal odyssey of "property and civil rights" begins with the conquest of New France. Following the cession of Canada to the United Kingdom, the king promulgated the Royal Proclamation, 1763.[17] Enacted under the royal prerogative power to legislate in conquered territories, the proclamation purported to sweep away the remnants of French civil law, replacing it with the common law.[18]

Formally speaking, the Royal Proclamation did indeed have this effect, though in practice it was not successful. The almost uniformly French residents of the new British colony were not familiar with the common law, and so they continued with their previous legal arrangements, resolving disputes where necessary through informal processes that followed the old law.[19] The law on the books did not match the law that parties actually adhered to, and continued to regard as legitimate and binding. This kind of mismatch between formal law and custom tends to undermine legal certainty and respect for the law.[20] This episode revealed just how closely intertwined legal principles governing interpersonal relations are with local norms and customs. In doing so, it foreshadowed the disastrous attempts by Canadian authorities to displace the legal systems of Indigenous communities in the nineteenth and twentieth centuries, which similarly created a gap between formal and customary law.[21]

British authorities responded to the failure to effectively impose the common law on the colony, and the resulting dissatisfaction among the colony's residents, by enacting the Quebec Act, 1774.[22] Among other things, the act provided that "in all Matters of Controversy, relative to Property and Civil Rights, Resort shall be had to the Laws of Canada, as the Rule for the Decision of the same."[23] The "Laws of Canada" meant the French civil law formerly in force in the colony.[24] The act specifically exempted criminal law from its ambit, meaning that British criminal laws continued to apply.[25] The accepted meaning of the act's provisions governing French laws, which came to be seen as one of the central bulwarks protecting French culture in the Americas, was that the French civil law would govern private law matters.[26] That presumptively included all legal relations among private parties. However, it did not include relations between citizens and the state acting in its sovereign capacity, including the criminal law, nor did it include the law relative to the administration of public bodies.

For almost a century following the Quebec Act, private law matters in what is now Quebec were governed by uncodified French civil law (more specifically, the *coutume de Paris*, one of the regional versions of customary French law).[27] The three traditional branches of French civil law are: the status of persons, property rights, and obligations (including contract law and delicts, which are extracontractual forms of liability that the common law would classify under the heading of "torts").[28] These headings encompass the full ambit of legal relations among private parties.

Following the division of Upper Canada from Lower Canada in 1791, the very first act of the new legislature of Upper Canada was the Property and Civil Rights Act, 1792.[29] That act provided that English common law would govern "all matters of controversy relative to Property Civil Rights," again understood to encompass the entire body of private law.[30] Like their French counterparts in Lower Canada, the English residents of Upper Canada did not want to be governed by a legal tradition that was alien to their own customs and practices.[31] Lower Canada and Upper Canada were re-unified in 1841 as the united Province of Canada.[32] A somewhat unusual situation existed following the re-unification: there was a single legislature for the colony, but half of it was governed in private law matters by French civil law, and the other half was governed by English common law. During this time, the range of matters on which the laws differed between "Canada East" and "Canada West" was encompassed by the phrase "property and civil rights," as used in the Quebec Act, 1774, on the one hand, and the Property and Civil Rights Act, 1792, on the other.[33]

In 1865, the legislature of the Province of Canada – the same legislators that passed the Quebec Resolutions in favour of Confederation – enacted the Civil Code of Lower Canada.[34] This inaugural codification of Quebec civil law is perhaps the single best piece of evidence regarding just how expansive the term "property and civil rights" was understood to be at the time of Confederation. As the preamble to the Civil Code makes abundantly clear, the code was intended to cover those subjects on which the laws differed between Canada East and Canada West.[35] In other words, the subjects covered by the code were the subjects that were understood to fall under the legal term of art, "property and civil rights," which served to delineate the areas in which the law of Canada East did not follow the common law.

The original 1866 text of the Civil Code of Lower Canada is expansive in its scope, covering the full range of matters that might be understood to fall under private law, including the status and capacity of persons, property rights, obligations (including contractual and delictual obligations), and "commercial law."[36] One of the basic principles applicable to the interpretation of civil codes is exhaustiveness.[37] Unlike a statute in a common law jurisdiction, a civil code is intended to be a complete statement of the law in the areas it addresses. Civil codes attempt to achieve this through the interplay between general and specific provisions, which in theory can provide an answer for every case.[38] The Civil Code was intended as an exhaustive statement of the law of property, contractual relations, as well as the legal implications of activities giving rise to harms suffered by third parties. The ample scope of the code demonstrates the breadth of the range of subjects that the term "property and civil rights" was understood to include at the time of Confederation.

There is thus strong support for the view that the Constitution Act, 1867 is best understood as placing authority over the basic structure of economic relations – including property, contract, and tort law – under provincial jurisdiction. The text then carves out a range of specific exceptions, subjects that would have fallen under this capacious understanding of "property and civil rights" except for the fact that they are expressly conferred on the federal Parliament. These include banking, bills of exchange and promissory notes, copyright, patents, navigation and shipping, and a number of others. In subsequent chapters, I will argue that these federal powers are consistent with the principle of subsidiarity. There are strong structural reasons why they could not have been effectively addressed by the provinces in a federation committed to free and integrated internal trade.

While "property and civil rights" is the most important source of provincial power, other heads of power reinforce the presumptive provincial jurisdiction over local matters, including powers over local works and undertakings, municipalities, the incorporation of provincial corporations, and the residual power over "matters of a merely local or private nature in the province."[39] Taken together, the allocation of these local matters to the provinces reflects a commitment to local autonomy and subsidiarity.[40]

Exclusivity and Subsidiarity

The Constitution's ability to deliver on the promise of local autonomy and subsidiarity depends ultimately on the exclusivity of provincial heads of power. Indeed, the exclusivity of provincial jurisdiction was repeatedly touted by the framers as a source of security for provinces, one that was reinforced in the later drafts of the Constitution.[41] The final text of the Constitution Act, 1867 makes abundantly clear that both federal and provincial powers are exclusive, meaning that when the relevant heads of power are properly construed, they should not overlap.

Exclusivity is crucial to local autonomy and subsidiarity. If federal powers under the Constitution are given an expansive interpretation that overlaps significantly with areas of provincial jurisdiction, then provincial authority in the areas of overlap is vulnerable.[42] Under the doctrine of federal paramountcy, valid provincial laws are rendered inoperative by conflicting federal laws.[43] Paramountcy in the Canadian context, as it relates to exclusive provincial powers, is a doctrine developed by the courts. However, doctrines equivalent to it are common features of federal systems, which require a way to resolve disputes in cases of valid conflicting laws from different orders of government.[44] Indeed, something like the doctrine of paramountcy is arguably close to a functional necessity in a federal system of government.[45] However, the reality of federal paramountcy means that in any area of overlap, Parliament has the upper hand. While the Supreme Court now generally favours restraint in the application of paramountcy, seeking to avoid a finding that laws conflict, that can only do so much to protect provincial jurisdiction. Oftentimes, conflicts are essentially undeniable. Parliament can always override provincial policy choices in areas of overlap simply by enacting conflicting legislation. Moreover, Parliament could also seek to fully occupy the field in its areas of jurisdiction, for instance by indicating that inconsistent provincial laws are contrary to its objectives. Accordingly, in areas of overlap, provincial laws may only be able to operate at the sufferance of a Parliament with the power to oust them.

This is a dark side of a "flexible" conception of federalism that allows for significant jurisdictional overlap: it brings with it a covert centralization that has the potential to undermine local autonomy and subsidiarity.[46] On such an approach, the principle that local governments are presumptively competent and that the central government's powers are limited to cases where they are necessary to be effective can come to be abandoned. That is effectively what has occurred in the United States. In the twentieth century, the Commerce Clause in the US Constitution was given an interpretation so expansive that there were few real limits on the scope of federal authority.[47] Though some exceptions to the scope of federal power under the Commerce Clause have emerged in more recent case law, Congress today has the power to overrule state legislation on most economic matters.[48]

One key difference between the US and Canadian Constitutions is that Canadian federalism is premised upon the mutual exclusivity of federal and provincial heads of power. In principle, that should help to check the kind of creeping expansion of federal authority that occurred in the US, since heads of provincial power are expressly excluded from Parliament's jurisdiction. However, the principle of jurisdictional exclusivity has fallen deeply out of fashion in contemporary Canadian constitutional thinking.[49] This is regrettable, since several vital constitutional principles are supported by exclusivity, including not only local autonomy and subsidiarity but also, as I argue in subsequent chapters, the commitment to economic integration and free internal trade.

It is worth emphasizing that the text of the Constitution could not be clearer in its endorsement of jurisdictional exclusivity.[50] The principle is reiterated at numerous points throughout the text of sections 91 and 92 of the Constitution Act, 1867, which outline the principal heads of power of the federal Parliament and provincial legislatures. Section 92 begins by stating that provincial legislatures may "exclusively" make laws in relation to the enumerated heads of provincial power.[51] Section 91, dealing with federal heads of power, specifically excludes matters coming within provincial heads of power from the federal power to make laws in relation to "Peace, Order, and Good Government," before declaring that the enumerated heads of federal power are themselves exclusive.[52] A separate "deeming provision" makes it clear that enumerated federal powers are not matters of a "local or private nature" falling under provincial jurisdiction.[53] The text of the Constitution reiterates the exclusivity of federal and provincial powers to the point of redundancy, a fact that should indicate its importance to the constitutional scheme.

The expectation of exclusivity is further reinforced by the sections of the Constitution dealing with the concurrent jurisdiction of Parliament and provincial legislatures over agriculture and immigration.[54] These are the explicit exceptions to the textual commitment to exclusivity, and on these matters alone, the text of the Constitution indicates that provincial laws will be in effect "as long and as far only as it is not repugnant to any Act of the Parliament of Canada."[55] The fact that the text of the Constitution is silent on the question of jurisdictional overlap outside of these two areas of concurrent jurisdiction reflects the expectation that in all other areas, there would not be any overlap at all.[56] This view was encapsulated by John A. Macdonald's statement during the Confederation debates that the allocation of exclusive federal and provincial jurisdiction had "avoided all conflict of jurisdiction and authority."[57]

That proved too optimistic, to put it mildly, as Macdonald himself might have suspected it would. The doctrine of federal paramountcy turned out to be necessary in relation to supposedly exclusive heads of power, even at a time when courts were still broadly committed to exclusivity in interpreting the division of powers.[58] However, the expectation at the time of Confederation was clearly that federal and provincial heads of power would be interpreted as being mutually exclusive.

It must be acknowledged that there are practical reasons to allow for limited jurisdictional overlap where otherwise valid laws have secondary effects on the powers of the other order of government. Real-world legislatures tackling real-world problems sometimes cannot stay perfectly within the lines imagined by the framers. This can lead to ancillary or incidental jurisdictional intrusions as part of an otherwise valid legislative scheme.[59] Moreover, some issues have a genuine "double aspect," and can be addressed by both orders of government acting within their own spheres of authority.[60] The activity of driving a car, for instance, involves both provincial aspects (the regulation of roads and highways) and federal aspects (criminal laws addressing matters such as dangerous driving).[61] In practice, it is sometimes not possible to completely seal off areas of provincial and federal jurisdiction, such that there is no jurisdictional overlap at all.

The inevitability of jurisdictional overlap became apparent through judicial interpretation of the Constitution by the courts, even if this outcome would not have necessarily been predicted by the framers or other informed contemporaries of Confederation.[62] Permitting limited jurisdictional overlap is pragmatic, allowing governments to fulfill their mandate in practically effective ways even if it involves limited jurisdictional intrusions. Such limited overlap is also consistent with a purposive interpretation of the division of powers. By not allowing heads of power to be hemmed in by an overly strict interpretation of jurisdictional boundaries, courts can help give effect to the purposes behind the allocation of a power to a given order of government.

Even so, the pragmatic and purposive impetus to allow for overlap must be reconciled with the unambiguous textual commitment to exclusivity. Failing to give exclusivity its due amounts to ignoring the text of the Constitution. Lord Atkin's metaphor of "watertight compartments" of federal and provincial jurisdiction has become something of a pejorative term in recent years.[63] Yet constitutional interpretation must strive to maintain a reasonable degree of exclusivity in order to remain consistent with the text and uphold important elements of the underlying vision, including the commitment to local autonomy and subsidiarity.[64] It may be better to say that the compartments should be "water-resistant," with incursions limited to those reasonably necessary to achieve a legislative purpose within the jurisdiction of the enacting body.[65] I discuss the mechanisms for how this can best be achieved in later chapters. At this stage, it is simply important to note the importance of exclusivity to the scheme of the Constitution Act, 1867, including the principles of local autonomy and subsidiarity.

Local Autonomy at the Founding

The Constitution's commitment to local autonomy and subsidiarity is amply supported by sources from the time of Confederation. While there was some disagreement on the degree of decentralization that would be desirable, essentially all the framers agreed that the text allowed for local subjects to be addressed at the provincial level while allocating subjects concerning the nation as a whole to Parliament. Moreover, a robust provincial jurisdiction was an objective sedulously pursued by legislators from Canada East and the Maritimes, resulting in drafting changes that clarified the exclusivity of provincial powers.[66] Politicians from Canada East were particularly concerned with preserving provincial jurisdiction over private law, including the range of topics covered by the Civil Code of Lower Canada.[67] And indeed, it was the shared understanding of the framers that the text of the Constitution did in fact achieve that objective, resulting in significant protections for the autonomy of the provinces in this domain.

During the 1865 Confederation debates in the Province of Canada, Hector Louis Langevin, the solicitor general for Canada East, gave the opinion that the term "property and civil rights" included within it "all the civil laws of Lower Canada."[68] These laws were on the eve of being codified in the Civil Code of Lower Canada, then in the final stages of ratification after a drafting process that took several years.[69]

John A. Macdonald, the arch-centralizer of Confederation, famously would have preferred a legislative (i.e., non-federalized) union to a federation, but he recognized that without a federal union, there could be no agreement among the colonies.[70] This political reality was underscored by a humorous exchange in the Canadian legislative assembly in 1864. Macdonald was in the process of outlining his preference for a centralized legislative union when he was interrupted by his French-Canadian political ally and cabinet colleague, George-Étienne Cartier. Cartier interjected with the blunt statement, "That is not my policy," to the laughter of the assembly.[71] Macdonald eventually came to acknowledge that a legislative union was unacceptable to large sections of British North America, including French-Canadian members of his own party. He noted in the 1865 Confederation debates that the need for a federal union derived in part from the fear among Lower Canadians that "their laws might be assailed," something the division of powers protected against.[72] He went on to conclude that while "all the great subjects which affect the general interests of the confederacy as a whole" are assigned to the federal Parliament, "the local interests and local laws of each section are preserved intact and entrusted to the care of local bodies."[73] Other participants in the debates commented that all local matters would be "banished" from the federal Parliament and that "the power of the federal government to interfere with the exclusively internal affairs of any of the confederated provinces would be of the most limited and inconsiderable character."[74]

Concerns were raised during the debates about the potential for federal heads of power to encroach on the local interests of the French Canadians in Canada East, including interests relating to religion, language, and civil law.[75] For instance, Louis Olivier, a member of the legislative council, argued that the Constitution did not adequately preserve local autonomy according to what we would today call the principle of subsidiarity: "As much power should have been entrusted to the local governments, and as little as is consistent with the functions it will have to discharge to the central government," since there is a tendency for central authorities to enlarge their power over time.[76] He feared the model laid down in the Quebec Resolutions did not adequately protect against federal encroachment, for instance, in relation to the property rights of religious corporations.[77]

The responses from the supporters of the Confederation project to concerns of this kind heavily emphasized jurisdictional exclusivity. For instance, Étienne Taché, a member of the legislative council aligned with the conservative Parti bleu, responded by arguing that fears of federal encroachment were misplaced in light of the exclusive provincial heads of power, and the language in the Quebec Resolutions indicating that federal heads of power did not include areas of provincial jurisdiction.[78] Macdonald, too, emphasized exclusivity in his speech touting the Quebec Resolutions.[79] However, concerns remained about whether the potential for federal encroachments would undermine the federal nature of the scheme.[80] As Asher Honickman has highlighted, these concerns were addressed through changes made at the 1866 London Conference leading up to the introduction of the legislation in the Imperial Parliament.[81] The relevant changes included the introduction of language in the preamble to section 91, specifically indicating that the federal peace, order, and good government power did not include subjects exclusively assigned to the province, as well as language in section 92 indicating that the provincial heads of power were to be exclusive.[82] These changes were pressed by representatives from Canada East and the Maritimes, concerned to secure local autonomy.[83] This additional language emphasizing exclusivity, some of it arguably redundant, was thus introduced into the Constitution specifically to address concerns about the security of provincial jurisdiction, including provincial jurisdiction over private law matters.

It is important to acknowledge that the Constitution also came with important centralizing features, partly in response to the perception that the US Constitution was unduly decentralized, which the framers blamed for the Civil War.[84] The federal residual power over peace, order, and good government remained in the constitutional text through the revisions at the London Conference, though it was tempered by the exclusivity of provincial heads of power. The Constitution also provided for the reservation of provincial laws by the federally appointed lieutenant governor and the disallowance of provincial laws by the governor general.[85] However, there was a recognition in the Confederation debates and other sources of the time that the use of the reservation and disallowance powers should be exceptional.[86] Indeed, as Paul Romney has noted, a *Globe* article during the Confederation debates compared the federal disallowance power to the Crown's power to withhold royal assent, a power that had already fallen into disuse by that time.[87]

It is not surprising that reservation and disallowance powers were intended to be used only in exceptional circumstances. Their use for ordinary policymaking by the federal government would have rendered the careful delineation of federal and provincial jurisdiction much less meaningful, turning provincial legislation into a matter of negotiation between provincial legislatures and the federal cabinet. The attempts to preserve provincial jurisdiction by politicians from Canada East and the Maritimes would have been largely in vain. These powers must have been understood to be designed for exceptional circumstances, in at least some sense, in order to fit with the scheme of the act.

The disallowance and reservation powers have since fallen into desuetude, having gone unused for many decades.[88] Their presence in the text, while anomalous according to a conventional understanding of federalism, does not necessarily undermine the commitment to local autonomy. The Constitution, after all, contains a number of powers that were expected to be subject to non-legal constraints. For instance, the significant formal powers of the governor general and lieutenant governors were to be exercised in a manner consistent with the conventions of responsible government. If one accepts that the reservation and disallowance powers were understood to be exceptional powers, their presence in the text might simply reflect the view that the courts did not have a monopoly on taking measures to preserve the constitutional order. The federal cabinet and vice-regal officers also had the power to check provincial measures that transgressed the proper boundaries of provincial authority.[89]

The instances in which these federal powers were used in the decades after Confederation mostly fit this model. Disallowance was primarily used to strike down provincial measures that the federal government regarded as being outside of provincial jurisdiction.[90] These included measures that undermined federal policies on interprovincial railways, intruded on federal banking powers, and violated civil liberties.[91] In the majority of cases where the power was used, it had a strong justification grounded in the Constitution. In other words, it is arguably the case that disallowance and reservation were never understood to be ordinary policy tools of the federal government, but rather exceptional powers to preserve the constitutional order.

If the reservation and disallowance powers had been used to the full extent apparently permitted by the text of the Constitution, they undoubtedly could have undermined the principles of local autonomy and subsidiarity, just as the unconstrained exercise of the governor general's power to dismiss a government could undermine the Constitution's commitment to democracy. Yet these powers were expected to be constrained by extralegal principles. In the case of the reservation and disallowance powers, they were initially used in ways that were at least plausibly consistent with the division of powers, before the extralegal constraints tightened and the powers fell into desuetude. When understood in context, then, the mere existence of the powers in the text are not inconsistent with a textual commitment to local autonomy and subsidiarity.

During the middle decades of the twentieth century, a number of historians and legal scholars advanced the view that Canada had been planned as a highly centralized nation and that this centralized vision was betrayed by judicial decisions from the Judicial Committee of the Privy Council.[92] The works advancing these views were based on heterodox legal interpretations and historical scholarship that gave heavy weight to the views of Upper Canadian establishment politicians like John A. Macdonald.[93] The historian Donald Creighton, for instance, argued that the framers intended to confer jurisdiction over commercial activity on Parliament, with the property and civil rights power being restricted to "certain rights and customs dependent on land," including "matters of minor economic, or of largely cultural, importance."[94] He went on to comment on the tensions created by the desire for the "preservation of the distinctive laws and customs of semi-feudal Quebec."[95] Respectfully, it is difficult to square any of this with the content and scope of the Civil Code of Lower Canada. The code was very much grounded in an ideology of economic liberalism on issues ranging from the powers of ownership to contractual autonomy.[96] And as discussed above, it covered the full range of matters connected to private law, including most commercial activity. If the code tracked the contemporary understanding of the scope of "property and civil rights," as I have argued that it did, then Creighton's argument could not possibly be right.

The views of Creighton and his contemporaries have come under fire in recent years. Indeed, as historian Donald Wright puts it, a "new academic consensus" has emerged, holding that the Canadian Constitution has always been rooted in provincial autonomy, and that the intention of most of the framers was not to create a highly centralized federation.[97] This renewed historical understanding is consistent with a commitment to principles of local autonomy and subsidiarity, including a presumption of provincial competency to address local matters. However, as I will outline in subsequent chapters, this presumption of local competency is rebutted in other areas, especially interprovincial trade and the systemic and structural features of the national economy, which transcend provincial boundaries.

Other Provincial Powers

While this chapter has focused primarily on the provincial power over property and civil rights, the Constitution also confers a range of other powers on provincial legislatures. The other significant provincial powers relevant to economic questions include: direct taxation; borrowing money on the credit of the province; the management and sale of public lands; hospitals (other than marine hospitals), asylums, and charities; municipal institutions; business licences; local works and undertakings (excluding a range of interprovincial and international projects assigned to the federal Parliament, as well as projects declared by Parliament to be for the general advantage of Canada); the incorporation of companies with provincial objects; the administration of justice within the province, including the establishment of courts and civil procedure; the imposition of penalties for provincial offences; and the residual power over "all matters of a merely local or private nature in the province."[98]

The provincial power over municipal institutions is worthy of special note. It might be suggested that a constitution committed to local autonomy and subsidiarity would take special steps to protect the jurisdiction of the most local level of government. However, provinces are generally understood to have plenary jurisdiction over municipal governments. Here it is useful to draw a distinction between ends and means. The Constitution is committed to the principles of local autonomy and subsidiarity. Yet this commitment is reflected through the means of the jurisdiction of the *provinces*, which have the power, but not necessarily the obligation, to sub-delegate to municipalities.

In addition to the provincial powers present in 1867, one might also add provincial control over natural resources in the province, which was originally conferred only on the four original provinces and those that later joined as colonies (rather than being created out of federal territories).[99] Authority over natural resources was later made generally applicable to the provinces in 1930 and eventually expanded in content through the addition of section 92A to the Constitution in 1982.[100]

The fact that western provinces were initially not granted jurisdiction over natural resources is best understood as an instance in which constitutional actors failed, for a time, to fully live up to the ideals of the constitutional order. However, the Constitution's commitment to local autonomy and subsidiarity was eventually extended fully to the western provinces, putting these political communities on an equal footing with the founding provinces. As discussed in later chapters, it was only much later that the Constitution's commitment to local autonomy and subsidiarity came to be extended to Indigenous communities, a process that remains incomplete.

The common thread running through these provincial powers is their local character. The exercise of these powers would not be expected to give rise to significant effects on parties in other provinces. They also do not relate to policy areas in which national coordination is necessary for economic integration, such as currency or the banking system. The provincial residual power over "generally all matters of a merely local or private nature in the province" sums up the ambit of the provincial heads of power.

Together with the expansive property and civil rights power, these provisions presumptively allocate economic jurisdiction over primarily local matters to the provinces, in keeping with the principle of subsidiarity. In subsequent chapters, I address the federal exceptions to provincial economic jurisdiction, dealing primarily with subjects that transcend the local context of a given province.

Conclusion

The two forms of decentralized economic authority discussed so far – property rights and local governance autonomy – can come into conflict. For instance, during the Confederation debates in the Province of Canada, members of the legislative council discussed a hypothetical provincial law taking property rights away from a religious corporation. The legislators debated whether the use of the federal disallowance power to prevent a province from engaging in such an action would amount to an *interference* with, or a *vindication* of, local rights.[101] At the heart of this disagreement were competing conceptions of local rights, one emphasizing property rights and the other the jurisdiction of the local legislature.[102] The disallowance power has of course fallen into desuetude, but the potential tension between property and local governance autonomy persists. As discussed in the previous chapter, the Constitution affords to legislatures the power to reconcile private property rights with the common good, including the power to infringe property rights. However, a range of protections apply, requiring the legislature to speak clearly when authorizing an expropriation, for instance. In a later chapter, I will discuss how best to reconcile the Constitution's commitment to secure property rights with the ultimate authority of the legislature to infringe those rights.

While support for secure property rights was essentially unanimous among the framers, we mostly have Quebec to thank for the extent to which principles of local autonomy and subsidiarity are expressed in the Constitution.[103] This turned out to be rather fortuitous, given the importance of decentralization to the governance of a large and complex society and economy. The decentralizing features of the Constitution have allowed for locally informed decision-making by regional political communities, some of which were only dimly contemplated by the framers themselves, if at all. These include not just the provinces of Alberta and Saskatchewan, which today formally have the same jurisdiction as Quebec, but also northern and Indigenous communities. As I pointed out at the outset of this chapter, the self-government powers of the Inuit-majority territory of Nunavut are today based primarily on the same legal term of art – "property and civil rights" – that was first set out in the Quebec Act, 1774 before being carried forward into the Constitution Act, 1867, and from there into the 1993 Nunavut Act.[104] As I argue later, the economic vision of the Constitution provides a useful model for how other Indigenous communities, which were previously largely excluded from the economic and political order, can be brought in as full and equal partners within a united Canada. Decentralization through the mechanisms of property rights and local autonomy are core components of that vision.

To argue that the Constitution is committed to principles of decentralization through property rights and local governance does not in itself resolve the tensions that can arise between these two competing principles or between decentralization and the parallel commitments to economic integration and free trade. The specifics of how these conflicts are to be resolved in a manner consistent with the text and principles of the Constitution are the subject of much of the remainder of this book.

Interjurisdictional Economic Relations

Positive and Negative Integration

Property rights and local autonomy are among the core commitments of the Constitution, but these objectives could have been pursued without Confederation.[1] The actual impetus for Confederation lay elsewhere, largely in the promise of economic integration and free trade among the colonies. The main economic challenge that the framers had to confront was finding a way to reconcile economic integration and free trade with the equally important commitments to decentralized economic decision-making. The central contention of this book is that the text of the Constitution reconciles these competing commitments in impressively thoughtful ways, arriving at solutions which remain relevant today. The next three chapters are about how the Constitution promotes economic integration, while balancing that integration with the parallel commitments to secure property rights and local autonomy.

As Michael Trebilcock has observed, there are essentially two main ways to lower the barriers to trade within a political community: "positive" integration, which involves positive steps to lower barriers, such as enacting uniform or harmonized laws in certain areas; and "negative" integration, which refers to restrictions against trade barriers.[2] The Constitution pursues both of these strategies, empowering the federal Parliament to enact laws that serve to integrate the national economy, and at the same time limiting the power of governments, particularly provincial and local governments, to create barriers to trade.[3] The next two chapters will focus on how the Constitution provides for positive integration. This chapter outlines the key aspects of federal powers relating to interjurisdictional economic relations, i.e., economic activity between and among different jurisdictions, including provinces,

Indigenous communities, and foreign nations. The next chapter will address federal powers relating to systemic and structural features of the national economy. Finally, chapter 6 will consider the features of the Constitution that provide for negative integration, explaining the restrictions the Constitution imposes on barriers to trade.

The Constitutional Commitment to Economic Integration

Confederation took place at a time of widespread belief in the virtues of free trade, in both the United Kingdom and Canada, an ideological outlook that the framers shared.[4] Moreover, the end of the Reciprocity Treaty with the United States in 1865 was an important aspect of the historical context of Confederation, providing an impetus for a British North American Union.[5] The proposed union of the colonies promised to compensate for the lost access to US markets by providing new channels for trade.[6] The pre-Confederation failure of the colonies to agree to terms for the building of the Intercolonial Railway linking Canada to the Maritimes, combined with the continued existence of tariffs and other trade barriers among the colonies, served to highlight the limitations of decentralized governance in bringing about the desired integration.[7] At the same time, the promise of a national market that could eventually include the Prairies and British Columbia further underscored the potential benefits of economic integration.[8] While there were other motives for Confederation, including improved defence against possible American military incursions, integrating the economies of the British North American colonies under a regime of free internal trade was a central purpose of the Constitution Act, 1867.[9]

The centrality of economic integration to Confederation is not a novel insight. Indeed, it is a point long acknowledged by historians. Donald Creighton put it this way: "The central economic ambition of the Fathers of Confederation was to increase the production, to hasten expansion and to promote the prosperity of the British North American provinces by the establishment of a new national economy. The other economic hopes of Confederation were, in the main, included within or dependent upon this major expectation; the other economic decisions taken at Confederation were meant, on the whole, to serve this major purpose. The creation of a national economy was the economic counterpart of the establishment of a new political nationality."[10]

While Creighton failed to fully appreciate the significance of other objectives of the Constitution, especially its simultaneous commitment to local autonomy, his identification of economic integration as a major purpose of Confederation is well-supported.[11] Indeed, in the Confederation debates, the economic benefits of trade among the colonies were perhaps the single most commonly advanced argument in favour of the new constitution.

For instance, John A. Macdonald emphasized the economic integration that the Constitution would promote, arguing that "if we wish ... to establish a commercial union, with unrestricted free trade, between people of the five provinces, belonging, as they do, to the same nation, obeying the Same Sovereign ... this can only be obtained by a union of some kind between the scattered and weak boundaries composing the British North American Provinces."[12] Alexander Galt, a leading architect of the Constitution who would go on to serve as Canada's first post-Confederation minister of finance, explained that one of "the chief benefits expected to flow from the Confederation was the free interchange of the products of the labor of each province."[13] He claimed that the Constitution would eliminate "restrictions on the free interchange of commodities as to prevent the manufactures of the rest from finding a market in any one province, and thus from sharing in the advantages of the extended Union."[14]

Peter Mitchell, member of the Legislative Council of New Brunswick and a delegate to the Quebec Conference, linked the economic integration promised by Confederation to a belief in material progress:

> Our people are industrious – our resources abundant – but union is necessary to our success. Association by national union with three or four millions of people, attached to the institutions of our parent state, would give us a strength and importance which we do not possess. We would have extended markets for our ships and other manufacturers, and by increased trade, an increased home market for the farmer ... Railroads ere long would connect our principal cities and towns with the world outside of us, and in course of time we might look forward to their extension across the continent.[15]

George-Étienne Cartier, one of the leading Quebec members of the pre-Confederation Canadian government and another principal architect of Confederation, touted the increased prosperity that would come from unifying the large territory and population of the province of Canada with the year-round ports of the Maritimes.[16] The differing comparative advantages of the colonies were a common theme in the

Confederation debates, which served to highlight the gains to be reaped from free trade among them.[17] Cartier went on to decry the barriers to trade that then existed among the colonies: "It was of no use whatsoever that New Brunswick, Nova Scotia and Newfoundland should have their several custom houses against our trade, or that we should have custom houses against the trade of those provinces."[18]

The framers' belief in the importance of free trade within British North America was unambiguous. Yet the text of the Constitution does not pursue economic integration at all costs, in light of its parallel commitments to local autonomy. Rather, the Constitution adopts a targeted strategy, providing for centralized decision-making in the key areas necessary to the structure of an integrated national economy, while establishing protections for free trade that also allow for local decision-making in areas of genuine local concern.

As I outlined above, the Constitution's commitment to economic integration has both a "positive" aspect, seen in the jurisdiction of the federal Parliament to enact uniform laws relating to the national economy, and a "negative" aspect, seen in the restrictions against barriers to trade.[19] With respect to positive integration, the subject of this chapter, the historian Andrew Smith argues that the collection of powers allocated to the federal Parliament "suggests that the creators of the British North America Act understood that a failure to harmonize the laws governing finance, weights and measures, currency, intellectual property, and various other matters would create *de facto* trade barriers."[20] Indeed, Lord Carnarvon, the colonial secretary who introduced the Constitution Act, 1867 in Parliament, specifically identified positive integration, in the form of federal jurisdiction over certain economic matters, as a core objective of the Constitution. During parliamentary debates regarding the Constitution Act, 1867, he summarized the pre-Confederation situation in these terms:

> There is no uniformity of banking, no common system of weights and measures, no identity of postal arrangements. The very currencies differ. In Canada the pound or the dollar are legal tender. In Nova Scotia the Peruvian, Mexican, Columbian dollars are all legal; in New Brunswick, British and American coins are recognised by law, though I believe that the shilling is taken at twenty-four cents, which is less than its value; in Newfoundland Peruvian, Mexican, Columbian, old Spanish dollars, are all equally legal; whilst in Prince Edward's Island the complexity of currencies and of their relative value is even greater. Such then

being the case, I can hardly understand that any one should seriously dispute the advantage of consolidating these different resources, and interests, and incidents of government under one common and manageable system.[21]

While the framers and other contemporaries were clear in their belief that the Constitution would promote economic integration, they were typically less forthcoming than Lord Carnarvon in linking this objective to specific heads of federal power. In this chapter and the next, I draw primarily on the text of sections 91 and 92 of the Constitution Act, 1867 in explaining how federal economic jurisdiction promotes economic integration. The powers conferred on Parliament are those that are reasonably necessary for effective economic integration, according to basic principles of political economy. While the Constitution reflects a balance between provincial autonomy and federal authority, most of the specific powers conferred on Parliament can be readily justified based on the constitutional objectives of economic integration and free internal trade.

On the question of which powers should be allocated to the federal Parliament, the framers were undoubtedly influenced by the US Constitution. Most of the framers were familiar with both the US Constitution and the political writings of the US founders, so it is not surprising that the US model of federalism was influential.[22] Interestingly, the framers looked to the US Constitution both as a model, on some issues, and as a cautionary tale, on others. The framers' ambivalent relationship with the US Constitution is encapsulated by Macdonald's speech in the 1865 Confederation debates. Noting that the drafters of the Quebec Resolutions "had the advantage of the experience of the United States," he continued:

I think and believe that [the US Constitution] is one of the most skilful works of human intelligence ever created; is one of the most perfect organizations that ever governed a free people. To say that it has some defects is but to say that it is not the work of Omniscience, but of human intellects ... We can now take advantage of the last seventy-eight years, during which that constitution has existed, and I am strongly of the belief that we have, in a great measure, avoided in this system which we propose for the adoption of the people of Canada the defects which time and events have shown to exist in the American Constitution.[23]

The defects Macdonald identified in the US Constitution – having an elected politician as head of state and leaving residual legislative powers with the state legislatures rather than Congress – were indeed "corrected" in the Quebec Resolutions and the eventual Constitution.[24] In other ways, though, the Constitution Act, 1867 mirrored the US Constitution, particularly with respect to the powers allocated to federal institutions. A number of Congressional powers under the US Constitution have clear analogues in the Constitution Act, 1867, including the powers over international and interstate commerce, commerce with Native American tribes, copyright, patents, currency, post offices, bankruptcy, defence, and taxation.[25]

The thinking that informed the recognition of these federal powers under the US Constitution is, in some cases, indirectly relevant to understanding the analogous provisions of the Canadian Constitution. Sources from the time of the enactment of the US Constitution, such as the *Federalist Papers*, reveal that these federal powers were intended to provide for positive economic integration through uniform federal laws in these areas, as well as to counter the incentives of state governments to serve local interests at the expense of those outside the state.[26] These objectives generally align with those underlying federal economic powers under the Canadian Constitution, discussed in this chapter and the next.

John Stuart Mill's influential 1861 work, *Considerations on Representative Government*, similarly underscored the benefits of federal union for promoting economic integration.[27] In his discussion of federal systems of government, Mill notes the particular importance of uniform national laws governing customs, currency, and the post office, in providing for free trade within a federation.[28] Mill's work was likely read by the framers, and may have had some influence, though on these points it largely echoes the justifications for federal powers under the US Constitution put forward in the *Federalist Papers*.[29]

The Constitution Act, 1867 confers significant, though strictly bounded, jurisdiction on the federal Parliament in relation to interjurisdictional economic relations, as well as the systemic and structural features of the national economy. These powers can be broken down into six broad headings, each of which can be justified as providing for economic integration consistent with principles of subsidiarity. The headings are: interjurisdictional economic relations, the infrastructure of exchange, federal fiscal powers, non-rivalrous national goods, activities with direct extraprovincial effects, and general, non-enumerated powers that permit the judicial recognition of federal authority on issues that transcend provincial boundaries in particular ways. The first of these categories is considered below, while the remaining categories, which pertain to what may be termed systemic and structural features of the national economy, are the subject of the next chapter.

Interjurisdictional Economic Relations: The Case for Centralization

Many of the enumerated heads of federal power under sections 91 and 92 of the Constitution Act, 1867 fit within the broad heading of interjurisdictional economic relations, which includes trade, communication, and transportation across jurisdictional lines. Indeed, interjurisdictional economic relations is the single largest conceptual category among the federal heads of power, accounting for roughly a third of the federal Parliament's exclusive enumerated powers. As I argue below, the federal powers that are best explained by their significance to interjurisdictional trade, communication, transportation, and other economic relations include:

- the regulation of trade and commerce (section 91(2));
- postal service (section 91(5));
- beacons, buoys, lighthouses, and Sable Island (section 91(9));
- navigation and shipping (section 91(10));
- quarantine and the establishment and maintenance of marine hospitals (section 91(11));
- ferries between a province and any British or foreign country or between two provinces (section 91(13));
- naturalization and aliens (section 91(25));
- lines of steam or other ships, railways, canals, telegraphs, and other works and undertakings connecting a province with any other or others of the provinces, or extending beyond the limits of the province (section 92(10)(a));
- lines of steam ships between a province and any British or foreign country (section 92(10)(b)); and
- Indians, and lands reserved for the Indians (to use the outdated language of section 91(24)).

Authority over economic relations that transcend jurisdictional boundaries is often best conferred on a central government due to the differing institutional incentives faced by central and local governments. In setting policy for commercial activity that crosses the boundaries of

subnational governments, those governments face incentives to prioritize local interests over the interests of parties in other jurisdictions. This
natural tendency of local governments is problematic with respect to
economic relations with other local jurisdictions, since these relations
create particularly ripe opportunities to benefit local interests at the
expense of outsiders. For instance, restrictive regulations applicable only
to imports from another province could benefit in-province producers
at the expense of producers in other provinces. Crucially, those outsiders
are not represented in the government of the local jurisdiction enacting
the regulation, and so the costs they bear are unlikely to be given significant weight in the government's deliberative process. Authority over
economic relations with other subnational jurisdictions would permit
local governments to transfer resources from unrepresented outsiders to
those inside the jurisdiction.[30] While this strategy might seem optimal
from the perspective of each local government, the cumulative effect
of beggar-thy-neighbour policies enacted by various local jurisdictions
would likely be to make them all worse off than they otherwise would
be. At the same time, local measures of this nature could give rise to
hostilities among local jurisdiction and escalating acts of retaliation,
undermining national unity.[31]

Similar concerns exist with respect to international economic
relations. Local governments could seek to regulate trade with other
countries in ways that serve local interests but that have negative impacts
on other parts of the country. Locally imposed barriers to international
trade, for instance, could increase the costs of imports flowing through
the local jurisdiction to other parts of the country. Such barriers to
trade could also spark retaliatory measures that end up impacting other
parts of the country. For instance, if British Columbia were able to
enact its own laws targeting imported goods from Vietnam, that could
increase the cost of those goods not only for British Columbians, but
also for Albertans purchasing goods imported through British Columbia. Yet Albertans would have had no say in the policy. The British
Columbia law could also potentially spark retaliatory trade measures by
Vietnam that would end up affecting Albertans, who again would not
have been represented in the institutions that enacted the initial policy.

Other points, besides the differing incentives of central versus local
governments, also favour the centralization of policies with respect to
international trade. A political community presenting a united front can
have greater leverage in international trade negotiations than smaller,
divided communities, something participants in the Confederation
debates pointed out.[32] Indeed, the absence of a coordinated international

trade policy among the British North American colonies was seen to be a pressing problem at the time of Confederation, one that the federal power in this area promised to solve.[33]

The problems associated with local regulation of interjurisdictional economic relations are not limited to intentional favouritism toward in-province interests. In regulating interjurisdictional economic relations, local governments could also create barriers to trade inadvertently, by simply failing to coordinate their approaches, or by failing to account for the cumulative impact of intersecting local laws relating to interjurisdictional commerce. Parties trading across jurisdictions might have to navigate several sets of local laws pertaining to trade, transportation, and communication, increasing the costs of transacting. There is no guarantee that these local laws would be consistent, and every likelihood that even well-intentioned laws would cumulatively create a disproportionate regulatory burden.

It should be apparent from the foregoing that interjurisdictional economic relations give rise to important collective action problems. All local jurisdictions are in principle better off if they agree not to engage in local favouritism and protectionism, and if they coordinate in the regulation of interjurisdictional trade. However, a group of fully autonomous local governments may be unable to credibly commit to doing so in the long run. In Canada, the Constitution provides a solution, in the form of centralized authority over interjurisdictional economic relations. The federal Parliament is less likely to be unduly swayed by regional interests, since all regions are represented. Moreover, Parliament is uniquely able to provide for standardization. This limits the costs that would otherwise be associated with multiple local regimes seeking to regulate interjurisdictional relations. Of course, if taken to its extreme, the logic of uniformity and harmonization would undermine the values of decentralization outlined in the previous chapters. And so, it is notable that the federal role is limited to particular categories of powers where the case for a centralized approach is strongest and where local laws are most likely to give rise to problems, including interjurisdictional economic relations.

The Trade and Commerce Power

The most broadly framed power pertaining to interjurisdictional economic relations is the section 91(2) federal trade and commerce power. There was famously some ambiguity as to the precise scope of this power at the time of Confederation, in light of the potential conceptual overlap between trade and commerce and the provincial power over property and civil rights.[34] However, the aspects of the trade and commerce power that have never been controversial are those that relate to interprovincial and international trade and commerce. While the trade and commerce power also contains a limited branch that covers intraprovincial activities – what the courts have termed the "general" trade and commerce power, discussed in the next chapter – the more significant branch relates to interprovincial and international trade and commerce.[35]

The judicial interpretations holding that the trade and commerce power relates primarily to interjurisdictional trade and commerce have been the subject of criticism, particularly by mid-twentieth-century historians and legal scholars who favoured a more centralized federation.[36] Yet the idea that the core of the power is about interjurisdictional economic relations is actually quite well-supported. Firstly, in interpreting the text of the Constitution, the exclusive federal power over trade and commerce has to be reconciled with the expansive and equally exclusive provincial power over property and civil rights. As the Privy Council recognized in its seminal decision in *Citizens Insurance v. Parsons*, a plenary federal power over intraprovincial "trade" and "commerce" would have ousted provincial jurisdiction over much of private law.[37] The term "trade and commerce," used in its widest possible sense, would capture most of the law of contract and large segments of tort and property. Such an interpretation would be inconsistent with the commitment to local autonomy and the preservation of Quebec's distinctive civilian private law, which were central to the Confederation bargain.

The use of "trade" and "commerce" in pre-Confederation enactments also supports the view that these terms were primarily directed at interjurisdictional economic relations. As the Privy Council noted in *Parsons*, the guarantees respecting "trade" in the 1707 Act of Union between England and Scotland were primarily directed at trade among regions of the United Kingdom or between those regions and British colonies.[38] There are also other relevant examples. For instance, the 1839 Durham Report, which was the basis for the unification of Upper and Lower Canada, recommended that the imperial government should continue to exercise jurisdiction over "the regulation of foreign relations, and of trade with the mother country, the other British colonies, and foreign nations."[39] In this report, well-known to contemporaries of Confederation and highly relevant to the pre-Confederation system of government in the Province of Canada, the "trade" that is appropriately the subject of centralized control by the imperial government is explicitly identified as *interjurisdictional* trade.

The Durham Report's emphasis on interjurisdictional trade is consistent with imperial practices of the eighteenth and nineteenth centuries. In arguing for an expansive interpretation of the trade and commerce power, Donald Creighton suggests that it should be considered analogous to the power over "trade" that the imperial government exercised through the Board of Trade in pursuit of mercantilist policies.[40] Yet most of Creighton's own examples of the interventions of the Board of Trade involved interjurisdictional economic relations, including tariffs, quotas, and prohibitions on exports and imports among colonies, between colonies and the United Kingdom, and between colonies and other nations.[41] Prior to the American Revolution, the United Kingdom did restrict certain forms of manufacturing in the American colonies, though it did so primarily in pursuit of an objective related to interjurisdictional trade, namely preserving export markets for British manufactured goods.[42] However, by the time of Confederation, British colonial policy had become less mercantilist and interventionist in nature, and more oriented toward free trade.[43] Accordingly, policies of this nature would no longer have been a necessary incident of trade policy. While the Board of Trade did also regulate matters such as banking and currency, these would be among the federal Parliament's specifically enumerated powers. The pre-Confederation role of the imperial government as a central authority regulating trade suggests a strong focus on interjurisdictional economic relations.

An understanding of the trade and commerce power that is centred primarily on interjurisdictional economic relations not only reconciles the power with the overall scheme and purpose of the Constitution Act, 1867, it also aligns with the meaning of the phrase as used in its constitutional context. Admittedly, section 91(2), unlike the Interstate Commerce Clause in the US Constitution, does not expressly limit the power to its interjurisdictional aspects. Accordingly, it is perfectly appropriate that the trade and commerce power has been recognized as having a "general," non-interjurisdictional branch that captures a limited number of systemic or structural features of the national economy that are not among the more specifically enumerated federal powers. However, the "general" branch must necessarily be limited in order to reconcile the trade and commerce power with the scheme of the Constitution. The more significant of the two branches of the trade and commerce power relates to interjurisdictional trade and commerce.

The interprovincial and international branch of the trade and commerce power captures those aspects of interprovincial and international trade not covered by more specific federal heads of power. While the

Privy Council took a highly restrictive view of the trade and commerce power, since the 1950s, the Supreme Court of Canada has upheld a number of measures aimed at regulating cross-border trade under this head of power, including laws relating to the marketing of grain and other agricultural products, the transport of oil from one part of the country to another, and the use of grade names for agricultural products in interprovincial and international trade.[44] The interprovincial and international branch of the trade and commerce power fits neatly into the category of interjurisdictional economic relations, based on the underlying vision of Parliament as the legislative body that is best situated to consider interests across the country and avoid local favouritism.

The use of the federal power over interprovincial and international trade and commerce has been hampered in some instances by a highly restrictive approach regarding the secondary effects that a law grounded in the trade and commerce power may permissibly have on economic relations within a province.[45] For instance, in *Dominion Stores v. The Queen*, the Supreme Court upheld requirements relating to the use of agricultural grade names in interprovincial and international trade.[46] However, the Court struck down a requirement that those same grade names could only be used for marketing *within* the province of production if the products complied with the standards associated with those grade names.[47] Arguably, this limited intraprovincial reach of the act was reasonably necessary for the law to be effective.[48] The use of the grade names by non-conforming products within the province of production could lead to confusion for purchasers in interprovincial and international markets, defeating the purpose of the statutory scheme. While courts in recent years have mostly taken an unduly flexible and permissive approach to secondary effects of laws outside of the jurisdiction of the enacting body, the trade and commerce jurisprudence has been marked by the opposite problem. As I will argue in later chapters, the appropriate standard for assessing intrusions of this nature is one of reasonable necessity in achieving a valid legislative objective. Once this is recognized, it becomes apparent that there is room for the federal Parliament to take a range of positive actions to lower interprovincial trade barriers, a topic discussed in chapter 10.

Specifically Defined Heads of Power

In addition to the trade and commerce power, Parliament also has jurisdiction over a number of more specific subjects tied to interjurisdictional economic relations. Some of the enumerated powers in this category are expressly or implicitly limited to the interprovincial and international dimensions of the subject in question. For instance, the federal power over lines of steam, railways, canals, telegraphs, and other interprovincial undertakings is limited by the text to interprovincial or international matters of this nature, though Parliament also has the power under section 92(10)(c) to declare intraprovincial works to be for the general advantage of Canada, or the advantage of two or more provinces, and thus bring them under federal jurisdiction.[49] Parliament's power over interprovincial undertakings has been naturally extended in the jurisprudence to include other interprovincial transportation projects, such as interprovincial pipelines and transmission lines.[50] The power over ferries is similarly expressly limited to interprovincial or international ferries.[51]

Parliament's power to declare intraprovincial works to be for the general advantage of Canada (or of two or more provinces) undoubtedly allows Parliament to extend its authority beyond strictly interprovincial projects. Yet there are two key aspects to note about this power. First, it is exceptional, requiring an express declaration from Parliament. Second, it requires a finding by Parliament that the work in question transcends the interests of a single province, thus invoking one of the recurring justifications for federal powers identified in this chapter and the next. A unilateral declaratory power may be anomalous by the standards of a classical conception of federalism (which is likely why the power has been used sparingly in recent years), but the required grounds for the declaration do fit with the basic commitments of the economic constitution.[52]

Other heads of power are, by their nature, principally about inter-provincial or international trade, communication, or transportation. The power over quarantine and marine hospitals is primarily about the health protocols governing new arrivals in the country.[53] The power over naturalization and aliens, along with the concurrent federal power over immigration, relate to the status of those who come to the country from other countries.[54] In many cases, of course, those who come to the country join the labour market or start businesses. The federal powers over immigration, naturalization, and aliens thus relate directly to an important form of international economic relations.

Other specific powers under this category are not expressly restricted to interprovincial and international aspects of the matter in question. The power over the postal service is not limited to service between provinces, for instance, nor is the power over navigation and shipping limited to navigation and shipping to destinations beyond provincial boundaries.[55] Federal jurisdiction over radio and televisual communications has been recognized primarily on the basis of the federal power over interprovincial undertakings, though the power has been extended to include intraprovincial communications.[56] The intraprovincial reach of these subjects is best understood as a matter of practicality and cost. It would be impractical to have a separate postal service for letters sent within the province, just as it would be impractical to have separate regulations for shipping that happened not to cross provincial boundaries or radiocommunications within a province.

Despite the intraprovincial reach of a number of these powers, the fact that they are within federal jurisdiction is best explained by their significance to interprovincial and international trade, communication, and transportation. The postal service is a good example. The postal service is an integrated communication and transportation network with national and international reach, and it was a vital tool for most forms of interprovincial or international trade at the time of Confederation. Federal jurisdiction served to ensure that the postal service fulfilled this function with respect to interprovincial and international communication and trade, with the intraprovincial reach of federal jurisdiction being essentially incidental, based on the obvious practical advantages of having a single, integrated postal network. Importantly, it is the scope of the network, not the relative quantities of intraprovincial versus extraprovincial mail, that explains the federal role. Even if most letters are sent to intraprovincial destinations, it is the need for an effective postal network with national and international reach, which would be harder to achieve with multiple provincial services, that best explains why the subject is under federal jurisdiction.[57]

Other subjects in this category that are not limited to interprovincial and international aspects include navigation and shipping, and beacons, buoys, lighthouses, and Sable Island (an uninhabited island off the Atlantic coast notable at the time of Confederation as the site of a marine rescue station).[58] These subjects meet the same basic criteria as the postal service: (1) They are closely related to interprovincial and international economic relations, including trade, communication, and transportation; and (2) it would be costly and highly impractical to limit the federal role to its interprovincial and international aspects. The same beacons, buoys, and lighthouses that are used for navigating between provinces and from other countries are naturally also used for traffic within a province. To have ships and crews subject to different rules governing navigation and shipping depending on the destination would be impractical, and would give rise to increased costs of regulatory compliance with little corresponding benefits. Conceptually, the federal role in these areas is best explained by their significance to interprovincial and international trade, communication, and transportation. The intraprovincial reach is ultimately an incidental matter of cost and practicality.

The federal power over aviation, recognized first under Parliament's now-defunct power to implement Imperial treaties, and then decades later under the residual federal peace, order, and good government power, also arguably fits within this category.[59] In the twentieth century, aviation became critically important to interprovincial and international trade, communication, and transportation. Even though not all flights have extraprovincial destinations, it would be costly, impractical, and arguably dangerous to have separate regulatory regimes depending on the destination of a flight.[60] Interestingly, while the 1932 case that first recognized the federal aviation power did so on the basis of the Imperial treaty power, Lord Sankey did note the strong connection to enumerated federal powers, specifically the power over interprovincial and international trade and commerce, and the postal service.[61]

Indigenous Relations

It may at first seem odd to see the federal power over Indigenous relations – or "Indians and lands reserved for the Indians," to use the language of the Constitution Act, 1867 – listed as part of the category of interjurisdictional economic relations.[62] After Confederation, this power was used by Parliament and the federal government as a kind of plenary authority to control the lives of Indigenous people, often in ways that threatened Indigenous nations' ability to sustain themselves as distinct, self-governing peoples.[63] Indeed, even before Confederation, a paternalistic and assimilationist approach to Indigenous relations had begun to take hold.[64] Indigenous people came to be thought of as wards or dependents of the government, and policies were directed toward suppressing Indigenous culture.[65] For more than a century after Confederation, this vision was used to justify the far-reaching control by the federal government over Indigenous people and communities.[66] However, the pre-Confederation origins of the federal power in this domain reveal that it was largely based on an older and much more limited conception of the Crown's role in Indigenous relations.

In the eighteenth century, the British Crown centralized control over relations with Indigenous nations, most notably depriving individual settlers and colonial governments of the power to enter directly into transactions for the acquisition of Indigenous lands.[67] The motivation for this centralization was complex, but much of it boiled down to the fact that relations with Indigenous societies were in some senses analogous to international relations, with notable implications for military and diplomatic strategy.[68] The British Crown had valuable alliances (and intermittent hostilities) with various Indigenous nations, and individual settlers and colonies were unlikely to share the overarching strategic perspective of the Crown.[69] Unchecked expansion into Indigenous territory had the potential to upset the Crown's interests and lead to unwanted (and expensive) hostilities.[70] At the same time, there was a sense that the Crown, as a more distant, centralized authority, was more likely to deal honourably with Indigenous nations than colonies and settlers that stood to gain from expansion into their lands.[71]

The Royal Proclamation, 1763, which crystallized the Crown's takeover of Indigenous relations from the American colonies, provided that the acquisition of land from Indigenous nations could only occur through a treaty between the British Crown and the Indigenous nation as a whole.[72] The Royal Proclamation was based on a vision of Indigenous nations as distinctive polities with collectively held rights protected under British law. While Indigenous nations were not recognized as fully independent sovereigns, they were taken to be internally self-governing political communities whose external legal relations were based on treaties entered into directly with the British Crown, rather than being subject to the local authority of the various colonies.[73] The Royal Proclamation, and the eighteenth-century Crown-Indigenous relations more broadly, were rooted in a "nation-to-nation" interjurisdictional conception of those relations.[74]

By the mid-nineteenth century, as alliances with Indigenous nations became less significant from a military and strategic perspective, new approaches to Indigenous relations took hold. These were largely based on the goal of assimilating Indigenous people into the dominant culture. At the same time, there was a move toward offloading the British Crown's role in Indigenous relations to individual colonies. In fact, the British North American colonies took over control of Indigenous relations in 1860.[75] Yet this raises an important question: if Indigenous relations were already being handled by individual colonies at the time of Confederation, why did the Constitution Act, 1867 allocate responsibility to the federal Parliament? The best answer is that the older, nation-to-nation conception of Indigenous relations reflected in the Royal Proclamation continued to be influential, even as newer, assimilationist strands of thinking were gaining ground.[76]

The Royal Proclamation continued to loom large at the time of Confederation and in the decades that followed. For instance, the post-Confederation numbered treaties entered into by the federal government in Ontario and the Prairies were based, formally at least, on the Royal Proclamation model of Indigenous relations.[77] The Crown entered into treaties with First Nations as political communities with a presumptive right to their lands that could only be ceded through such treaties (even if the implementation of the treaties often left much to be desired).[78] This approach was based on having a central authority, independent of local settler communities, that was responsible for Indigenous relations and treaty-making. Section 91(24) of the Constitution Act, 1867 effectively provided that the federal government would take over the role that had previously been occupied by the British Crown as the central authority managing interjurisdictional relations between settler and Indigenous communities. The US Constitution's allocation to Congress of a power over "commerce ... with the Indian tribes" may also have influenced section 91(24).[79] However, the federal power over Indigenous relations in the US was based on some of the same considerations. These included the need for an independent central authority to manage relations between particular states and Indigenous nations, which had important implications for the entire country.[80]

Parliament's power under section 91(24) is thus best explained by the interjurisdictional nature of relations, including economic relations, with Indigenous societies. Since Indigenous nations are internally self-governing, their relations with those outside the community tend to transcend jurisdictional boundaries. Centralized authorities like Parliament are, in theory, better positioned to address such interjurisdictional matters than local governments. For instance, in governing Indigenous relations, Parliament is less likely than the provinces to be beholden to particular regional political interests. Historically, these regional interests would have included the desire of local settlers to acquire more land.[81] Today they might include provincial and municipal governments' desire not to lose portions of their tax base to Indigenous governments.[82]

While the federal power over Indigenous relations is not expressly limited to its interjurisdictional aspects, the federal role fits the same logic as federal powers over interprovincial and international economic relations, namely that relations among different local jurisdictions are best managed by a central authority. In reality, for most of Canada's history, section 91(24) was taken by the federal government as a plenary power over Indigenous people, which admittedly the broadly worded text of the provision would seem to permit. However, recovering the older, and more limited, understanding of the federal role in Indigenous relations aligns with a vision of reconciliation based on Indigenous self-government within a united Canada.[83] Going forward, the federal government's legislative authority in this area is most readily justified if it is limited to setting the interface between Indigenous and other governments. That would include economic relations that transcend the boundaries of those governments. The core of the federal Indigenous relations power, today more than ever, seems to lie in its interjurisdictional aspect, which notably includes interjurisdictional economic relations involving Indigenous communities.

Federal Fiscal Powers

While provincial legislatures are limited to levying "direct" taxes, Parliament may impose either "direct" or "indirect" taxes. The distinction between direct and indirect taxes is based on now-outmoded thinking on the incidence of taxes. The basic idea behind the distinction is that a direct tax is levied on the person who ultimately bears the burden of the tax, while an indirect tax is levied on a party other than the one who ultimately bears the burden.[84] The prevailing thinking at the time of Confederation was that the question of who bears the burden of a tax depended largely on how the tax was designed, such that it made· sense to rely on a binary distinction between direct and indirect taxes. It is now better understood that the incidence of taxes can vary along a spectrum based on a range of contingent factors other than the legal design of the tax, such as the characteristics of the demand curve for a given good.[85] As a purely descriptive matter, taxes are not inherently direct or indirect based on their legal characteristics alone.

However, if one looks past the reasoning behind the definition of the categories to examine the specific forms of taxation that were understood to be indirect versus direct, Parliament's exclusive jurisdiction over indirect taxation makes a good deal of sense. The core examples of taxes that were understood as being indirect at the time of Confederation were customs and excise duties.[86] A customs duty is a tax paid for importing a good into a jurisdiction, while an excise duty is a tax paid by the manufacturer or distributor of a good.[87] Both of these forms of taxes are notable for their potential impact on the flow of interprovincial and international trade, though the connection is clearer with respect to customs duties. A customs duty is imposed on importing across jurisdictional lines specifically, whereas an excise duty is likely to be passed on to businesses and consumers in other jurisdictions (though admittedly this is more contingent on the nature of the market in question). Export taxes, imposed on the exportation of a good from a given jurisdiction, are also understood to be indirect.[88] The restriction against provincially imposed customs and export taxes is further reinforced by section 121, which requires that goods be "admitted free" from one province to another, a requirement that precludes interprovincial tariffs (as well as other forms of trade barriers).[89]

By conferring on Parliament the exclusive power over customs duties, export taxes, and, less significantly, excise taxes, the Constitution puts taxes that are especially likely to affect interprovincial and international trade under the control of a body that represents the entire country. Provincial legislatures, representing only in-province interests, might be tempted to enact fiscal measures that benefit local interests at the expense of those outside the province. The Constitution deprives them of the very fiscal measures that are most likely to do this. The plenary scope of federal fiscal powers in comparison with the more limited power of provincial legislatures is thus explained, in part, by the effect that certain kinds of tax can have on interjurisdictional trade.

Section 94 and Uniform Private Law

The commonly overlooked section 94 of the Constitution Act, 1867 grants a federal power to provide for uniform private law among the common law provinces, with their consent.[90] While this provision was never acted upon, its presence in the constitutional text can be explained by its relationship to interprovincial trade. Harmonizing private law lowers the costs to doing business across jurisdictional boundaries. Accordingly, section 94 reflects some of the same logic as other provisions dealing with interjurisdictional economic relations, though of course it would have been much more far-reaching, capturing within its ambit all in-province transactions rather than just the aspects of economic relations that are most likely to straddle provincial boundaries. The fact that this provision required provincial consent, and was never acted upon, demonstrates the extent to which federal economic authority was constrained by countervailing forces of local autonomy, both within the text of the Constitution and in the political dynamics that existed after Confederation.

Federal Constitutional Obligations

In addition to the federal economic powers, the federal government is also subject to constitutional obligations that reflect the importance of its role in promoting economic integration among the provinces.

Section 145 of the Constitution Act, 1867 required Parliament and the federal government to complete the Intercolonial Railway, linking Quebec to the Maritimes.[91] The 1871 British Columbia Terms of Union and the 1873 Prince Edward Island Terms of Union, both of which are part of the Constitution, also contain federal obligations relating to economic integration.[92] The British Columbia Terms of Union obliged the federal government to complete a railway to the Pacific within ten years,[93] while the Prince Edward Island Terms of Union required the federal government to maintain year-round ferry service to the island (a requirement that was modified by bilateral a constitutional amendment in 1993 to clarify that the maintenance of a bridge would also satisfy the federal government's obligations).[94] An analogous constitutional obligation relating to ferry service is also contained in the Newfoundland Act, which also forms part of the Constitution of Canada.[95] These obligations, which relate to federal powers over interjurisdictional economic relations, serve to underscore just how important economic integration is to the constitutional mandate of Parliament and the federal government.

Conclusion

Subjects relating to interjurisdictional economic relations together form the largest single conceptual category of federal economic powers. Federal jurisdiction in this area is grounded in a basic set of political and economic assumptions that are as valid today as they were in 1867. Firstly, where economic relations transcend the boundaries of local political communities, a central authority is better placed to account for the interests of parties across the country. It is less likely that a central authority will promote the interests of one region at the expense of others, for instance. Secondly, a central authority is better able to provide for national coordination and standardization. This is particularly important for interjurisdictional relations because parties would otherwise have to navigate the intersecting laws of the different local jurisdictions. While the category of interjurisdictional economic relations is the largest conceptual grouping of federal economic power, it is not the only one. In the next chapter, I will consider the other categories of federal powers, which generally relate to systemic and structural features of the national economy.

Systemic and Structural Features
of the National Economy

In addition to its powers pertaining to interjurisdictional economic relations, the federal Parliament also exercises jurisdiction over systemic and structural features of the national economy. The broad categories of federal power in this area include: the infrastructure of exchange, national fiscal policy, non-rivalrous national goods, economic activity with direct extraprovincial effects, as well as general economic powers that permit courts to recognize federal jurisdiction in areas that transcend local jurisdictions in particular ways. The federal role with respect to each of these categories can be explained based on fundamental principles of political economy, in a manner that is consistent with the principle of subsidiarity. Generally speaking, matters falling under these categories either require national coordination for effective governance or involve effects on extraprovincial interests. As a result, they cannot be effectively regulated at the local level in a manner consistent with the integrated national economy to which the Constitution is committed. This chapter considers each of the categories of federal jurisdiction relating to systemic and structural features of the national economy, completing the overview of the features of the Constitution that serve to promote positive economic integration.

The Infrastructure of Exchange

The second largest category of enumerated federal powers, after interjurisdictional economic relations, relates to what may be termed the "infrastructure of exchange." This category consists of powers that address the country's financial infrastructure and the physical units on which transactions are based. Parliament's jurisdiction over these subjects allows for national uniformity, creating standardized mediums of exchange and a common vocabulary for transactions across the country. This serves to lower the costs of transacting, particularly across provincial boundaries, without unduly limiting provincial autonomy with respect to private law. The powers over what I call the "infrastructure of exchange" form a consecutive list from sections 91(14) to 91(20) of the Constitution Act, 1867:[1]

- currency and coinage;
- banking, incorporation of banks, and the issue of paper money;
- savings banks;
- weights and measures;
- bills of exchange and promissory notes;
- interest; and
- legal tender.

The federal Parliament's powers over the financial system give it the authority necessary to designate a single currency whose value is stable and uniform across the country. This helps lower transaction costs. The overlapping powers over currency and coinage, the issue of paper money, and legal tender are obviously related to this function. They allow Parliament to provide for a standardized national approach to currency in its various forms. The powers over bills of exchange and promissory notes are closely related, since these types of instruments are capable of serving the same functions as currency, including as a store of value and a means of transacting.

The federal banking power also relates to monetary policy since banks affect the money supply in important ways. When fractional reserve banks lend out money, they introduce new currency into the financial system, by lending out to one party from the funds deposited by another.[2] Banks also act in other ways that affect the value and availability of the currency on which transactions depend, including through their interest rates and lending policies.[3] Regulatory authority over banks is thus closely related to monetary policy. Standardized banking laws can also help to lower the cost of transactions, particularly across jurisdictional boundaries, by limiting compliance costs of banks and ensuring consistent procedures regardless of where a financial transaction takes place.

The federal interest power also relates to the infrastructure of exchange in at least two important ways. Firstly, prevailing interest rates affect the money supply and, consequently, the value of currency.[4] Secondly, the interest rate applicable under a contract can affect the true price of the contract paid by the purchaser. A contract that ostensibly sets one price could in fact have a much higher price depending on the interest rate applicable to payments. This difference between the apparent price and the true price could take an unsuspecting party by surprise if payments were subject to interest rates not communicated clearly.[5] The federal Interest Act, enacted under the section 91(19) interest power, addresses this issue by setting a default interest rate applicable to most contracts, and requiring interest rates that depart from the default standard to be communicated as an annual rate.[6] Clear and predictable interest rates serve some of the same functions as a stable and uniform currency. They are both means of lowering the information barriers and other transaction costs associated with doing business by allowing parties to readily ascertain the true value of the transaction.

There is one subject on the list of powers relating to the "infrastructure of exchange" that is not financial in nature – namely, the power over weights and measures. This power also relates to how transactions are denominated, though it relates to the measurement of physical things rather than the measurement of financial value. The weights and measures power provides for the establishment of uniform national standards of measurement. This can lower the information barriers to transacting across jurisdictions, since it avoids the need for parties to understand different measurement systems. Since all systems of measurement are in some sense arbitrary, there is little value in maintaining different local measurement systems, at least not under a constitution that aspires to provide for an integrated national economy. The most that one can hope for in a measurement system is that it allows parties to clearly communicate physical properties, such that they can be readily understood by as many other parties as possible. A uniform national measurement system is best able to achieve that.

Together, the federal powers over the financial system and measurement standards provide a common national vocabulary for exchange. A dollar means the same thing in one part of the country as another. Moreover, the federal government usually has the tools it needs to ensure that the value of a dollar a year from now will be reasonably predictable (at least under normal economic conditions), and that parties will have access to the currency needed to facilitate transactions. At the time of Confederation, the different British North American colonies maintained different currencies, which created barriers to trading across jurisdictional lines.[7] These barriers would have included the information costs associated with ascertaining the value of a given amount of currency, but also the additional risk associated with transacting in a currency whose value could shift relative to the local currency.[8]

It should be noted that while the federal Parliament has a range of enumerated powers related to the financial system, it does not have a plenary power over anything connected with monetary policy. For instance, it does not follow from the foregoing that the Parliament should have the power to directly regulate the prices and wages agreed to in everyday transactions in order to control inflation.[9] Such a power was rejected by the Supreme Court, outside of emergencies, in the *Inflation Reference*.[10] The federal government had argued that combating inflation fell under the "national concern" branch of the federal residual power with respect to peace, order, and good government, an argument which the Court rejected.[11] The outcome in the *Inflation Reference* serves as a reminder that the Constitution pursues its objectives primarily through the specific powers enumerated in the text of the Constitution. That remains true even if Parliament's general economic powers – including the peace, order, and good government power – are best understood in light of the same underlying justifications that explain the enumerated powers.

There is a modern economic literature on the "optimal" size of a currency area, based on factors that include the degree of economic integration and the differences in the fiscal policies of the governments within the currency area.[12] To give one modern-day example, it may not have been ideal for Germany and Greece to share a currency, since this limited the flexibility of the latter to devalue its currency in response to its relatively loose fiscal policy.[13] Of course, the contemporaries of Confederation would not have been familiar with the twenty-first century literature on the optimal size of currency areas. That said, the expectation at the time of Confederation was that the economy would be highly integrated, and that the federal government would take the lead in setting a common fiscal policy. Accordingly, the economic case for Canadians to share a common currency was (and remains) reasonably strong, although differences between resource-based Western economies and those in the East can sometimes lead to macroeconomic policy tensions.[14]

Uniform weights and measures also lower transaction costs by providing a common vocabulary for exchange. A kilogram means the same thing across the country, and provides a common unit within which to denominate weights. It must be acknowledged that Canada's transition to the metric system, which in practice was only partially achieved, underscores the limits of legislation in dictating the terms of everyday transactions.[15] Custom can be persistent in this and many other areas of economic life. Many Canadians continue to think and transact using the old imperial units of measurement. It may be that the shift to the metric system was a misguided policy if it failed to fully alter the vocabulary of everyday transactions, resulting in two competing measurement systems. The issue becomes even more complex when one takes account of the relative benefits of aligning with the many countries that use the metric system versus the benefits of aligning with the United States, Canada's largest trading partner. However, regardless of whether Parliament has exercised its weights and measures power wisely, it is difficult to dispute the claim that it is better positioned than the provinces to provide for a uniform approach across the country.

The exclusivity of federal powers governing the infrastructure of exchange can be understood as being necessary to achieve the economic integration to which the Constitution is committed. Competing currencies or measurement systems at the provincial level would undermine the common vocabulary and mediums of exchange that uniform national policies in these areas can achieve. Provincial legislatures are simply not well placed to weigh the costs and benefits of departures from a standardized infrastructure of exchange, since inevitably some of the costs would be borne by parties outside the enacting province. Incidentally, concerns about provincial intrusions in these areas are not purely hypothetical. Alberta's Social Credit government in the 1930s attempted to create what amounted to a parallel financial system, which would have threatened federally imposed uniformity with respect to banking and currency.[16] The measures in question were either struck down by the courts or disallowed by the federal cabinet.[17] This episode is perhaps best understood as an example of our institutions working to maintain the standardized infrastructure of exchange envisaged by the text of the Constitution.

National Fiscal Policy

The taxation and spending powers of the federal Parliament are substantial. Parliament is accorded power over "the Public Debt and Property," the "borrowing of Money on the Public Credit," and the "fixing of and providing for the Salaries and Allowances of Civil and other Officers of the Government of Canada."[18] With respect to taxation, section 91(3) allocates to Parliament the power to raise funds "by any Mode or System of Taxation," with no express limitation.[19] This stands in contrast to provincial legislatures, which are only accorded power over "Direct

Taxation within the Province in order to the raising of a Revenue for Provincial Purposes."[20]

The plenary nature of federal fiscal powers is worthy of note. The federal power is not limited by the text of the Constitution, in contrast to the provincial taxation power, which is limited by mode ("direct taxation"), location ("in the province"), and purpose ("for provincial purposes").[21] As discussed in the previous chapter, one effect of these provisions is to reserve jurisdiction over customs and tariffs to Parliament, which can be linked to Parliament's broad powers over interjurisdictional economic relations. However, Parliament's taxation powers also allow it to take the lead in setting fiscal policy for the nation as a whole. Given the overwhelming significance of indirect taxes to government revenue at the time of Confederation, that was likely part of its intended purpose.[22] The plenary federal taxation power puts significant fiscal levers in the hands of the order of government that also establishes the monetary policy for the country. This is generally a desirable state of affairs, in that it allows for the coordination of fiscal and monetary policy.[23]

Admittedly, the federal government has not been quite as fiscally dominant as might have been intended, given the growth over time in the importance of direct taxes such as the income tax and sales taxes levied directly on consumers, as well as provincial revenues from natural resources.[24] Yet the federal fiscal position is still quite strong relative to the provinces.[25] The fiscal dominance of the federal government is not without its downsides, including the relative lack of political accountability with respect to federal transfers to the provinces.[26] Yet as the experiences of "looser" monetary unions have shown, there are also large risks to sharing a currency while pursuing divergent fiscal policies, and the plenary fiscal powers of Parliament help to mitigate this risk in Canada's case.[27]

While the federal fiscal powers are not expressly limited by the text of the Constitution, there are still possible questions that may be raised regarding the use of federal fiscal levers in a manner that is unduly coercive toward the provinces.[28] Provinces may be induced to align their policies with federal priorities through the use of conditional grants or even conditional taxes. Under certain circumstances, these policies could amount to a threat, leaving a province with little choice but to conform to federal priorities in an area of provincial jurisdiction. This is an issue that remains relatively underdeveloped in Canadian constitutional jurisprudence.[29] The text of the Constitution is clear in according Parliament with significant fiscal powers, but the use of those powers to undermine the federal nature of the Constitution could lead the courts to recognize some legal limits on the use of the federal spending or taxation powers. The transformation of provinces into unwilling agents of federal policy, through the unduly coercive exercise of federal fiscal powers, arguably contravenes implicit limits on the powers accorded to Parliament in the text of the Constitution.

Non-Rivalrous National Goods

A number of the federal powers relate to economic goods that are inherently national (or global) in scope. In the language of economic theory, these goods are *non-rivalrous* at the national level, meaning that once they are produced they can be simultaneously enjoyed by individuals across the country at no additional cost.[30] The enumerated federal powers that relate to non-rivalrous national goods include those dealing with national defence ("militia, military and naval service, and defence"), intellectual property ("patents of invention and discovery" and "copyrights"), and statistical data ("the census and statistics").[31]

The economic case for non-rivalrous national goods to be regulated by a central authority is intuitively quite strong. These goods are inherently scalable, meaning they can in principle be scaled up across the country (and beyond). Once such a good is provided, it can be of benefit to anyone in the country, at an additional or "marginal" cost of zero. Accordingly, it is prima facie desirable to have an order of government in charge of these goods that will take account of the benefits received by all Canadians, and not just those living in a particular region. A legislative body with national representation is more likely to weigh the cost of the good against the full benefits received across the country, rather than weighing benefits and costs only accruing in a particular province.

National defence provides an instructive example. Once defence from outside military threats is provided in a jurisdiction, it immediately benefits everyone in the jurisdiction. To the extent that it is part of a coordinated defence policy, an army base in Ontario and a naval ship in the Atlantic Ocean can "benefit" a resident of Alberta by enhancing national security. In theory, these military resources deter attacks and provide resources that can be drawn upon to respond to a variety of threats. The peace and security dividend from military resources benefits all Canadians. Moreover, the enjoyment of that dividend does not diminish with the number of residents of the country who benefit from it, meaning the good is non-rivalrous. If the legislature of Ontario were in charge of allocating resources to military bases in Ontario, one might expect that it would only take account of the benefits that would accrue to Ontario residents, and not the peace and security benefits that other Canadians would receive due to the non-rivalrous nature of the good at the national level. The expected result would be an underinvestment in national defence. The allocation of defence to the federal Parliament means that the full scope of the benefits is more likely to be accounted for in policy decisions. The non-rivalrous nature of defence, combined with the strategic advantages of coordinated defence policy, explains the federal role in this area. These features of defence policy were known to the contemporaries of Confederation and, indeed, improved defence was one of the key motivating factors leading to the enactment of the Constitution Act, 1867.[32]

The enumerated federal intellectual property powers over copyright and patents also relate to goods that are non-rivalrous at the national level. Copyright deals with creative works, including books, music, plays, television shows, and films. Patent law deals with useful inventions. Both of these types of goods are non-rivalrous.[33] Once a book has been written, or a song recorded, it can be enjoyed by an unlimited number of consumers simultaneously, without any diminishment in others' enjoyment of the work. Similarly, once something has been invented, that invention can be used by anyone without diminishing the use of those already using the invention.

The non-rivalrous nature of these intellectual property rights makes them fundamentally different from property rights in physical resources, which are generally under provincial jurisdiction. When one family is already living in a house, additional families that come to live in the house will tend to impose costs on each other and diminish their enjoyment of the house. The house is therefore a rivalrous good. By contrast, the enjoyment I derive from reading Hugh MacLennan's *Two Solitudes* is in no way lessened by the fact that there may be many other people simultaneously reading the same work elsewhere in the country. Nor is my enjoyment of a smartphone lessened by the fact that others are also enjoying the product of the inventions that made the smartphone possible. These are non-rivalrous goods, and that feature makes a big difference to the question of which order of government is best placed to regulate them.

Copyright and patent serve to promote the creation of products of human creativity and ingenuity.[34] The public benefits of these products are not localized in any meaningful sense, unlike the benefits associated with property rights in physical resources. The greater the potential market for the work or invention, the greater the incentive to create or invent, a fact that was alluded to in the Confederation debates as an argument for federal power over intellectual property.[35] Parliament can take account of the benefits to the country as a whole of a given set of intellectual property policies, along with the costs of granting temporary monopolies to copyright and patent holders. A local government might be tempted either to underestimate the benefits of creativity and innovation by failing to account for benefits that accrue to parties in other jurisdictions, or to unduly weigh the private benefits that accrue to local copyright and patent holders.

Localized intellectual property policy is also less likely to be effective, for related reasons. Once a work is created or an invention revealed, it can be copied elsewhere, often at a negligible cost. Intellectual property rights confined to a single jurisdiction can be easily circumvented by copying the work or adopting the invention in another jurisdiction. This explains why in the twenty-first century, intellectual property is the subject of international agreements aiming to ensure the uniformity of intellectual property policy across countries.[36] While federal jurisdiction does not solve the problem of international coordination, the allocation of copyright and patent powers to the federal Parliament solves these problems within Canada, and gives the federal Parliament the power to readily implement commitments stemming from international agreements on intellectual property policy.

The collection of relevant statistics about the country, including through the census, also provides non-rivalrous national goods. Once the data have been gathered and presented, they can be used by an unlimited number of people across the country at no additional cost. Since the benefits of this process are not localized, it makes sense that Parliament, with representation from across the country, should make decisions about what data to collect and what resources to put into the process of collecting it. It must be acknowledged, though, that the allocation of the census power to Parliament was also likely based on the need for an impartial account of provincial populations for the purposes of allocating seats in the House of Commons.

Economic Activity with Direct Extraprovincial Effects

A small number of activities involve substantial, direct effects that extend beyond the territory of the jurisdiction in which the activity takes place. The clearest example among the enumerated powers is the federal power over fisheries.[37] The essential fact necessary to understanding the federal fisheries power is that fish move around. Many fish, both freshwater and marine, migrate over large distances, such that they are quite likely to cross provincial or international boundaries during their lives.[38] Moreover, fish in the ocean often spend much of their time far from shore, outside of the jurisdiction of a given province or country.[39] A fish caught in one jurisdiction, or in an offshore area, will not be available to the fishermen and women of other jurisdictions. The interprovincial and international effects of fisheries policies were well-known to contemporaries of Confederation. For instance, the joint management of Atlantic fisheries under the Reciprocity Treaty with the United States was a prominent issue in the Maritimes, and served to underscore the connection between fisheries and international relations.[40] Indeed, the exclusive nature of the federal power over fisheries was not initially reflected in the Quebec Resolutions, and was only established at the London Conference, largely in recognition of the international dimensions of fisheries management.[41]

The direct, tangible effects of fisheries on parties in other jurisdictions distinguishes it from most other areas of economic activity in a way that justifies the role of a central authority. The federal Parliament is uniquely positioned to take account of the interests of the multiple provinces that could be affected by decisions related to fisheries management. It is also best placed to present a united front in international relations relating to offshore fisheries.

The federal power over bankruptcy and insolvency is also arguably best understood in light of the effects of bankruptcy law on other jurisdictions, though the argument is less straightforward than the one with respect to fisheries. In order to be effective, bankruptcy laws cannot be territorially limited.[42] If a party declares bankruptcy in jurisdiction A, that bankruptcy has to be able to affect the legal status of the property owned by the party in jurisdiction B. Otherwise, parties could shield assets from creditors simply by keeping them in another jurisdiction. This is essentially the justification that James Madison offered in *Federalist 42* for the federal bankruptcy power in the US Constitution, which may have served as a model for Parliament's bankruptcy power under the Constitution Act, 1867.[43] Under any reasonably effective bankruptcy regime, a bankruptcy declared in one province must be capable of affecting property rights and the rights of third-party creditors in other provinces. These necessary extraprovincial effects may help explain the federal bankruptcy power.

Of course, ordinary private law adjudication can also affect the rights of parties outside a province – for instance, through litigation over a contract involving extraprovincial parties. The crucial difference between ordinary private law adjudication and bankruptcy may lie in the unpredictable and non-consensual nature of the effect that bankruptcy law can have on out-of-province creditors. The potential for legal effects of this nature may enhance the case for a single regime that is seen as credible by extraprovincial and international creditors.[44] Other explanations for the federal bankruptcy power are also possible. Bankruptcy law can involve tensions between in-province debtors and potentially unpopular out-of-province interests, especially banks. Accordingly, it may be particularly susceptible to local populist impulses that would seek to benefit provincial residents at the expense of outside creditors.[45] Parliament may be less susceptible to regional populism of this nature, since its constituents are more likely to reflect a balance of creditors and debtors. Bankruptcy may also have been understood to be linked to public morality, including the idea of a moral obligation to pay one's debts. And so, the federal bankruptcy power could exist in part for reasons similar to the federal criminal law power, which, as discussed below, may have been based on the belief that questions of public morality are best dealt with by a centralized body.[46]

It may be that the justifications for the federal bankruptcy power are not as straightforward and persuasive as those of other federal powers. Provincial coordination, on issues like the extraprovincial enforcement of bankruptcy judgments, may be capable of solving the problems that decentralized bankruptcy law would create. In this respect, it is noteworthy that post-Confederation Parliaments had an ambivalent relationship with the bankruptcy power. After initially passing insolvency legislation in 1869 and 1875, Parliament repealed the legislation in 1880, abandoning the field of bankruptcy and insolvency for a period of almost forty years, until 1919.[47] While it is possible to explain the federal bankruptcy power in terms of extraprovincial effects, it may be that this power is better understood as simply an exception to the economic vision, in that it provides for centralization of a matter that could, in principle, be dealt with reasonably effectively at the provincial level.

There are other areas of economic activity that tend to have direct and substantial effects that transcend jurisdictional lines. Increasing awareness of the effects of pollution has brought some of these issues to the fore in the twentieth and twenty-first centuries. The extraprovincial effects of marine pollution, for instance, formed part of the basis for the recognition of federal jurisdiction over that matter under Parliament's residual peace, order, and good government power.[48] Another relevant example is the problem posed by emissions of greenhouse gases.

Emissions from one province affect parties in other provinces (and in other countries) to the same extent as they affect the residents of the emitting province.[49] As discussed below, extraprovincial effects of this nature are quite properly relevant to the recognition of new matters under Parliament's residual peace, order, and good government power.

The limitation of this category to activities with "direct" effects on other jurisdictions is noteworthy. All economic activity can have effects on other jurisdictions, but often those effects are mediated through human agency. For example, the failure of one province to recognize a given contract as being enforceable could lead to financial difficulties for a company, causing it to restrict operations in another province. If any and all extraprovincial effects were admitted as a basis for federal authority, the provincial property and civil rights power could be quickly whittled away.

What, then, is special about direct extraprovincial effects, such that singling only them out for federal control does not amount to an arbitrary limit on the logic of centralization? The answer likely lies in the relative simplicity of direct effects. The cause of the extraprovincial effect of over-fishing or pollution is generally known and understood. This fact means that these problems can be readily addressed by policy interventions, such as limits on the number of fish caught or the quantity of emissions. By contrast, extraprovincial effects that are mediated by human agency are complex and uncertain, and tend to intersect with other issues that may have local salience. Changing the law to make a given contract enforceable might address certain extraprovincial economic effects, but at the same time it might also bring local private law out of line with local customs and values. Such a change could also give rise to a range of localized effects that are more likely to be understood by those in the community in question. In other words, because of its complexity and intersections with other aspects of life in a community, private law as a whole is not a good subject for centralization, though centralization may be permitted for more straightforward and discrete subjects that directly affect other jurisdictions, like fisheries and extraprovincial pollution.

General Economic Powers

Most federal economic powers are defined with a fairly high degree of specificity. This is to be expected, given that they typically operate as exceptions to the general provincial power over property and civil rights. There are two important exceptions to the specificity of federal

economic powers, both of which have been important sites of contestation in Canadian federalism: (1) the "general" branch of the trade
and commerce power, which refers to the aspects of the trade and
commerce power that do not relate specifically to interprovincial and
international trade and commerce; and (2) the federal residual power
over peace, order, and good government.

As the Privy Council recognized long ago, the federal power over
"trade and commerce" cannot be given its largest possible meaning
without eviscerating the provincial power over "property and civil
rights."[50] A federal power over anything connected to trade or commercial activity would encompass much of private law within its ambit,
including the law of contract and large segments of tort and property.
An approach along these lines would resemble the courts' interpretation of the Interstate Commerce Clause under the US Constitution,
which during the twentieth century came to operate as a kind of federal
plenary power, based on the logic that most activity is in some way
connected to interstate commerce.[51] By contrast, in the 1881 case of
Citizens Insurance Company v. Parson, the Privy Council famously, and
correctly, held that the federal trade and commerce clause had to be
given a restricted meaning in order for it to fit within the broader
scheme of the Constitution Act, 1867.[52]

The interprovincial and international branch of the trade and
commerce power has always been relatively uncontroversial. A federal
power over trade that crosses jurisdictional lines fits with the broader
scheme of the Constitution, as described previously, and is aligned with
the underlying purpose of facilitating free trade among the provinces.
However, in the Parsons case, the Privy Council also indicated that
there was another branch of the Trade and Commerce power, not specifically rooted in interjurisdictional economic relations. The Court
held in obiter that "it may be that [the words "regulation of Trade and
Commerce"] would include general regulation of trade affecting the
whole dominion."[53] However, the so-called general trade and commerce
power was consistently rejected as a source of federal authority for
many decades following the Parsons decision.[54] In more recent times,
it has been found as the source of federal authority over a narrow set
of matters, including competition law, trademarks, systemic risk in
financial markets, and, most recently, anti-spam legislation.[55]

The test the Supreme Court established for the general trade and
commerce power is based on five indicators of federal authority:
(1) Is the law part of a general regulatory scheme? (2) Is the scheme
under the oversight of a regulatory agency? (3) Is the law concerned

with trade as a whole rather than with a particular industry? (4) Is the scheme of such a nature that the provinces, acting alone or in concert, would be incapable of enacting it? And (5) would the failure to include one or more provinces or localities in the scheme jeopardize its successful operation in other parts of the country?[56] These factors emphasize the regulatory, or public-law nature of the power, which is relevant given the provincial power over private law, as well as the functional problems that would arise from a failure to impose a uniform national scheme. Yet the core of the test is conceptual, rather than functional.[57] The requirement that the matter concern "trade as a whole," rather than particular industries, has been a crucial factor in the long line of cases rejecting federal authority under the general trade and commerce power, including in the 2011 *Securities Reference*, which rejected a proposed national securities regulator.[58]

While the courts have been quite restrictive in recognizing federal authority under the general trade and commerce power, the areas of federal jurisdiction that are clearly grounded in it – including competition law, trademarks, and systemic risk in financial markets – are not insignificant. Moreover, these issues fit with the scheme of the Constitution Act, 1867 remarkably well.

Trademarks are perhaps best understood as an example of the "infrastructure of exchange," one of the categories of enumerated powers outlined previously. The central purpose of trademark law is to provide reliable information to purchasers about the identity of the suppliers of goods and services with whom they transact. Trademark law protects identifying names and marks in order to avoid the confusion that would arise if the use of these names and marks were unrestricted.[59] When a consumer sees the name "Stanfield's" on a pair of underwear, he can reliably assume they were made by the Stanfield's whose products he is familiar with, and not by some fly-by-night operation that has appropriated the name in order to confuse buyers. The identity of the supplier is a key piece of information in many transactions. Having standardized national rules about trademarks lowers the information costs of exchange in a manner analogous to having a uniform national currency and standardized weights and measures. Similarly, trademarks contribute to a common national vocabulary of exchange, a feature which would be undermined by inconsistent provincial regimes.

Anti-spam legislation, the most recent matter held to fall under the general trade and commerce power, also arguably relates to the infrastructure of exchange.[60] Federal legislation in this area aims to preserve channels of communication that are important to electronic commerce. In so doing, it promotes a national and international platform for transactions, facilitating exchange across different industries.

Competition law and systemic risk in financial markets transcend particular localities in a different way. These matters relate to emergent properties of the national economy, which are not reducible to particular transactions, industries, and local markets.[61] Competition law seeks to regulate market power, which is a property that emerges from the overall organization of the economy. Determining whether a firm has market power – that is, the power to unilaterally affect equilibrium prices or other attributes of transactions in a market – requires a policy lens that transcends particular transactions, industries, and local markets. A firm that is the only supplier in a particular industry in a local market may not actually have significant market power if there are firms in other local markets that could hypothetically compete for business.[62] Similarly, the only supplier in a given industry may not have significant market power if there are other related industries that can produce substitutable goods.[63] Competition law focuses primarily on one of the emergent properties of the organization of the national economy – namely, market power. Provinces are unable to effectively regulate competition in national markets because market power in an integrated national economy is a concept that transcends provincial boundaries. The inability of provinces to effectively regulate in this area follows from this conceptual feature of the matter, which by its nature relates to "trade as a whole."

Systemic risk in financial markets similarly relates to emergent properties of the national economy. Systemic risk refers to the risk of a chain reaction of defaults that threatens the stability of the entire financial system.[64] Risk of this nature does not derive solely from a given transaction, nor can it often be fully appreciated based on the structure of a single industry in a single locality. Rather, systemic risk is a supervening feature of the national economy, requiring analysis of data across industries and local markets.[65] Because it is an emergent property of the national economy, irreducible to particular transactions, industries, or local markets, systemic risk can only be effectively regulated from a national perspective.[66] The federal power over national securities data collection, recognized by the Supreme Court in the same decision, is related to systemic risk, since national data is necessary to identifying and addressing systemic risk.

The recognition of federal authority over discrete issues that relate to emergent properties of the national economy is a natural extension of the scheme of the division of powers over the economy. These are matters that by their nature must be regulated nationally or not at all. At the same time, they are conceptually well-defined and limited, such that they do not pose a major threat to the overall federal structure and the principle of subsidiarity in economic matters identified previously.

The other general economic power under federal jurisdiction is the residual power over peace, order, and good government (commonly and somewhat regrettably abbreviated as the POGG power). This power, too, has been the source of controversy, particularly among the mid-twentieth-century historians and legal scholars who argued that the framers intended a highly centralized federation, and who objected to the limited scope given to this power by the courts.[67]

Judicial interpretation has identified three branches of the POGG power: (1) the "gap" power; (2) the "emergency" power; and (3) the "national concern" power. The gap power relates to a very narrow set of matters on which there is an identifiable textual gap in the division of powers. For instance, section 92(11) assigns authority to the provinces over "The Incorporation of Companies with Provincial Objects." Jurisdiction over the incorporation of companies with national objects is not expressly assigned to Parliament, but it has been recognized under the POGG "gap" power, based on an inference from the gap in the division of powers that would otherwise exist.[68] The emergency power allows for Parliament to assume temporary authority in what are normally areas of provincial jurisdiction during emergencies. The federal emergency power was invoked successfully during the two world wars and the inflation crisis of the 1970s.[69] The recognition of such a power is based on the fairly intuitive idea that during a temporary emergency, the need for centralized coordination of societal efforts toward a singular goal – such as winning a war – can outweigh the normal arguments in favour of subsidiarity and local autonomy.

The most significant branch of the POGG power to the permanent economic structure of the Constitution is the so-called "national concern" branch of POGG. This power, first identified by the Privy Council in the 1882 case of *Russell v. The Queen*, refers to matters which have "ceased to be merely local or provincial" and have become matters of "national concern," as well as to certain kinds of new matters which did not exist at Confederation.[70] While the Privy Council was slow to recognize matters as falling under this branch, even for a time holding that the POGG power was actually restricted to emergencies, a number of matters with economic significance have been held to fall under the POGG national concern branch, beginning in the 1940s.[71]

The case law on the recognition of new matters falling under the POGG "national concern" branch is framed in quite general terms. The recognition of such matters tends to be controversial and to reveal strongly held judicial disagreements.[72] The Supreme Court recently revisited the test for recognizing a matter under POGG in the *Greenhouse Gas Reference*, drawing heavily on prior case law. In that case, the Court set out a three-part test for establishing a new matter under the national concern branch of POGG. Firstly, the matter must be of sufficient concern to the country as a whole to warrant its recognition under the national concern branch of POGG.[73] Secondly, the matter must have a "singleness, distinctiveness, and indivisibility" that distinguishes it from matters of provincial concern.[74] And thirdly, the matter must have a scale of impact on provincial jurisdiction that is reconcilable with the division of powers.[75] With respect to singleness, distinctiveness, and indivisibility, the Court held that jurisdiction should be found only over a specific and identifiable matter that is qualitatively different from matters of provincial concern.[76] Moreover, federal jurisdiction should only exist where evidence establishes provincial inability to deal with the matter.[77]

Provincial inability is arguably the heart of the POGG national concern test. On this point, the Court set out three distinct subrequirements: (1) the legislation must be such that the provinces would be constitutionally incapable of enacting it; (2) the failure to include one or more provinces would jeopardize the operation of the scheme in other provinces; and (3) a province's failure to deal with the matter would have grave extraprovincial consequences.[78]

The emphasis on provincial inability, and extraprovincial effects in particular, is notable, given that it largely aligns with one of the categories of enumerated federal powers identified above. Indeed, the specific matters that are today understood to clearly fall under the POGG national concern branch are all closely connected to one or more of those categories. These matters include: aviation, nuclear power, the national capital commission, marine pollution, and establishing minimum national standards of greenhouse gas price stringency.[79]

Aviation relates to at least two of the categories of enumerated powers. In addition to its obvious connection with interprovincial and international economic relations, aviation is also a matter with direct extraprovincial effects, since an airplane travelling within a province could affect the route and safety of airplanes from other provinces or countries. Nuclear power also has strong links to the categories or enumerated powers. The unique risks associated with nuclear power include the potential for significant and direct interprovincial effects from a nuclear meltdown or other accident, which can cause radiation to spread over large distances. In addition, the regulation of nuclear power has national security implications, due to the potential for the fuel and technology used in nuclear power generation to be repurposed for use in nuclear weapons. The threat of the proliferation of nuclear weapons is obviously a serious matter related to national defence, one of the national non-rivalrous goods with which Parliament is entrusted.

The need for a federal national capital commission emerged in part because the physical footprint of the headquarters of the federal government spans two provinces, on either side of the Ottawa River, which increased the challenges associated with coordinating land use and other policies.[80] Having a well-planned national capital region that reflects the interests of the country as a whole is arguably a non-rivalrous national good, since all Canadians can (in principle) derive pride and satisfaction from it.

Finally, direct extraprovincial effects loom large with respect to marine pollution and carbon emissions. Marine pollution emitted within the province can affect areas outside the territorial limits of provincial waters. Even though not all marine pollution crosses provincial borders, the practical challenges of distinguishing between intraprovincial and extraprovincial pollution for regulatory purposes would likely be unmanageable. And carbon emissions from activities in one province affect other provinces (and other countries) just as much as the emitting province itself.

As I discuss later, the recognition of new federal powers must be strictly limited in order to properly uphold the scheme of the division of powers, as well as the Constitution's commitment to local autonomy and subsidiarity. However, the case law on Parliament's general economic powers has largely been faithful to the Constitution's vision of economic integration, subject to principles of subsidiarity. This is perhaps seen most clearly in the strong analogies between the categories of Parliament's enumerated powers and the matters that have been recognized as falling under the general trade and commerce power and the national concern branch of POGG.

Other Federal Powers

There are other federal powers relevant to economic regulation that are not clearly linked to the underlying economic vision. These powers mostly relate to the one major category of enumerated federal power not canvassed above: public morality. The three heads of power which most clearly fall under this category are the powers over criminal law and

procedure, marriage and divorce, and, possibly, bankruptcy and insolvency.[81] The Canadian Constitution is unusual among federations in
assigning exclusive jurisdiction over criminal law to the central government.[82] The power over bankruptcy and insolvency is also somewhat
anomalous. It is part of the body of private law, and so would have likely
been understood to fall under provincial jurisdiction if not specifically
enumerated as a federal power. As outlined above, it is possible that the
federal bankruptcy power is explained in part by the extraprovincial
effects of bankruptcy, though these are not as obviously significant in
the case of bankruptcy as they are for other federal powers grounded
in extraprovincial effects.

The best explanation for the federal criminal law and marriage
and divorce powers, as well as possibly the bankruptcy power, is likely
non-economic. These were seen as matters of public morality at the
time of Confederation, and the more central government was seen as
being less susceptible to populist impulses that might "abuse" power
in these areas.[83] The federal criminal law power in particular may also
be linked to the importance of ensuring secure protections for civil
liberties.[84] The thinking may have been that civil liberties would be
more responsibly protected by the federal Parliament than by provincial
legislatures. There may also have been an element of path dependency
at play. English criminal law had been applied in Lower Canada since
the time of the British conquest, in contrast to private law, which was
subject to a distinct body of French civil law. Accordingly, the idea of
a uniform pan-Canadian criminal law would have been much easier
to contemplate than uniform private law.

While there is no doubt that the criminal law and marriage and
divorce powers are economically significant, they are not necessary
elements of the economic vision of the Constitution as I have conceptualized it. Indeed, the federal powers in these areas are also arguably
exceptions to the constitutional commitment to subsidiarity. While
the Constitution is generally committed to subsidiarity on economic
questions, that commitment does not seem to apply in these areas
connected with public morality. It would be difficult to argue that
criminal law and marriage and divorce could not have been addressed
effectively at a more local level. The economic vision of the Constitution
is the dominant theme that explains the powers allocated to Parliament,
but it is important to acknowledge the influence of other ideas where
they apply. The federal criminal law and marriage and divorce powers
are simply exceptions to the economic vision of the Constitution, best
explained by non-economic ideas relating to public morality.

It must be acknowledged that in his *Considerations on Representative Government,* John Stuart Mill put forward an argument for centralized control of criminal law and the police on the basis of the external effects of local policies in this area.[85] Loose criminal laws could give rise to criminality and immoral behaviour that spreads to other parts of the country, according to Mill. However, if these kinds of external effects mediated by human agency were accepted as a basis for federal control, then the Constitution's commitment to local autonomy would be completely undermined. Private law also shapes interpersonal morality in important ways, for instance, and Mill's argument also extends to other areas of provincial jurisdiction, such as the administration of justice. Accordingly, the better view is that the criminal law and marriage and divorce powers are exceptions to the economic vision of the Constitution, rather than examples of subjects with extraprovincial effects that justify federal control.

Conclusion

Over the past two chapters, I have sought to outline how the Constitution provides for positive economic integration through the economic jurisdiction of the federal Parliament. The Constitution pursues a targeted approach to positive economic integration, defining federal powers in formal, conceptual terms, which in turn reflect an underlying economic vision.

The Constitution balances subsidiarity with economic integration by assigning to the federal Parliament subjects over which centralization is supported by enduring principles of political economy. These include subjects where the approach of one jurisdiction tends to significantly affect the interests of other jurisdictions, including interjurisdictional economic relations, fiscal policies such as tariffs that tend to impact those outside the jurisdiction, and activities with direct interjurisdictional effects such as fisheries. The logic supporting centralization on these matters is fairly straightforward: in the absence of centralization, local governments would be tempted to enact policies that would benefit their own residents at the expense of outsiders. Parliament, representing the entire country rather than one region or locality, is less likely to act based on local interests (though of course it is not entirely immune from doing so, particularly when it favours larger and more electorally significant regions).

The differing political incentives of local versus national governments can also explain the federal role in relation to non-rivalrous national goods, such as national defence, creative works protected by copyright, and inventions protected by patents. Because their benefits are infinitely scalable, these subjects are best addressed by a government that has incentives to account for the full range of benefits across the country, rather than only those that accrue to one region.

Federal authority also extends to matters on which national coordination is of special importance, such that it overcomes the Constitution's general presumption in favour of local authority on economic issues. National coordination is important on issues, such as competition policy and systemic risk, that relate to the emergent properties of the national economy. On these matters, a unified national approach is demanded by the qualitative nature of the subject matter, which transcends particular transactions, industries, and local markets.

National coordination can also allow for standardization, which is particularly important in certain areas of policy. Arguments based on standardization can provide an additional justification for the federal role over interjurisdictional economic relations, since the absence of uniform laws applicable to these relations could give rise to information and transaction costs associated with navigating multiple intersecting local regimes. The special importance of standardization also explains federal authority over the infrastructure of exchange, including currency, the banking system, and weights and measures. Standardization is important on these subjects because they determine how the financial and physical features of transactions are measured and communicated. On these issues, standardization is prized because it increases the pool of parties that can trade with relatively low information and transaction costs.

The principle of jurisdictional exclusivity is vital to each of these economic justifications for federal authority. The same arguments that support a federal role on these matters also support the exclusivity of federal power. The federal role is grounded primarily in the need for policies in certain areas to reflect the interests and perspective of the nation as a whole, as well as in special arguments favouring coordination and standardization on certain issues. Those goals are undermined by provincial incursions into these subjects, just as they would be by an absence of federal authority. In this sense, the arguments for positive integration through federal economic jurisdiction dovetail with those for negative integration, which are about restrictions on the power of provincial and local governments to interfere with features of the national economy, including free internal trade. The next chapter deals with the elements of negative integration incorporated into the Constitution.

Constitutional Protections
for Free Trade

Decentralization and Economic Integration

Decentralization gives rise to a persistent challenge that all well-functioning federations must address: how to ensure that local government powers are not used in a way that harms fellow citizens living in other jurisdictions. In the Canadian context, provincial legislatures have clear incentives to put the interests of their own residents first. On many issues, this feature of federalism does not create significant problems. Provincial legislatures and governments can act on the basis of local knowledge and local values and priorities to enhance the well-being of their residents, often without affecting the interests of outsiders to any significant extent. However, in some areas of policymaking, including notably those relating to interjurisdictional trade, there are opportunities for local authorities to seek to promote in-province interests at the expense of outsiders.

For instance, a province might seek to shelter a local industry from out-of-province competition, at the expense of producers in other provinces (as well as consumers). On issues of this nature, local officials face a constant temptation to prioritize the interests of their own residents, even where the costs, including those borne by outsiders, exceed the local benefits. Outside parties do not have a significant voice in the local legislature, and so their interests tend to be discounted.[1] If every local jurisdiction pursued such policies, they would all be worse off than they would be if they collectively committed to free internal trade. In other words, localized barriers to cross-border trade are a structural collective action problem that is more or less inherent in a federal system of government.

Constitutional limits on locally imposed trade barriers can be understood as a commitment mechanism that addresses this collective action
problem. Each local jurisdiction agrees to restrictions on local action,
on the understanding that the other jurisdictions will also be bound
by the same restrictions. The constitutional nature of the restrictions
is important, since it helps guarantee that local governments will not
renege whenever doing so appears to be in their interest (at least in
the short run). Most successful federations have adopted constitutional
restrictions on internal trade barriers, including the United States,
Australia, and Canada.[2] The European Union has also committed
to limits on member states' ability to restrict internal trade.[3] Indeed,
the EU's restrictions on internal trade barriers are more robust than
Canada's. Constitutional limits on trade barriers are common within
well-functioning federations because they respond to a fundamental
challenge created by federal systems of government. Specifically, such
restrictions help ensure that local jurisdiction is not exercised in a way
that harms outside interests.

The harm imposed by local trade barriers can be understood in a
number of different ways. The issue can be approached from a bloodless
economic perspective, as a means of ensuring that the aggregate welfare
of the population is not undermined by local policies. Discriminatory
trade barriers tend to make parties materially worse off in the long
run. Accordingly, a constitutional commitment mechanism should in
principle improve overall welfare. Alternatively, local trade barriers can
be understood as threats to national unity that are inconsistent with
the ideal of common citizenship.[4] Restrictions on trade that target
other jurisdictions are acts of hostility, "the economic equivalent of
war."[5] They have the potential to give rise to escalating disputes between
jurisdictions, through a process of tit for tat, ultimately leading to
a full-on trade war. Apart from their effect on economic well-being,
then, these kinds of acts may be simply inconsistent with common
membership in a national political community.

These problems are far from hypothetical. Indeed, at various points
in Canadian history, including quite recently, provinces have engaged
in tit-for-tat trade disputes, in which they have imposed restrictions on
each other's products in response to local interests. The "chicken-and-
egg war" of the 1970s is one example, in which provinces imposed rival
agricultural quotas that benefited their own producers.[6] More recently,
British Columbia proposed restrictions on the transport of particular
forms of petroleum that just happened to be produced in Alberta, to
which the Alberta government responded by threatening to "turn off

the taps" to the existing sources of Alberta oil on which the economy of British Columbia relied.[7] Incidentally, both of these disputes were effectively resolved by the courts on the basis of jurisdictional limits on provincially enacted trade barriers.[8]

Restrictions on government policy that impair trade are forms of negative integration, in contrast to the positive integration canvassed in the previous two chapters.[9] These doctrines restrict what governments can do, rather than providing scope for positive action. The Canadian Constitution contains two broad forms of negative integration: (1) the denial of provincial jurisdiction over economic heads of power assigned exclusively to the federal Parliament, including, in particular, the federal powers over interprovincial trade, transportation, and communication, and indirect taxes; and (2) stand-alone constitutional guarantees relating to trade, including the requirement that goods be "admitted free" from one province to another under section 121 of the Constitution Act, 1867.[10]

Trade Barriers at the Founding

It was the shared understanding of the framers that the Constitution would promote free trade by removing interprovincial trade barriers.[11] Recent scholarship has highlighted the fact that Confederation came about following the end of the Reciprocity Treaty that provided for free trade between British North American colonies and the United States. One of the motivating factors behind Confederation was the desire to provide for alternative markets to replace the lost access to the US market.[12] In speeches supporting the Constitution, leading political actors often touted forms of negative integration associated with the proposed Constitution. For instance, George Brown argued: "If a Canadian goes now to Nova Scotia or New Brunswick, or if a citizen of these provinces comes here, it is like going to a foreign country. The customs officer meets you at the frontier, arrests your progress, and levies his imposts on your effects. But the proposal now before us is to throw down all barriers between the provinces – to make a citizen of one, citizen of the whole."[13]

John McMillan of the New Brunswick House of Assembly similarly touted the importance of breaking down trade barriers:

[There] are objects that should animate us with a spirit of progress. What is the cry of England? "Free trade, free trade with the world": and this should be our motto, not as I said, the other day, to build a China wall around us and crop us up in our little

eggshell, and call all outside of us barbarians. This is not the
principle of the day; this should not be our policy, but to enter
into an alliance that will enable us to have free trade with our
neighbours; and this union of the provinces, I maintain, would be
commercially the best step we could take.[14]

The framers sometimes explicitly invoked the United States Constitution as a model for how a federation could provide for enhanced
trade by breaking down barriers. For instance, George Brown made
the following observation in the 1865 debates: "I go heartily for the
union, because it will throw down the barriers to trade and give us
control of a market of four millions of people. What one thing has
contributed so much to the wondrous material progress of the United
States as the free passage of their products from one state to another?"[15]
The framers were clearly influenced by the US Constitution, as well
as by the writings of the American founders.[16] It is noteworthy, then,
that the US Constitution, as interpreted by the US Supreme Court up
to the time of Confederation, was understood to place important limits
on states' ability to interfere with interstate commerce.[17] By the 1850s,
it had already been established that the federal power over interstate
commerce was a partially exclusive power, at least as it related to topics
demanding a unified national approach.[18] The accepted rationale for
exclusive federal authority over interstate commerce lay in the potential for state-level policies to interfere with the flow of trade, either
incidentally or on the basis of overt hostility to out-of-state interests.[19]

The text of the Constitution Act, 1867 embraces the exclusivity of
legislative powers in a much more clear and explicit way than the US
Constitution. As in the United States, the exclusive federal power over
interjurisdictional trade has been the principal mechanism by which
internal trade barriers have been characterized and policed through
constitutional doctrine.[20] By allocating exclusive powers over these
matters to the federal Parliament, the Constitution denies provincial
jurisdiction over them. As discussed below, negative integration also
takes other forms, including the exclusive federal powers over indirect
taxes, as well as the stand-alone protections for trade, of which section 121 is the key exemplar.

The Negative Dimension of Federal Economic Powers

In recent years, much of the attention of those interested in interprovincial trade barriers has been focused on section 121, the "free trade" clause

of the Constitution Act, 1867.[21] However, in the broad span of Canadian constitutional history, the exclusivity of federal economic powers has been a far more significant restraint on trade barriers erected by the provinces.[22] Since jurisdiction over interprovincial trade, for example, belongs exclusively to Parliament, any provincial measure that is in pith and substance about interprovincial trade is ultra vires, or beyond the jurisdiction of the province. On its own, this feature of the Constitution is sufficient to capture many overt acts of protectionism. If a province adopts a regulatory measure whose primary purpose and effect is to restrict imports from outside the province, the measure is presumptively beyond the jurisdiction of the province.[23] By making federal authority exclusive, the Constitution restricts provincially enacted trade barriers.

This is one of the ways in which the principle of jurisdictional exclusivity is crucial to the achievement of the Constitution's objectives. It is worth reiterating that the text of sections 91 and 92 are clear to the point of redundancy in emphasizing the exclusive nature of federal powers, including the trade and commerce power.[24] As such, federal economic powers can be understood to have both a positive and a negative dimension: they each constitute both a grant of authority to Parliament over a subject and a corresponding denial of authority over that same subject to the provinces. The negative dimension of the federal powers is important to the constitutional scheme. As argued in the previous chapter, almost all federal economic powers can be explained by principles of political economy that point to the desirability of a national approach on these subjects. The same considerations that justify the grant of federal power also indicate that overlapping provincial policymaking in these areas is likely to be harmful to the economic union.

In some areas, federal jurisdiction is justified primarily by special arguments favouring coordination and standardization, which would be undermined by provincial policymaking. For instance, the federal powers over banking and currency make sense in light of the especially significant role that standardization in these areas can play in reducing transaction costs. Provincial policies in these areas would be likely to undo some of the standardization benefits of federal jurisdiction, giving rise to trade barriers whose costs are likely to outweigh any benefits from provincial policymaking.

Other federal powers are justified primarily by the differing incentives faced by centralized versus local governments. A number of federal powers relate to subjects, such as interjurisdictional economic relations, in which policies enacted in one part of the country would have appreciable effects on other parts of the country. In these areas, there are special considerations favouring centralized control due to the greater likelihood that the federal Parliament will consider costs and benefits across the country, rather than in one particular locality. With respect to interjurisdictional economic relations, including interprovincial trade, provinces face incentives to shift costs to those outside the province. The national representation in the federal Parliament means that it is less likely to be swayed by these kinds of regional considerations. Again, the same considerations that justify federal jurisdiction also justify the denial of jurisdiction to the provinces, which are more likely to enact protectionist policies that externalize costs onto other jurisdictions.

There are four principal ways in which federal economic powers provide a check against provincially enacted trade barriers. Firstly, as previously noted, a provincial law whose dominant features relate to a federal head of power is ultra vires. For example, this means that a measure whose dominant feature is to restrict the flow of trade across provincial lines is ultra vires, since it relates in pith and substance to interprovincial trade.[25] Pith and substance review of provincial laws has been a significant check on provincially enacted trade barriers, invalidating most overt acts of provincial protectionism, as well as other significant intrusions into areas of federal jurisdiction over interjurisdictional trade, transportation, and communication.[26]

Secondly, a degree of scrutiny is applied in cases where a provincial measure intrudes into areas of federal jurisdiction as part of a broader statutory scheme that is otherwise within provincial jurisdiction. For instance, a provincial law that primarily regulates intraprovincial transactions may also affect transactions that cross the provincial boundaries. Factors relevant to the analysis include the degree of connection between the impugned measure and the statutory scheme as a whole, as well as the significance of the intrusion into federal jurisdiction.[27] How, specifically, this inquiry should be structured has been a point of some contention in Canadian constitutional law, and is addressed in later chapters. However, the exclusivity of federal powers demands that incidental or ancillary intrusions of this nature be given at least some meaningful scrutiny. If such intrusions were to be given a free pass, then the cumulative effect of multiple provincial statutes could amount to significant provincial regulation of supposedly exclusive areas of federal jurisdiction. The clear textual commitment to exclusivity demands that there be some limits on incidental or ancillary provincial intrusions into areas of federal responsibility (and vice versa).

Thirdly, there are aspects of exclusive federal heads of power that should not be regulated at all by the provinces, even where there is a close connection between the impugned measure and a valid provincial objective. This has been recognized in Canadian constitutional law under the doctrine of interjurisdictional immunity (sometimes referred to as IJI), according to which some heads of federal power are recognized as having a "core" that is immune from provincial laws.[28] The Supreme Court has had a conflicted relationship with interjurisdictional immunity in recent years, in some cases disparaging it as a relic of the bygone days of watertight compartments and in others embracing it as a valid feature of the constitutional regime of exclusive federal powers.[29]

Many examples of interjurisdictional immunity in constitutional case law involve provincial measures that could give rise to barriers to trade, communication, and transportation, such as provincial zoning laws limiting which sites could be recognized as aerodromes.[30] Though it is underappreciated in this respect, interjurisdictional immunity has been a significant source of case law promoting negative economic integration.[31] Interjurisdictional immunity is quite similar to the "dormant Commerce Clause" under the US Constitution, which restricts state action that impedes interstate trade, even in the absence of an inconsistent federal law.[32] However, unlike the Dormant Commerce Clause, which only restricts state action relevant to the Commerce Clause, interjurisdictional immunity can protect the core jurisdiction under any federal head of power. I will argue in chapter 10 that the economic purposes associated with negative integration can assist in the heretofore fraught question of identifying what constitutes the unassailable core of federal economic powers.

The fourth mechanism by which the Constitution provides for negative economic integration is through the doctrine of paramountcy, which applies in cases involving valid federal and provincial laws that are inconsistent with each other. The federal law renders the provincial law inoperative to the extent of the inconsistency. While federal paramountcy with respect to exclusive (as opposed to concurrent) powers is not provided for explicitly in the constitutional text, it is arguably a functional requirement of a federal regime and thus implicit in the constitutional order.[33] By rendering inconsistent provincial laws inoperative, the doctrine ensures that the policy choices of Parliament prevail over those of the provinces in areas of federal jurisdiction. Federal paramountcy serves to reinforce the economic purposes of the Constitution by deferring to Parliament's determinations on issues that may often involve significant benefits to national coordination or considerations of extraprovincial effects. Paramountcy also gives Parliament a powerful tool to oust provincial measures that interfere with federal initiatives promoting economic integration, one that it could use strategically to curb provincially enacted trade barriers if the political will existed to do so.[34]

Interprovincial Trade, Communication, and Transportation

The negative dimension of federal powers is particularly significant to achieving the Constitution's economic purposes in two areas: (1) interprovincial trade, communication, and transportation and (2) indirect taxes. In these policy areas, measures enacted in one jurisdiction can impose clear and immediate costs on parties in other jurisdictions. These are thus subjects that are particularly vulnerable to the parochial temptation to serve in-province interests at the expense of outsiders. Provincial enactments in these areas are likely to fail to account for out-of-province interests, either intentionally or inadvertently. Some of these subjects also require national coordination in order to be effective, such as with respect to aviation policy, and such coordination could be impaired by the application of provincial laws. Accordingly, the exclusivity of these federal powers is particularly important to achieving the economic vision of the Constitution.

The federal powers over interprovincial trade, communication, and transportation all deal with economic relations that cross jurisdictional boundaries. Protectionist policies by their nature seek to regulate and limit such relations, drawing a distinction between those inside the jurisdiction and those outside. For instance, a provincial enactment that restricts the importation of goods into the province could be found to relate to interprovincial trade rather than a valid intraprovincial objective.[35] Similarly, restrictions on the transport of goods produced out of province may be found to relate in pith and substance to exclusive federal heads of power relating to interprovincial transportation.[36] By depriving provinces of the power to directly regulate interprovincial economic relations, the Constitution creates an important safeguard against protectionism, one that reflects the text's commitment to free internal trade.

The negative dimension of the interprovincial branch of the federal trade and commerce power has the potential to be particularly significant in promoting economic integration. Indeed, given the relative dearth of federal initiatives that have been upheld on the basis of the trade and commerce power, that power has arguably, up to this point, been more important for what it *denies* to the provinces than for what it grants to Parliament. The fact that the Constitution implicitly withholds from the provinces the power to enact laws in relation to interprovincial trade is one of the central features that mark the commitment to free internal trade.

Indirect Taxes

The negative dimension of the federal taxation power is also a significant manifestation of the Constitution's economic vision. Under section 91(3), Parliament has exclusive power over "the raising of Money by any Mode or System of Taxation."[37] By contrast, the tax jurisdiction of provincial legislatures is limited to "Direct Taxation within the Province in order to the raising of a Revenue for Provincial Purposes."[38] There are three limits built into the provincial power when it is read alongside the exclusive federal power.[39] The first, the restriction of the provincial taxation power to "provincial purposes," is not necessarily an important substantive limit.[40] However, the "provincial purposes" specification is necessary as a formal matter to make the provincial taxation power consistent with the scheme of mutual exclusivity. Without that specification, the provincial power would overlap with the federal taxation power, which is protected by language in the preamble of section 91 stating that it is an exclusive power that exists "notwithstanding anything in this Act."[41] "Provincial purposes" are simply whatever purposes are determined by the provincial legislature, but this is sufficient to distinguish the provincial taxation power from the federal power, the revenue of which is directed to purposes determined in the first instance by Parliament, not the provincial legislatures.

The second limit on the provincial taxation power is geographic. The provincial taxation power only extends to taxes "within the province." This is an important limitation that directly relates to negative economic integration. Taxes imposed on persons, property, transactions, or benefits outside of the territory of a province by their nature have important extraprovincial effects.

A core structural problem of federalism is that local governments are unlikely to properly account for costs imposed on those outside the local jurisdiction. The restriction on extraterritorial provincial taxation helps to address this problem when it comes to taxation. However, even a tax imposed within the geographic boundaries of a province can impose significant costs on those outside the province. The third limit on provincial taxation power is meant to address this concern. Provincial taxation power is limited to "direct" taxation, which implicitly excludes indirect taxation. As discussed in chapter 4, the distinction between direct and indirect taxation is based on nineteenth-century understandings of where the burden of a tax ultimately falls.[42] With respect to a direct tax, the party who remits the tax is the party who actually incurs the cost of the tax. By contrast, taxes are considered indirect if the burden tends to fall on someone other than the party who pays the tax to the government. Read together with the geographic limitation on provincial taxation authority, the restriction against indirect provincial taxes reflects an intention to ensure that the burden of provincial taxes falls within the province imposing the tax.[43] More specifically, the restriction against indirect taxes clearly rules out the establishment of customs duties or tariffs by the provinces.[44] These restrictions respond to the structural problem of provincial authorities failing to properly account for costs incurred outside the province, including those associated with barriers to trade.

In the twentieth century, economists came to understand that distinguishing between direct and indirect taxes is not an analytically useful way to classify taxes. The incidence of a tax depends on contingent factors other than how the tax is formally structured, which inform how parties change their behaviour in response to a tax.[45] In other words, it is simply not possible to state definitively what the incidence of a tax will be based on its formal legal characteristics alone. Nonetheless, the forms of taxes that have been commonly understood to be indirect taxes are precisely those that are most likely to burden the flow of trade across jurisdictional lines: customs duties, export taxes, and excise taxes.[46] Customs duties and export taxes are triggered by crossing jurisdictional lines and thus create barriers to interjurisdictional trade by design. Excise taxes are imposed on the manufacture or distribution of a commodity. In the case of goods primarily produced for export, excise taxes can function like an export tax in burdening the flow of trade. In the case of imported goods, excise taxes can function like a tariff. During the Confederation debates, a number of speakers railed against the existence of customs duties among the British North American colonies.[47] The denial to the provinces of the power to levy indirect taxes (along with section 121, discussed below), ensured that there would be no provincially imposed customs duties after Confederation.

The underlying ideas behind the allocation of taxation power under the Constitution were sound, even if the specific concepts used to implement them were flawed. The limits on provincial taxation power sought to internalize, to the extent possible, the burdens of provincial taxes, so that they would be incurred by members of the provincial political community imposing the tax, and not by outsiders. At the same time, the specific forms of tax denied to the provinces are those most likely to burden the flow of interprovincial trade. A particular fiscal barrier to trade might seem appealing to a provincial legislature, based on the in-province interests it might serve. However, the cumulative effect of provincially imposed tariffs would be likely to harm the country as a whole, depriving it of the gains from interprovincial trade that would otherwise exist. The allocation of taxation power thus responds directly to the collective action problem discussed above. It is a core feature of the economic Constitution that reflects the commitment to free internal trade.

The effectiveness of the Constitution in achieving negative economic integration through the division of powers depends largely on the exclusivity principle. The move in recent decades toward a more flexible conception of the division of powers, in addition to being inconsistent with the text of the Constitution, also threatens mechanisms of negative economic integration that are central to the economic vision of the Constitution. In chapters 9 and 10, I will address the question of how the important purposes supported by exclusivity are best balanced with the pragmatic impulse to allow for some limited jurisdictional overlap.

Stand-Alone Constitutional Protections for Free Trade

In addition to the negative integration provided for by the division of powers, the Constitution also contains other, more direct protections for free internal trade. The most significant such provision is section 121, which states: "All Articles of the Growth, Produce, or Manufacture of any one of the Provinces shall, from and after the Union, be admitted free into each of the other Provinces."[48] The ordinary meaning of this provision would seem to be that goods should be admitted without restrictions. Notably, the words of section 121 do not limit the scope of the restrictions on trade that it prohibits.

Section 121 is contained in Part VIII of the Constitution Act, 1867, the title of which is "Revenues; Debts; Assets; Taxation." Part VIII contains an assortment of provisions dealing with fiscal matters. It might be inferred from this that section 121 is primarily concerned with prohibiting inter-provincial customs duties. As I have previously argued, however, limiting the meaning of the provision based on the title of Part VIII would not be consistent with the principles of statutory interpretation that were

accepted at the time of Confederation.[49] Moreover, the location of
section 121 within this part sends a mixed signal at best. The simplest
explanation for the location of section 121 in Part VIII is that there was
no other part of the Constitution that would have been a better fit.
Section 121 undoubtedly deals in part with fiscal barriers to trade like
customs duties.

The meaning of the phrase "admitted free" is the key to understanding section 121. On this point, the legislative context of the provision
matters. Pre-Confederation statutes providing for free trade among
British North American colonies used language that closely mirrored
section 121, with one important difference. The pre-Confederation
statutes required that goods be admitted "free from duty" rather than
simply being "admitted free."[50] The historical context, in turn, reinforces
the significance of the absence of "from duty" from section 121. As the
historian Andrew Smith has explained, non-tariff trade barriers erected
by the United States were a major public policy challenge in the years
leading up to Confederation.[51] For example, goods were detained at the
border for long periods of time, even though they were not subject to
tariffs. Given that it was well understood at the time that trade could be
restricted not only through tariffs but also through regulatory measures,
the absence of the "from duty" qualifier appears significant. When
section 121 provides that goods will be "admitted free," it serves to restrict
not only customs duties or tariffs but also other forms of trade barriers.

In the *Comeau* case, the Supreme Court clarified that, in addition
to tariffs, section 121 also prohibits non-fiscal regulatory measures that
restrict trade in a manner analogous to tariffs.[52] This was in spite of
older case law suggesting the provision only prohibited tariffs.[53] The
extension of section 121 to include non-tariff trade barriers was undoubtedly a positive development, in that it precludes governments from
doing indirectly what they cannot do directly. In my view, the difficult
question in interpreting section 121 is not so much whether it extends
to non-tariff trade barriers, but rather how demanding the judicial
scrutiny of trade barriers should be. It simply cannot be the case that any
regulatory measure that burdens trade in any way is unconstitutional, no
matter how minor or incidental the burden. Such an approach would
seriously undermine provincial autonomy within areas of provincial
jurisdiction. At the same time, though, the text and purpose of section
121 have to be given meaningful effect. For instance, barriers to trade
that discriminate against out-of-province goods are inconsistent with
section 121, and should be held to be unconstitutional unless justified
according to reasonably demanding criteria.[54]

In its decision in *Comeau*, the Supreme Court adopted a highly permissive approach to assessing trade barriers under section 121, one that essentially mirrors a division of powers analysis on a flexible approach to federalism. According to the Court, a trade barrier is only inconsistent with section 121 if its primary purpose is to restrict inter-provincial trade, and if it is not rationally connected to a larger statutory scheme serving a valid legislative objective.[55] Ironically enough, on this approach, customs duties at a provincial border could conceivably be upheld as long as they were rationally connected to a valid statutory scheme otherwise within provincial jurisdiction (though they would still likely be invalid as an indirect tax).[56] I argue in chapter 10 that the Supreme Court's unduly permissive approach to section 121 is misguided, serving to further undermine an economic vision already threatened by the move away from the principle of exclusivity in the division of powers.

The Court's conflation of section 121 with a division of powers analysis does highlight an important feature of the constitutional structure: with respect to both fiscal and non-fiscal trade barriers, section 121 overlaps considerably with the restrictions against provincially enacted trade barriers created by the division of powers. An interprovincial tariff would be an indirect tax, and thus presumptively ultra vires the provinces (unless it could be upheld as an incidental or ancillary feature of an otherwise valid statutory scheme under a modern "flexible" approach to the division of powers). Similarly, a regulatory measure intended to restrict interprovincial trade would be presumptively ultra vires the provinces since it would relate in pith and substance to interprovincial trade (again, subject to more flexible approaches that would allow such a measure to be upheld as an incidental or ancillary feature of a larger statutory scheme). Indeed, for most of Canada's constitutional history, provincially enacted trade barriers were kept in check primarily by the division of powers, leaving relatively little room for section 121.

The question of how section 121 should relate to the restrictions against trade barriers provided for by the division of powers is addressed more fully later. Regardless of the specifics of constitutional construc-tion, the very existence of section 121 is an important marker of the purposes underlying the Constitution. Section 121 is one of only a few independent restrictions on the legislative powers allocated to Parlia-ment or provincial legislatures in the Constitution Act, 1867. The act contains hardly any other provisions that directly restrict what can be done in policy terms, as opposed to allocating jurisdiction and setting up procedures for governance.[57] This fact should serve to underline just how important economic integration and free trade are within the scheme of the Constitution.

There are other constitutional provisions that restrict trade barriers, though none as significant as section 121. Sections 122 and 123 were transitional provisions intended to immediately lower trade barriers from the time of Confederation. Section 122 provided that pre-Confederation customs and excise laws applicable to international goods would continue in force until they were altered by Parliament. Section 123, in turn, provided that where the customs or excise had been paid on goods in one province, they would receive credit for those payments if they were then later moved to another province. Thus section 123 served to lower interprovincial trade barriers from the time of Confederation, even before Parliament enacted uniform customs and excise laws for the new dominion. Again, this feature serves to reinforce the priority the Constitution accorded to the objective of free internal trade.

Certain constitutional provisions adopted after 1867 also reflect a commitment to negative economic integration. Section 92A of the Constitution Act, 1867, incorporated in 1982, clarified and expanded provincial jurisdiction over natural resources. However, the provision also included important restrictions on the power of provinces to burden the flow of interprovincial trade in natural resources. Section 92A(1) allocates exclusive jurisdiction to the provinces over the exploration, development, management, and conservation of natural resources.[58] Section 92A(2) provides that provinces may make laws in relation to the export of natural resources from the province, but it then limits this power in an important way, stating that "such laws may not authorize or provide for discrimination in prices or in supplies exported to another part of Canada."[59] Similarly, section 92A(4) provides for provincial taxation of natural resources, subject to the requirement that "such laws may not authorize or provide for taxation that differentiates between production exported to another part of Canada and production not exported from the province."[60] Together, these restrictions prevent provinces from adopting measures that are directed toward burdening the flow of trade in natural resource products, either through fiscal or non-fiscal means. In this sense, they are consistent with the vision of economic integration reflected elsewhere in the Constitution Act, 1867.

The mobility rights provided for in section 6 of the Charter also deserve mention.[61] While obviously not part of the Constitution Act, 1867, this provision does address a gap that previously existed in the constitutional regime providing for negative economic integration. While section 121 and the division of powers provided for free trade in goods, the rights of individuals to move and work across the country were not clearly protected. Section 6(2), which relates to internal mobility, provides: "Every citizen of Canada and every person who has the status of a permanent resident of Canada has the right (a) to move to and take up residence in any province; and (b) to pursue the gaining of a livelihood in any province."[62] Section 6(2)(b), which addresses the gaining of a livelihood in other provinces, seems to serve an economic purpose relating to economic integration, though unfortunately this is something the Supreme Court denied in its leading decision dealing with section 6.[63] I will argue in chapter 10 that the Court's reasoning in that case is symptomatic of a broader failure of judges to understand and appreciate the economic structure of the Constitution.

Conclusion

The Constitution's commitment to negative economic integration and free trade is manifested in both the exclusive nature of federal economic powers and in stand-alone protections for free trade, like section 121. These structural features of the Constitution give effect to the unanimous expectation of the framers that Confederation would lower barriers to trade within Canada. As with the other features of the economic constitution, the commitment to free trade is not without limits. The scope of the commitment to free trade is framed by the text of the Constitution, as well as countervailing principles of the economic constitution, in particular the commitment to local autonomy and subsidiarity. The question of how best to reconcile these competing principles will be addressed in chapters 9 and 10. Before that, however, I will seek to establish the continuing relevance of the economic vision of Constitution. It is to that subject that I now turn.

Continuity and Change
in the Economic Constitution

Canada's Living Constitutional Order

Up to this point, the primary focus has been on the economic vision reflected in the text of the Constitution Act, 1867. Yet a constitutional order consists of much more than just a text and its original purposes. The Constitution has been a site of political, economic, and legal contestation since its enactment, a process that has helped to shape the governance structures established by the text. At the same time, the country has obviously undergone significant social, political, and economic changes since Confederation. The development of the constitutional order by legal and political actors, combined with changed circumstances, may lead one to doubt the continuing relevance of the economic vision reflected in the text. The purpose of this chapter is to address these doubts. I argue that the basic elements of the Constitution's economic vision remain relevant today, in spite of the development and change over the past century and a half.

For most of Canada's history, there has been a remarkable fidelity to the economic vision of the Constitution, on the part of both courts and political actors. The commitments to secure property rights, local autonomy and subsidiarity, national economic integration, and free internal trade have been consistent themes, even as the constitutional order changed and developed over time. As I argue below, it is only in the past few decades that courts have begun to lose touch with this vision. Moreover, while some of the normative foundations of the economic vision have shifted, its basic features are broadly supported by Canadians. The economic vision thus retains its relevance, even on a progressive or "living tree" approach to constitutional interpretation.

In this chapter, I track some of the key developments in the constitutional order that have been brought about by both the courts and political actors, seeking to identify elements of continuity and change in how the Constitution structures economic relations. While of course much has changed since the enactment of the Constitution Act, 1867, the basic governance structures it established have largely been upheld over time. In other words, the text of the Constitution, which has been the focus of the analysis up to this point, is not a mere historical artifact. The text has provided the structure for a living constitutional order that reflects the economic vision of the Constitution.

Judicial Interpretation of the Economic Constitution

From the time of Confederation until 1949, the Privy Council in London was the final court of appeal for Canada.[1] It has long been acknowledged that the decisions of the Privy Council in federalism cases tended to favour the provinces.[2] In the mid-twentieth century, however, a group of English-Canadian academics made a much stronger claim, arguing that the Privy Council's interpretation of the division of powers was fundamentally inconsistent with the centralist vision of the framers as reflected in the text of the Constitution.[3] Those arguments have been re-evaluated in recent decades. Work by Alan Cairns, Paul Romney, Peter Hogg and Wade Wright, among others, argues that those mid-century English-Canadian academics greatly overstated the case.[4] There was in fact a great deal of continuity between the federal structure envisaged by the framers and the federation that emerged through the interpretation of the Privy Council.

As I argued in chapter 3, the Constitution is strongly committed to principles of local autonomy and subsidiarity. The arguments in that chapter help to establish that there was no fundamental disjunct between the Constitution as enacted and the relatively decentralized federation reflected in the Privy Council's decisions. Indeed, even the most controversial aspects of the Privy Council's federalism jurisprudence favouring the provinces – its narrow reading of the federal peace, order, and good government (POGG) and trade and commerce powers – were within the scope of interpretive discretion afforded by the text when read in its context and according to its underlying purposes. The limited and residual nature of the federal peace, order, and good government power is clearly indicated in the text of section 91, which expressly excludes all heads of provincial power from its ambit and only gives priority ("notwithstanding anything in this Act") to enumerated federal powers, not the POGG power.[5]

Similarly, the scope of the federal trade and commerce power was appropriately limited by the exclusive provincial power over property and civil rights, a term which was properly read in light of Canada's constitutional history to encompass the full range of private law.[6] While the Privy Council may have been overly restrictive in denying any ability to regulate intraprovincial trade as an incidental or ancillary feature of regulations directed at interprovincial and international trade, the fundamental thrust of its approach was grounded in the text of the Constitution as read in its historical context and according to its original purposes.

The Privy Council did affirm federal jurisdiction in the subjects essential to the economic vision of the Constitution, including with respect to interprovincial transportation and communication and financial institutions.[7] While strongly emphasizing aspects of the Constitution that promote local autonomy, the Privy Council's decisions were consistent with the overall economic vision, which includes federal jurisdiction over interprovincial and international economic relations, as well as systemic and structural features of the national economy. Importantly, the Privy Council's federalism jurisprudence adhered closely to the principle of jurisdictional exclusivity, a linchpin of the Constitution's economic vision.[8] Exclusivity protects local autonomy and upholds the principle of subsidiarity, while at the same time placing restrictions on provincial measures that impede interprovincial trade or interfere with federal regulation of systemic and structural features of the national economy. The Privy Council's fidelity to jurisdictional exclusivity aligned with an economic vision that protects local control while simultaneously promoting economic integration and free internal trade.

In other areas of public law as well, legal developments from London affirmed the principles of the economic Constitution. The House of Lords was the highest court in the United Kingdom during the time when Privy Council appeals were heard from Canada, and its judicial personnel overlapped considerably with the Privy Council. Decisions of the House of Lords on matters of common law were closely followed in Canada at this time. The Lords generally developed common law doctrine in ways that reinforced the security of property rights. The landmark 1920 decision in *Attorney-General v. De Keyser's Royal Hotel Limited*, in particular, firmly established that clear statutory language is required in order to authorize the taking of property without compensation.[9] This decision was in many ways the culmination of centuries of common law developments protecting property rights in a manner consistent with a parallel commitment to parliamentary supremacy. In limiting the scope of executive power to interfere with property rights, the decision in *De Keyser's Royal Hotel* reinforced the constitutional commitment to secure property rights. The decision also provided the basis for the Supreme Court of Canada's later jurisprudence dealing with "de facto" expropriation, discussed below.[10]

It is generally acknowledged that from 1949, when the Supreme Court of Canada became the final court of appeal in all matters, judicial decisions in federalism cases tended to allow more jurisdictional space for Parliament on economic issues. Both the federal trade and commerce power and the POGG power were given a more liberal interpretation. However, intrusions on provincial jurisdiction, particularly with respect to property and civil rights, were still policed with some rigour. As discussed in chapter 5, the expansion of federal authority after 1949 primarily related to matters – such as trademarks, competition law, and marine pollution – that are consistent with the constitutional principles of subsidiarity and with the general categories of Parliament's enumerated powers.

The Supreme Court continued to uphold the principle of jurisdictional exclusivity in the decades following the end of Privy Council appeals, while at the same time allowing for limited jurisdictional overlap where pragmatism and a purposive reading of federal and provincial powers seemed to require it. The Court's approach included allowance for ancillary intrusions closely connected with an otherwise valid statutory scheme, as well as the recognition of policy areas with a genuine "double aspect."[11] During this period, the Supreme Court formalized some of the features of jurisdictional exclusivity that had been underdeveloped by the Privy Council, including the concept of "interjurisdictional immunity," which identifies core features of one order of government's jurisdiction that cannot be affected by legislation from the other order of government, even if the intrusion is connected to a valid statutory scheme.[12]

The Supreme Court's jurisprudence did retain some aspects of apparent inconsistency with the economic vision that were inherited from the Privy Council. The Court's steadfast refusal to allow federal legislation to have secondary effects on intraprovincial trade, even when such effects were necessary to achieve a federal purpose relating to interprovincial trade, was a mistake. This approach unduly restrained the federal power to regulate interprovincial trade in the national interest.[13] While jurisdictional exclusivity is vital to the economic vision, a limited degree of jurisdictional overlap may be necessary for the effective exercise of certain heads of powers, including the power over interprovincial trade. In practical terms, it is difficult to regulate aspects of interprovincial trade without having any effect whatsoever on trade within the province. On this point, both the Privy Council and the Supreme Court were overly protective of provincial jurisdiction, to the point of undermining this important federal head of power. Broadly speaking, though, the Supreme Court's federalism jurisprudence in the decades following 1949 remained consistent with the economic vision of the Constitution.

In other areas, too, such as public law protections for property rights, the Supreme Court's jurisprudence affirmed the economic vision of the Constitution. For instance, the 1978 case of *Manitoba Fisheries Ltd. v. The Queen* may have been the high-water mark for property rights protections in the Supreme Court of Canada.[14] In that case, the Court required the government to pay compensation to affected parties after a statute nationalized the freshwater fishing industry. The statute in question had rendered valueless the business interests of participants in the freshwater fishing industry. The Court held that since legislation is presumed not to effect a taking of property rights without compensation, such a statute should be read to require compensation unless it indicates an intention *not* to compensate.[15] This decision reaffirmed the constitutional commitment to property rights and the limits on government interference with property in the absence of a clear statutory authorization, even while it acknowledged the existence of a statutory power to authorize uncompensated expropriation where a legislature clearly indicates an intent to do so.

Unwritten Principles of the Constitution

In recent decades, the Supreme Court has recognized a series of unwritten principles of the Canadian Constitution, some of which align with the economic vision of the Constitution. For instance, one of the earliest underlying principles of the Constitution that the Supreme Court recognized was the rule of law. The rule of law was recognized as an unwritten principle of the Constitution, in part, on the basis of the preamble's commitment to a constitution "similar in Principle to that of the United Kingdom."[16] In English legal history, the development of the rule of law was closely tied to secure protections for property rights, particularly protections against government interference.[17] From the perspective of the individual, a principal benefit of the rule of law is that government interference with one's liberty or property is constrained by predictable rules announced in advance.[18] Constraints of this nature create a predictable sphere of autonomy for the individual, allowing one to make plans for the future free from the threat of arbitrary interference.[19] Canadian courts have not yet explicitly acknowledged the connection between secure property rights and a "stable, predictable and ordered society" in which individuals can reliably plan their affairs, which the Supreme Court in the *Secession Reference* identified as the most basic guarantee of the rule of law.[20] However, doing so would be an appropriate extension of the principle of the rule of law, in keeping with its history and, as I have argued, the commitments in the text of the Constitution.

The Supreme Court has also recognized federalism as one of the underlying principles of the Constitution. Federalism "recognizes the diversity of the component parts of Confederation, and the autonomy of provincial governments to develop their societies within their respective spheres of jurisdiction."[21] The federal structure of the Constitution is said to assign power over a matter to the order of government "most suited to achieving the particular societal objective" associated with a subject, having regard to the country's diversity.[22] In recent years, the Court has gone further by also recognizing the principle of subsidiarity as a guide to constitutional interpretation.[23] Here as well, the Court's statements align with the economic vision, though as I will discuss in chapter 9, their actual decisions in recent years do not always reflect a strong adherence to it.

Besides these principles, the Court at one time recognized the principle of Canadian economic union as a guide to constitutional interpretation.[24] This position was most clearly endorsed in Justice La Forest's majority reasons in *Black v. Law Society of Alberta*, a 1989 case interpreting the section 6 guarantee of mobility rights under the Charter.[25] In drawing support for the importance of economic union to the Canadian constitutional order, Justice La Forest refers to the section 121 free trade clause as "one of the pillars of the Confederation scheme for achieving the economic union sought by the Fathers of Confederation."[26] Justice La Forest's inspired opinion in *Black* was undoubtedly the high point for the judicial recognition of the Constitution's commitment to an economic union.[27] Unfortunately, later developments in the Court's section 6 jurisprudence moved decisively away from recognizing the economic purposes reflected in that provision.[28] In the more recent *Comeau* decision dealing with section 121, the Court quoted approvingly from La Forest's discussion in *Black*, in which he identified economic union as a purpose of the Constitution.[29] Unfortunately, the narrow reading that the Court gave to section 121 did not seem to fully reflect this principle. As with other principles, the Court continues to refer to economic union, though the results do not necessarily align with that principle.

As a whole, the unwritten principles recognized by the courts in recent decades are consistent with, and are capable of encompassing, the elements of the economic vision outlined in this book. As I will describe in chapters 9 and 10, however, the Court's actual decisions in recent decades reveal an increasing lack of commitment to the economic vision of the Constitution.

Political Practice and the Economic Constitution

Canada's constitutional structure has not just been developed by the courts, of course, but also by political actors working within the structure set out in the Constitution Act, 1867. The developments led by politicians – including emergent political conventions and constitutional and quasi-constitutional changes – have largely served to reinforce the economic vision of the Constitution.

The trajectory of the federal disallowance and reservation powers provides an instructive example. These powers allowed the federal government to invalidate laws passed by a provincial legislative assembly. They remain in the text of the Constitution, though they have not been used for decades.

The disallowance and reservation powers were used dozens of times in the decades following Confederation to invalidate provincial laws.[30] On its face, this might seem to support the view that Canada was really intended to be a centralized federation, in which provincial authority existed at the sufferance of the federal government. However, when one digs deeper into the federal government's disallowance and reservation decisions, they tell another story.

In the vast majority of cases, the federal government's stated reason for exercising its disallowance or reservation power was that the provincial law in question was unconstitutional, in most cases on the basis that it infringed the federal Parliament's jurisdiction over economic subjects.[31] A brief review of the disallowed laws reveals that the federal government's constitutional concerns had a genuine basis in most cases and were not merely pretextual. For instance, the federal government disallowed laws that attempted to regulate interprovincial and international railways, steamships, trade, and the banking sector.[32] In other words, the disallowance and reservation powers were not used as a plenary federal authority to influence the exercise of law-making within areas of provincial jurisdiction. On the contrary, the federal government generally felt the need to justify the exercise of these powers in *constitutional* terms.[33] According to the governments that exercised these powers, they were being used to uphold the constitutional order, including the division of powers reflected in the Constitution Act, 1867, not to undermine it. If one starts from the premise that courts do not have a monopoly on constitutional interpretation, a view that would have been more common in the nineteenth century than today, the federal government's self-restrained use of these powers can be understood to be consistent with the constitutional division of powers.

The justifications offered by the federal government for the use of the reservation and disallowance powers reveal a significant degree of commitment to the legitimacy of the division of powers. If the division of powers had not been viewed as legitimate and binding in some sense, there presumably would have been no need for the federal government to justify its use of these powers in constitutional terms. The federal government has not invalidated a provincial law under its reservation or disallowance powers since 1943.[34] Since that time, the courts have exercised an effective monopoly on policing the division of powers. Yet, even before the 1940s, federal political actors apparently felt constrained by the legitimacy of the division of powers in exercising what was on its face a purely discretionary power to strike down provincial laws.

Political actors also helped to reinforce the economic constitution in other ways. Assertive provincial governments aggressively occupied the full extent of their jurisdiction over matters connected to "property and civil rights," and federal governments have largely been ambivalent about challenging provincial authority in these domains.[35] Yet, at the same time, Parliament generally sought to occupy the most important domains of economic regulation under its jurisdiction, including with respect to banking; interprovincial and international trade, transportation, and communication; and, somewhat belatedly, bankruptcy.[36]

The growth of federal transfers to the provinces, from relatively ad hoc measures to permanent features of the federation, also deserves mention. Equalization payments to provinces with lower fiscal capacity, in particular, have become strongly entrenched as a matter of political practice. Equalization now also enjoys some level of constitutional recognition, in the form of section 36 of the Constitution Act, 1982, though it is at best ambiguous whether the terms of that provision create a legally enforceable federal obligation to provide equalization payments.[37] While there has undoubtedly been a shift over time in the nature and scope of federal transfers, they have not altered the fundamental commitments of the economic constitution. Using federal fiscal capacity to stabilize provincial budgets and enhance national solidarity is consistent with the normative commitments of the economic constitution, especially if the transfers are unconditional. As long as the federal spending power is not used to effectively coerce or unduly influence provincial action in areas of provincial jurisdiction, federal transfers are not out of line with the essential features of the economic constitution.

Constitutional Amendment and the Economic Constitution

Constitutional and quasi-constitutional developments since Confederation have in some cases extended the economic vision of the Constitution, or at least remained consistent with it. The constitutional amendment granting federal jurisdiction over unemployment insurance is a notable example.[38] From the perspective of the individual, unemployment insurance is a form of insurance against risk and thus would naturally seem to fall under provincial jurisdiction over insurance markets.[39] However, from the perspective of the national economy as a whole, unemployment insurance serves another function, as a macroeconomic stabilizer that maintains household spending power during difficult economic times.[40] The federal government is best positioned to provide this service because it can draw upon the economic base of the entire country rather than potentially-more-volatile local economies. The amendment recognizing federal jurisdiction over unemployment insurance fits with the theme of federal jurisdiction over systemic and structural features of the national economy, including macroeconomic stability. The historical context of the amendment, coming in the aftermath of the Great Depression, reinforces the connection between this power and systemic economic considerations.[41]

A constitutional amendment also granted a non-exclusive federal power over old-age pensions.[42] The case for federal pensions similarly rests on the broader and less volatile economic base that the federal government can draw upon, providing a more credible commitment to future pensioners than would generally be possible for a provincial government subject to local economic fluctuations. A national pension scheme also facilitates interprovincial labour mobility through the portability of pension obligations, though, as the example of the Quebec Pension Plan shows, there are other ways to achieve that mobility.

The human rights protections enacted in the twentieth century were also at least consistent with the economic vision, and in some cases, they affirmed important aspects of it. The 1960 Canadian Bill of Rights sought to protect a range of fundamental rights, notably including property rights.[43] While the Charter famously failed to protect property rights, this was not so much a rejection of the *importance* of property rights as an expression of the desire of the provinces to maintain the full scope of their jurisdiction over economic matters.[44] Property rights were included in the federal government's early drafts of the Charter, but they were later removed as part of the process of building a consensus among the provinces.[45] The exclusion of property protections from the Charter is arguably best understood as a decision to favour one aspect of the economic constitution (local governance autonomy and subsidiarity) over another – namely, the commitment to secure property rights.[46] That said, even though property rights were left out of the Charter, the constitutional settlement of 1982 left in place the common law, constitutional, and quasi-constitutional protections for property discussed in chapter 2. While courts engaged in constitutional interpretation must respect the legislative choice to leave property rights out of the Charter, it is important not to overstate the significance of this exclusion. Canadian constitutional law still reflects a commitment to secure property rights, even if that commitment takes a form other than an entrenched individual right to property.

The final version of the Charter mostly focused on rights whose primary content and justification were non-economic, such as criminal procedural protections, fundamental personal freedoms, and equality rights. That said, some rights, such as the section 6 mobility rights, have an overt economic dimension. Section 6 expressly protects the right of citizens and permanent residents "to pursue the gaining of a livelihood in any province," subject to the authority of provinces to regulate professions in a manner that does not discriminate based on province of current or previous residence.[47] The provision provides for an important economic right connected to economic integration: the right to earn a livelihood in any province. At the same time, it seeks to reconcile the right with local regulatory authority by stating the right is subject to "any laws or practices of general application in force in a province other than those that discriminate among persons primarily on the basis of province of present or previous residence."[48] The requirement for non-discriminatory treatment is a commonly used tool in both domestic and international law for reconciling local regulation with trade and mobility protections.[49] Within the context of section 6, it reflects the parallel commitments to local autonomy, on the one hand, and national economic integration, on the other.

Section 92A of the Constitution Act, 1867, which was enacted along with the Charter, similarly reinforces the economic vision of the Constitution.[50] It affirms provincial control over natural resources, while at the same time seeking to protect interprovincial economic relations by prohibiting provinces from engaging in discriminatory treatment of out-of-province regions to which natural resources may be exported. This provision, too, reflects an intention to reconcile local autonomy with protections for interprovincial trade and economic integration.

Continuity and Change

Of course, much has changed in Canadian society since 1867. Perhaps most notable for the economic structure of Confederation has been the growth of the administrative and welfare state. A vast bureaucracy at the federal and provincial levels regulates economic activity to a far greater degree than was the case in 1867. Moreover, the growth in transfers to individuals has extended the role of government in ways that may not have been foreseeable at Confederation. Yet these changes do not necessarily conflict with the economic vision as outlined in the previous chapters. Indeed, they reflect the adaptability of the governance structures established by the Constitution, subject to important limits. Provincial taxation, spending, and economic regulation are manifestations of local governance autonomy. These provincial powers can be exercised to regulate economic activity and support individual residents while still respecting the largely procedural protections for property rights, as well as limits on interfering with areas of federal jurisdiction. Federal regulatory regimes and social programs within areas of federal jurisdiction similarly pose no inherent threat to the economic vision, though, as I have previously identified, the coercive use of the federal spending power in areas of provincial jurisdiction may raise legitimate concerns for local autonomy.

Remarkably, despite the significant changes over the past century and a half, the basic elements of the economic vision of the Constitution remain relevant. Property rights continue to be of foundational importance to the social and economic life of the country, though of course they are subject to extensive regulation, mainly by provincial and local governments.[51] Regional differences across this vast country continue to point to the need for significant local autonomy, not only on the part of provinces, but also territories and Indigenous nations. At the same time, there is significant economic integration across provincial lines, with a strong, cross-party consensus in favour of even freer interprovincial trade.[52]

Despite the continuing relevance of the economic vision of the Constitution, however, courts in recent years have started to lose touch with it. This trend, discussed in the final chapters of the book, includes a number of interrelated developments. Firstly, courts have attempted to move away from an adherence to jurisdictional exclusivity in federalism cases. This move has made the local autonomy of provinces and municipalities increasingly vulnerable to federal incursions, while simultaneously undermining the protections for interjurisdictional trade and economic integration that are provided by the exclusive nature of federal powers. The judicial trend away from jurisdictional exclusivity is flatly at odds with the text of the Constitution, as well as its underlying economic vision. Interestingly, the Supreme Court's stance on jurisdictional exclusivity has exhibited a kind of ambivalence, with the Court in some cases adopting the full-throated rhetoric of flexible federalism, while in others recoiling from following through on those ideas, since doing so would unravel important aspects of the current political and economic order of the country.[53]

Other recent legal developments have tended to undermine the economic vision as well. In recent years, courts have adopted a narrow understanding of constitutional protections for interprovincial labour mobility and trade, in particular section 6 of the Charter and section 121 of the Constitution Act, 1867.[54] The judicial reading down of these express constitutional protections reflects the diminished place of the economic vision in judicial thinking. At the same time, courts have weakened protections for property rights in constitutional, quasi-constitutional, and common law doctrines. Section 53 of the Constitution Act, 1867, which requires that taxation measures originate in the House of Commons, has been found not to apply to revenue-generating charges linked to a regulatory scheme, and to permit quite broad delegation of taxing powers to the executive.[55] Furthermore, common law protections against "de facto" expropriation, which were developed into robust form by the Supreme Court in the 1970s and the 1980s, were effectively neutered by the Supreme Court's 2006 decision in

CPR v. Vancouver.[56] Following the CPR decision, government actions could potentially deprive an owner of all of the tangible benefits of property ownership and still not trigger a presumptive entitlement to compensation.

Conclusion

While courts and political decision-makers have mostly remained faithful to the economic Constitution, at least until recent decades, it may still be argued that this economic vision is out of line with contemporary values. In the next chapter, I will outline a justification for the economic vision of the Constitution that is based on values and ideals that have broad resonance within contemporary Canadian society. While some of the grounds of justification for the economic Constitution may have shifted to varying degrees over the course of Canada's history, I argue that there is a strong case for our continued adherence to its basic features.

Justifying the Economic Vision in the Twenty-First Century

Centralization and Decentralization

This book seeks to argue that the economic vision of the Constitution is not just a subject of historical interest. In the previous chapter, I sought to establish the continuity between the governance structures envisaged by the text of the Constitution and the living constitutional order that has emerged over the past century and a half. In this chapter, I aim to show how the economic Constitution can be justified in terms that are aligned with contemporary values and commitments. The economic vision retains its relevance and can serve as the basis for a renewed understanding of the Constitution that responds to the policy challenges of today.

So far, I have argued that there are essentially two broad themes to the economic vision of the Constitution. First, there are the elements that promote decentralization of economic decision-making – namely, the commitments to the security of property, on the one hand, and local governance autonomy and subsidiarity, on the other. Second, there are elements that tend to promote centralization and economic integration, including the commitments to economic integration and free internal trade.

While each element remains relevant today, the specific justifications for the decentralizing features of the economic Constitution have arguably shifted and expanded over time. The arguments for decentralized decision-making that are most likely to resonate with Canadians today differ to some extent from those that would have been broadly accepted in 1867. New arguments have emerged, including a more pluralistic understanding of the justification for property rights, and a greater appreciation for the importance of the diverse values of local communities in government decision-making. By contrast, the basic justification for the centralizing features of the economic constitution has remained remarkably constant over time, even if our understanding of the implications of these arguments has evolved – for instance, with respect to the regulation of pollution that affects other jurisdictions. In what follows, I address the justifications for the decentralizing and centralizing features of the economic constitution in turn, including how the justifications have shifted over time. Ultimately, I seek to show that the economic constitution continues to present a compelling normative vision for Canada in the twenty-first century.

Expanding Justifications of Property and Contemporary Property Pluralism

At the time of Confederation, there were essentially two leading justifications for property rights, each of which informed the constitutional commitment to the security of property. The first justification was based on natural rights to property, particularly as they were conceptualized in the work of John Locke.[1] As Janet Ajzenstat has persuasively argued, the framers were strongly influenced by Lockean ideas, including the claim that property is grounded in natural rights which governments exist to protect.[2]

A separate argument (though one also present in Locke's work, to some degree)[3] holds that secure property rights create incentives to produce and improve resources.[4] Parties are more likely to work and invest when they have a secure claim to resources, leading to greater societal welfare in societies in which property rights are protected. For example, you would be more likely to sow seeds today if you were reasonably secure in knowing that you would be able to exclude others from harvesting the crop in the future. By creating incentives of this nature, property rights lead to greater productivity and, ultimately, prosperity. This argument, present in classic texts in law and political economy, including William Blackstone's *Commentaries on the Law of England* and Adam Smith's *Wealth of Nations*, would also have been familiar to informed contemporaries of Confederation.[5] Arguments based on natural rights to property and property's role in promoting economic prosperity are likely the two most significant arguments that would have been understood to justify a commitment to secure property rights in mid-nineteenth-century British North America. And indeed, these lines of argument are both represented in the Confederation debates.[6]

Property rights are arguably just as fundamental to the political and economic order of contemporary Canadian society as they were in 1867, yet the range of accepted justifications for property rights has shifted and expanded. The idea of natural rights in property no longer has the same degree of acceptance, either among the public or among scholars, though arguments based on Lockean natural rights to property are still sometimes advanced.[7] Arguments for natural rights to property today are perhaps more often advanced in non-Lockean terms. For instance, the contemporary legal philosopher Jeremy Waldron has put forward an influential argument for a general right of individuals to acquire and own property.[8] The essence of the argument is that property rights are an important aspect of individual well-being, and so property ownership should be available to all.[9] This argument stands in contrast to Lockean arguments for natural rights to property, which seek to justify the rights of particular owners to particular resources. In emphasizing the general nature of the right to property, this approach justifies property institutions that are available to all, rather than seeking to establish the inviolability of the rights of the present ownership class.

Economic justifications for property rights remain highly influential, though those that hold sway today are broader and more nuanced than before. In addition to arguments about incentives to work and produce, contemporary economic justifications for property also include the idea that property rights create incentives to avoid the overuse of resources. By internalizing the costs and benefits of parties' behaviour, property rights can help avoid a "tragedy of the commons."[10] Exclusive rights to particular resources help align parties' incentives to look after the long-term value of the resource, whether it is land, housing, fish, or something else.[11] For instance, you will be less likely to put too many sheep in the pasture if the pasture belongs to you, as opposed to being open to anyone. However, it is worth noting that the property rights in question need not necessarily be individual rights. Exclusive property rights held by defined communities can also facilitate effective resource management under the right circumstances.[12] The exclusive nature of the community's property rights is still vital, though, ensuring that access is limited to community members committed to the governance rules laid down by the group.[13]

Other economic justifications for property have gained acceptance in recent years. For instance, owners can often draw upon widely dispersed local knowledge in making decisions about their resource. Given the importance of local knowledge to effective resource-based decision-making, this can lead to better decisions and better outcomes than more centralized resource management systems, according to a range of criteria.[14] Parties "on the ground" are often better placed to make decisions about resources, and a property system with widely distributed interests provides a means of achieving that decentralized decision-making. Importantly, as with the newer arguments about solving collective action problems in resource management, the local knowledge argument does not necessarily require strict adherence to the model of individual ownership. Collective property interests held by members of a local community can also effectively channel local knowledge, at least under the right institutional circumstances.[15] The collective property interest of an Indigenous community in its traditional lands, for instance, can enable that community to make decisions about those lands based on locally held knowledge. Along with local governance powers, discussed below, the proprietary interests of Indigenous communities are a means of enabling local decision-making, an important corrective against the undue centralization of power in Indigenous affairs bureaucracies that took place in the nineteenth and twentieth centuries.[16]

There has also been a proliferation of other theories justifying property rights in recent decades, some of them new and others renewed interpretations of past work. For instance, arguments have been advanced based on individuals' personal connection to certain objects of property. Property interests closely connected to one's personal identity, or indeed, to the collective identity of a community such as an Indigenous nation, are said to deserve special legal protection on this approach.[17] This line of arguments may serve to justify special protection for a family home, for instance, or the traditional lands of an Indigenous community. There has also been renewed interest in Aristotelian arguments for property, based on the view that appropriately calibrated property systems can create conditions that promote virtue and human flourishing.[18] These approaches often tend to emphasize the idea that property involves both rights and social obligations.[19] Accordingly, they point toward a conception of property that is "progressive" and attentive to the needs and interests of non-owners.[20] The connection between property and autonomy has also received renewed attention in recent years. Property rights are said to form part of a sphere of autonomy for the individual.[21] Secure protections for individual property rights thus enhance an individual's liberty interests. Moreover, under the right circumstances, collectively held property can also facilitate the collective autonomy of distinctive groups, including Indigenous communities.[22]

As I have argued elsewhere, the best position today may be that property rights are justified on multiple, overlapping grounds that reflect the pluralistic normative commitments of contemporary societies.[23] There simply is no single theory of property that justifies the institution in all settings. Yet the diverse property theories outlined above do still overlap in identifying certain core features of property. Each of these accounts of property serves to justify an institution that decentralizes decision-making about resources in important ways. While there is certainly some disagreement about the proper scope of owner autonomy, these approaches each relate to an institution that puts a broad range of decision-making authority in the hands of a dispersed pool of owners. Property serves to decentralize decision-making about resources, which is particularly important in a large and diverse country.

It should be emphasized that the core, overlapping features of these contemporary accounts of property do not require that property rights be absolute or immune from regulation, modification, and even expropriation under a fair process within democratic political communities. However, all leading accepted justifications for property require that the rights in question be reasonably secure under normal circumstances. Property simply cannot fulfill its diverse functions – enhancing economic efficiency, promoting individual and collective autonomy, creating conditions for human flourishing, or protecting personal connections to objects of property – if owners live perpetually under the threat of arbitrary or unexpected interference with their rights.

In the twenty-first century, the constitutional commitment to the security of property rights is best understood in light of this pluralistic understanding of the justifications for property. As discussed in the next chapter, however, even on this broader understanding of the relevant justifications, Canadian courts have lost touch with the significance of secure property rights under our constitutional order.

A constitutional commitment to secure property rights is not necessarily a threat to the supremacy of legislatures. In the Canadian constitutional order, the protections that exist for property are aligned with the ultimate supremacy of the legislative branch. These protections include requirements for clear statutory language authorizing an expropriation, including regulations that are so far-reaching that they amount to a de facto expropriation; a presumptive right to compensation in the event of a de facto or de jure expropriation, unless there is statutory language to the contrary; requirements for fair procedures where property rights are infringed, subject to statutory language indicating those procedural requirements do not apply; and the requirement that taxation and spending measures be approved by the elected representatives of the people. Even on a robust understanding of these protections, they do not undermine the ultimate authority of the legislature to limit property rights based on democratically elected legislators' conception of the common good. The commitment to secure property rights is presumptive rather than mandatory and must yield when the legislature determines that another aspect of the public interest should take priority.

Justifications for Local Autonomy and Subsidiarity

Like the arguments for secure property rights, accepted justifications for the constitutional commitment to local autonomy and subsidiarity have also expanded since Confederation. Indeed, the term subsidiarity itself would likely not have been familiar to contemporaries of Confederation. The idea of subsidiarity grew out of Catholic social thought and only came to prominence in constitutional theory in the twentieth century, in part due to its adoption as part of the law of the European Union.[24] However, as recently noted by Dwight Newman, John Stuart Mill's 1861 work, *Considerations on Representative Government*, contains arguments that foreshadow some aspects of contemporary theories of subsidiarity.[25] Mill writes, "[i]t is but a small portion of the public business of a country which can be well done or safely attempted by the central authorities."[26] His reasons for making this claim include the greater local experience and knowledge wielded by local authorities, as well as the role that experience in local government can have in the formation of responsible and informed citizens.[27] As I have previously noted, there is some evidence that Mill's *Considerations on Representative Government*, written on the eve of Confederation by a prominent political economist, did have some influence on the framers.[28]

Yet, despite making some points in favour of local control, Mill's overall argument tends to favour governance that contemporary Canadian constitutional scholars would regard as relatively centralized. Mill views local governments as being principally suited to implementing policy directions emanating from the centre.[29] He points to the supposedly superior intellectual abilities of those working in the central government, and the greater ability of a central authority to ensure the uniform application of legal principles throughout a state's territory.[30] Indeed, Mill's vision of the role of local government tends to align most clearly with the centralizing voices at Confederation, such as John A. Macdonald.[31]

The decentralized structure of the Canadian federation likely owes less to theoretical arguments about the virtues of local government than it does to the claims of particular political communities that had the clout and motivation to resist the centralizing impulses of Macdonald and others. Preeminent among those political communities, of course, was the future province Quebec. Francophone politicians hoped that the provincial government of Quebec would serve as a bulwark to maintain the distinctive language, religion, legal system, and culture of French Canada.[32] However, the inclination toward decentralization was not limited to the Québécois. Prominent Maritimers also resisted centralization in the name of local control based on distinctive local values and priorities, as did Upper Canadian Grits committed to the ideal of local democratic self-government.[33] Thus Canada's decentralized federal structure was primarily the result of a compromise among the founding political communities. However, in the twentieth and twenty-first centuries, a richer and broader theoretical understanding of the importance of local governance autonomy has emerged.[34]

Today, the subsidiarity principle in constitutional theory is seen to be grounded in a number of interrelated arguments. As discussed in previous chapters, subsidiarity simply means that more centralized authorities should have a subsidiary function, performing tasks that cannot effectively be performed at a more local level.[35] This yields a presumptive preference for local autonomy except where local decision-making is not reasonably effective. Subsidiarity can be defended on several distinct grounds: the value inherent in meaningful participation in the decisions that affect an individual and her community, which is more likely to be possible at the local level; the superior knowledge of local circumstances likely to be available to local decision-makers; superior awareness of local norms, law, and customs on the part of local decision-makers; the greater accountability that is possible when those making the decisions are part of the communities affected by those decisions; the greater ability of local decisions to take account of the distinctive values of local communities; and the ability of local institutions to reflect and embody the distinctive cultural identity of local communities.[36]

As with justifications for property, the normative appeal of local governance autonomy and subsidiarity rests on multiple overlapping grounds. Taken together, they amount to a presumptive case for decentralization, absent countervailing considerations requiring centralized decision-making for effective policymaking. Since local political communities in a pluralistic society tend to have diverse values and priorities, the justifications for centralization that can rebut the presumption of decentralization should ideally be grounded in interests that transcend local difference. To the extent possible, justifications for centralization should be based on universal or at least broadly applicable human interests. As I argue below, the categories of federal economic jurisdiction can be explained through principles of political economy that are rooted in enduring features of human nature and human interests. While perhaps not universal, these principles are capable of appealing to political communities whose normative commitments may vary considerably in other respects.

While the Canadian federation initially took on a decentralized structure largely to satisfy the demands of colonial political interests, particularly the French Canadians in Quebec, arguments for local autonomy today are advanced by a much broader range of political communities. These include provinces, such as Alberta and Saskatchewan, that did not exist as distinct polities at the time of Confederation but today arguably reflect a distinctive culture within Canada. Yet the arguments in favour of local autonomy and subsidiarity also extend to other political communities, including Indigenous nations. Canada has always been far more diverse than the framers were prepared to acknowledge in 1867. While Indigenous nations were not taken to be full participants in the broader nineteenth-century Canadian state, today the Canadian legal system continues to adapt to the demands of Indigenous self-government. As I argue in the next chapter, the principles reflected in the Constitution Act, 1867 provide a valuable model for structuring governance relations between a central government and diverse local political communities, including Indigenous nations.

It may be suggested that the Constitution's commitment to political decentralization should also extend to the jurisdiction of municipalities.[37] Municipalities are conventionally understood as creatures of the provinces, acting on the basis of authority delegated from the legislature. While Charter rights could indirectly protect the autonomy of municipalities in certain circumstances, any move to give robust constitutional recognition to municipal governments would likely require a constitutional amendment.[38] As discussed in chapter 3, the Constitution pursues the objective of local autonomy principally through the mechanism of the jurisdiction of provincial legislatures. While the role and significance of municipalities have undoubtedly grown since Confederation, a constitutional amendment protecting their jurisdiction would present complexities. For one thing, the nature and extent of the delegation of jurisdiction by a province to a municipality appropriately varies with context. The powers that make sense for Ontario (population 15 million) to delegate to the City of Toronto (population 2.8 million) will be different from the powers that Prince Edward Island (population 150,000) chooses to delegate to a rural municipality. A certain degree of flexibility is required in determining what powers a legislature should delegate. For all its potential flaws, the Constitution's current affirmation of plenary provincial jurisdiction over municipalities provides such flexibility.

A constitutional amendment protecting municipalities would limit, at least to some degree, legislatures' discretion to determine what forms of delegation are appropriate in the circumstances. A case could be made that the benefits of more secure municipal jurisdiction would not outweigh the costs due to lost policymaking flexibility. Nevertheless, it must be acknowledged that any move in the future to constitutionally entrench the status of municipalities would indeed be broadly consistent with the Constitution's underlying commitment to local autonomy and subsidiarity.

The Renewed Appreciation for Decentralized Decision-Making

The decentralized nature of the Canadian federation was highly fortuitous. Without the influence of Quebec, and, to a lesser extent, certain voices in the Maritimes and Ontario, Canada likely would have had a much more centralized structure, which would arguably have been maladapted to governing a culturally diverse transcontinental state. Interestingly, appreciation for decentralized decision-making has varied during the time since Confederation. While there was a broad commitment to secure property rights and local autonomy in 1867, that commitment tended to wane in the middle of the twentieth century, under the influence of what has been called "high-modernist ideology," favouring top-down, centralized planning.[39] During this time, there were glaring examples of overreach on the part of centralized authorities – such as the expropriation and complete removal of a historic Acadian community of 1,200 people to create a national park at Kouchibouguac, as well as the forced relocation of Inuit communities in the North – that would be all but inconceivable today.[40] It is fair to say that there has been a renewed understanding of the importance of decentralized decision-making in recent decades, though the grounds are somewhat different from those that would have been accepted in 1867, with respect to both property rights and local government.

Both property rights and local governance autonomy can be justified
on overlapping, pluralistic grounds that appeal to those holding a
relatively broad range of normative commitments. Notably, neither
form of decentralization is absolute. The security of property rights is
important, but property rights must yield to other interests related to
the common good where the people's elected representatives express
themselves clearly. Similarly, the commitment to local autonomy is
limited by the principle of subsidiarity, which provides for more centralized administration on matters where centralization is necessary for
governance to be effective. Of course, the question of when a matter
falls under federal jurisdiction is determined primarily by the text of the
Constitution. As I argue below, that text reflects a conception of effective decision-making that is grounded in basic principles of political
economy. It is to the justification of these centralizing features of the
Constitution that I now turn.

The Assumptions Underlying Centralization

The centralizing features of the economic constitution consist of two
categories: those that provide for positive integration by granting
authority to Parliament, and those that provide for negative integration
by restricting barriers to trade. Within the larger category of positive
integration, the grants of federal jurisdiction can be said to reflect two
distinct rationales. Firstly, federal jurisdiction tends to extend to subjects
in which polices in one locality significantly affect interests in others.
These include subjects in which measures can impose significant costs
on those in other jurisdictions (such as interprovincial and international
trade, transportation and communication, and fisheries), as well as subjects in which policies give rise to benefits that are not easily confined
to one jurisdiction (such as national defence, creative works protected
by copyright, and inventions protected by patents). Secondly, federal
jurisdiction tends to include subjects in which national coordination
is important, either because of significant benefits to standardization
(such as with respect to currency and weights and measures) or because
the qualitative nature of the subject matter requires a national policy
lens (such as with respect to competition law and the regulation of
systemic risk). At the same time, the Constitution provides for negative
integration by restricting the ability of provincial legislatures and other
local governments to enact laws in areas of exclusive federal jurisdiction,
while also setting out stand-alone protections for interprovincial trade
and mobility.

The justification for these centralizing features of the Constitution is grounded in some fairly basic arguments of political economy. The primary assumptions on which these arguments rest relate to enduring features of human nature. In particular, the arguments assume limited altruism and a degree of rationality in decision-making, such that parties' behaviour tends to be influenced by incentives.[41] Limited altruism simply means that parties tend to value their own interests ahead of those of others. Rationality in this context reflects the idea that the means adopted by parties tend to be intelligible in relation to their ends. Perfect rationality is not required for the arguments to work. The assumption is rather a weaker one to the effect that much of the time parties' conduct tends to respond to the incentives they face, based on those parties' desired ends.

Building on these behavioural assumptions grounded in human nature, the centralizing features of the Constitution are also supported by arguments about the gains associated with trade, both at the micro level of trade among individual parties, as well as at the macro level, with respect to larger trade flows among different regions. The most basic arguments for gains from trade are quite simple. Trade between two consenting parties will tend to make both parties better off than they otherwise would be, or else they would not both consent to the transaction.[42] While this argument may not hold true with respect to all transactions – for instance, where parties are not adequately informed or where their conduct is not rational – it does describe a fairly intuitive general tendency, one that is at the foundation of much of contemporary economic analysis. Trade also facilitates specialization through the division of labour.[43] Parties can specialize in producing goods and services they are relatively better at producing, while relying on trade for other goods and services.[44] This specialization increases the productivity of market participants.

With respect to trade flows among different regions, gains from trade derive from the differing comparative advantages of the regions. Each region is able to benefit from the relative advantages of the other through trade, ultimately making both regions better off.[45] If one region has an abundance of natural resources, and the other can produce manufactured goods relatively cheaply, then trade will increase productivity since each region can specialize in producing what it is relatively better at while relying on trade for access to other goods.

These arguments have been widely understood since at least the early nineteenth century.[46] There are circumstances in which the applicability of the arguments needs to be qualified, but as general tendencies, they retain widespread acceptance. In the twentieth century, the analysis of gains from trade was further refined by a better understanding of the role of transaction costs.[47] Mutually beneficial transactions will not proceed in cases where the costs of the transaction exceed the gains from trade. If a seller values a case of Alberta craft beer at ten dollars and a potential buyer in British Columbia values it at twenty-five dollars, the possible gains from trade from the transaction amount to fifteen dollars. But if the costs of completing the transaction exceed fifteen dollars, then the transaction will not go ahead. Some transaction costs might be difficult to avoid, like the costs of transportation. However, transaction costs could also include regulatory barriers, such as the costs associated with navigating the liquor regulation and distribution regime in British Columbia. (As it happens, Alberta craft beer is almost entirely unavailable in British Columbia, for reasons relating to the structure of liquor distribution regime in British Columbia.[48]) Since mutually beneficial transactions are welfare-enhancing almost by definition, lowering transaction costs tends to make all parties better off, other things being equal.

The concept of transaction costs allows for a more precise description of certain features of the economic constitution, particularly those that provide for national standardization. Standardization in certain areas, such as currency and banking, can reduce transaction costs, allowing more mutually beneficial, welfare-enhancing transactions to proceed. Sharing a currency with trading partners on the other side of the country lowers the costs of transacting with them, including the cost of buying and selling currency and the risk of a change in the exchange rate. The related concept of information costs is also useful. Information costs are the costs incurred to acquire information relevant to a transaction. Some aspects of standardization are best understood as reducing information costs. For instance, nationally standardized weights and measures can help lower the cost of acquiring information relevant to a transaction, which in turn facilitates trade.

The arguments justifying the centralizing features of the Constitution assume that politicians respond to incentives, just as any other economic actor would. For instance, provincial leaders will tend to prioritize interests within their province over those in other provinces since they are elected by in-province voters only. While the idea that government actors respond to incentives is an old one, the understanding of the role of incentives in government decision-making was enhanced in the twentieth century by the school of thought known as public choice theory. Public choice theory essentially builds upon economic behavioural assumptions, such as rationality and limited altruism, and applies them to government decision-making.[49] While this work has allowed for much more sophisticated modelling of political processes, the basic idea that government actors respond to incentives was already present in influential eighteenth- and nineteenth-century works dealing with constitutional design, including the *Federalist Papers* and Mill's *Considerations on Representative Government*.[50] Indeed, as I argue in the next section, several of the main centralizing features of the Constitution can be explained by arguments based on the differing incentives of political actors at the local and national levels.

Justifying Centralization in the Constitution

The justification for centralized decision-making over policies involving significant extrajurisdictional effects is relatively straightforward. Whenever a policy involves significant costs or benefits to those outside of a given jurisdiction, principles of political economy will tend to favour centralization. This is due primarily to the tendency for political leaders of a local jurisdiction to prioritize the interests of those inside the jurisdiction.[51] There are at least three possible reasons for this. Firstly, those inside the jurisdiction are able to vote in local elections, while those outside the jurisdiction are not. The electoral incentives of local politicians thus strongly favour prioritizing the interests of those inside the jurisdiction. Secondly, political leaders may have more natural sympathy for those closer to them than those living in other jurisdictions.[52] Thirdly, local leaders will tend to be more *aware* of localized costs and benefits, giving them a greater saliency to decision-making than costs and benefits that arise in other jurisdictions.

The net effect is a tendency for local politicians to enact policies that externalize costs and internalize benefits. Examples might include seeking to tax out-of-province producers, overusing common-pool resources such as fish, or setting intellectual property policies that fail to account for the benefits of innovation that accrue in other jurisdictions. If every local jurisdiction in a federation pursued policies like this, the cumulative costs would be significant. Of course, the local jurisdictions might try to come together and agree not to pursue policies of this nature. However, collective action problems would bedevil any approach based on mutual agreement. Each jurisdiction would want the other jurisdictions to comply with the rules, but at the same time, it would constantly face incentives to defect from the agreement. Ultimately, a commitment mechanism is needed that can guarantee all local jurisdictions will comply with the rules.[53] An entrenched constitution that assigns exclusive jurisdiction to a federal Parliament over matters likely to involve extrajurisdictional costs and benefits is just such a commitment mechanism. Exclusive federal jurisdiction in these areas precludes local policies that could fail to account for external effects, while at the same time helping to ensure that policy in these areas is made by a nationally representative legislature that is more likely to consider costs and benefits across the country.

The Constitution also confers jurisdiction over subjects in which national coordination is of particular importance. These include areas, such as currency and weights and measures, in which the benefits of national standardization are significant relative to the benefits of localized specification. A federal order of government with national territorial jurisdiction is better placed to provide for national standardization in these areas, a point recognized by Mill in his discussion of federalism in *Considerations on Representative Government*.[54] Today we might frame the argument as follows: standardization lowers transaction and information costs associated with trading across jurisdictional lines, which enhances the available gains from trade. Parties contracting with a common currency, financial system, and system of measurement can acquire and process relevant information more efficiently than would otherwise be the case. At the same time, other kinds of transaction costs, such as the risk of a change in the relative values of two local currencies, are eliminated, further lowering the barriers to trade.[55] While standardization in these areas could in theory be achieved by interprovincial coordination, it is quite possible that multiple governments would not always be able to achieve unanimity, with each seeking to prioritize their own divergent local interests. The federal role in these areas is most clearly justified on the basis of the benefits of standardization in facilitating transactions, which in turn enhances welfare.

A distinct justification for positive integration applies in a narrow range of subjects that require a coordinated national approach due to the qualitative nature of the subject matter. Competition policy and systemic risk in the national financial system are examples of matters that relate to the emergent properties of the national economy.[56] Policy in these areas relates to phenomena that are irreducible to particular local economies or industries. "Systemic risk" and the competition-law concept of "market power" are not necessarily present at the level of individual transactions. Rather, these phenomena supervene on the overall structure of the national economy as a whole. They emerge from the multitude of transactions, industries, and local economies that comprise the national economy and accordingly require a coordinated national approach, which a central government is best able to provide. Again, interprovincial coordination could, in theory, achieve the same result, but the risk of provincial defection from the regime based on local interests means that the policies are best pursued nationally.

The arguments set out here serve to justify both a grant of federal jurisdiction in these areas and a limit on overlapping provincial or local jurisdiction. In each of these areas, it is desirable to have policy-making from the centre and correspondingly *un*desirable to have local policymaking, which is likely to fail to account for the national interest. The principle of jurisdictional exclusivity in the division of powers secures both of these outcomes since a grant of exclusive jurisdiction to Parliament on a given subject, in theory, deprives provinces of the jurisdiction to legislate on that subject.

Arguments based on the benefits of free trade serve to further reinforce the case for negative integration and, in particular, restrictions against locally imposed barriers to trade. These take two broad forms in the Constitution – namely: (1) the denial of provincial jurisdiction over exclusive heads of federal power; and (2) stand-alone guarantees of interprovincial trade and labour mobility, including section 121 of the Constitution Act, 1867 and section 6 of the Charter. The principal argument for free internal trade is that free trade among local jurisdictions enhances overall welfare. Local governments may be tempted to enact protectionist measures that serve local interests, but that simultaneously hamper interjurisdictional trade. This sets up a classic collective action problem: if all local jurisdictions pursued such policies, the cumulative effect would reduce the welfare of all of them. Constitutionally entrenched restrictions against trade barriers provide a commitment mechanism that helps to ensure local jurisdictions cannot defect from a commitment to free trade, a result that is in the best interests of each of them in the long run.

While based on realistic assumptions about enduring features of human nature, the arguments above are not value-neutral. They generally assume that enhanced material wealth is desirable, for instance. Nevertheless, even if these arguments do involve certain value commitments, they can in principle appeal to parties with a relatively wide range of other beliefs and values. Material wealth is desirable, in part, because it allows for greater satisfaction of parties' subjective preferences, whatever those preferences may be. A larger economic pie means more to go around, regardless of what one wishes to do with one's slice. Arguments based on enhanced material welfare can thus be defended on highly relativistic grounds that affirm the validity of a wide range of potential individual preferences.[57] While this aspect of welfare economics has been subject to criticism, it may well be a desirable feature in the justification of centralized authority in a highly diverse transcontinental federation. Though different parts of the country may have deeper value commitments that vary from region to region, the economic union provides an appropriately shallow set of unifying objectives for the country as a whole. Canadians living in Quebec, the West, or in Indigenous communities may have differing beliefs on a range of matters, but economic union under a federal Parliament provides a platform for cooperation on an issue of genuine common interest, including material economic progress.

This points to other complementary justifications for the economic union. By providing for the pursuit of common economic objectives, and preventing regionally divisive acts of protectionism, the centralizing features of the Constitution can help promote national unity.[58] Indeed, economic protectionism can be understood as "the economic equivalent of war," involving acts of hostility inconsistent with common citizenship.[59] By restricting such hostile acts, the Canadian economic union makes peaceful cooperation among differing regions of the country more likely, providing the conditions for the continuing development of a common national identity rooted in genuine common commitments. A strong and integrated national economy can also be understood to enhance national security, a consideration that weighed on the framers' minds in enacting the Constitution in the wake of the US Civil War.[60] The national security implications of a vibrant and integrated national economy have been the subject of renewed interest in recent years, particularly in light of concerns about the reliability of international supply chains during times of crisis.[61]

While our understanding of the decentralizing features of the Constitution has evolved somewhat over time to include a richer and more nuanced account of the justifications for secure property rights and local governance autonomy, the basic features of the justification for the economic vision have remained consistent over time. The remarkable durability of the justifications for both the positive and negative integration provided for under the Constitution is likely due to their source. These arguments are grounded in principles of political economy that are themselves based on enduring features of human nature. They are as true today as they were in 1867.

Conclusion

My ultimate goal in the preceding two chapters has been to establish that the economic vision of the Constitution remains relevant to constitutional interpretation today. Despite the evolution in our constitutional order since 1867, and despite developments in the accepted justifications for certain features of the economic vision, it retains its appeal. The economic vision aligns with the constitutional structure that political and judicial branches of the Canadian state have built over time. Moreover, a compelling justification can be advanced for the economic vision of the Constitution that resonates in the present day. Interpreting the Constitution in keeping with this economic vision would not be a case of allowing the dead hand of the framers to reach into the present and impose their values. Rather, the economic vision provides a normatively compelling account of the structural features of the Constitution that is in line with contemporary values. Even on a "living tree" approach, then, the economic vision is an appropriate guide to interpreting the text of the Constitution. In the remaining chapters of the book, I consider some of the implications of the economic vision to contemporary constitutional issues. While courts in recent years have lost touch with the economic vision of the Constitution, I seek to show what a renewed understanding of that vision would look like in the twenty-first century.

Renewing the Economic Constitution

Property Rights, Local Autonomy, and Subsidiarity

The central contention of this book is that the Constitution reflects a vision of economic relations that remains relevant today. The constitutional commitments to secure property rights, local autonomy and subsidiarity, economic integration, and free trade are not relics of the past. They are reflected not just in the text of the Constitution, but also in the living constitutional order that grew out of it. Moreover, they are aligned with current values and ideals, and point to solutions to contemporary legal and policy challenges. In these concluding chapters, I seek to outline the ways in which courts have begun to lose touch with the economic vision of the Constitution, as well as some of the problems this trend has created. At the same time, I will examine the implications of a renewed understanding of the economic constitution for the development of Canadian law, and how such renewal can address the challenges of today. This chapter addresses the implications of a renewed understanding of the decentralizing elements of the economic constitution – namely, the commitments to secure property rights and local autonomy and subsidiarity – while the final chapter addresses the centralizing commitments to economic integration and free trade.

While the Constitution's centralizing commitments to economic integration and free trade are important, I have been at pains in this book to emphasize that those centralizing features co-exist with countervailing commitments to decentralization. Canada's constitutional order decentralizes economic decision-making through two separate, intersecting mechanisms: the commitment to secure property rights and the commitment to local autonomy and subsidiarity. Property systems decentralize control over resources, putting primary responsibility for decision-making in the hands of a dispersed multitude of owners.[1] The terms on which these owners hold their property are set principally by the prevailing local system of private law, and by regulations imposed mainly at the provincial and local levels of government. This is one aspect of the Constitution's commitment to local governance autonomy. Moreover, as I have argued in this book, the Constitution's division of powers is committed to local autonomy and subsidiarity on economic policy more broadly. The Constitution presumptively allocates jurisdiction over economic questions to the provinces, with federal jurisdiction limited to subjects that cannot be effectively addressed at a local level.

These decentralizing features are vital to Canada's constitutional identity. A Canada without systems of secure property rights or significant local governance autonomy would be largely unrecognizable. The decentralizing features of the Constitution are adapted to the challenges of governing a large and diverse transcontinental nation, in which circumstances, values, and priorities differ across regions and localities. While these features remain firmly embedded in our constitutional order, the need for a renewed understanding of them has become increasingly clear. With respect to property rights, there is declining awareness, among members of the judiciary and others, of the common law traditions and constitutional provisions that protect property owners from state interference. When it comes to local governance autonomy, courts have failed to grapple with the ways in which the increasing trend toward a "flexible" conception of federalism renders provincial jurisdiction vulnerable to federal intrusion. These two issues will be considered in turn, together with a positive vision for how the economic Constitution can inform constitutional interpretation in these areas going forward.

Property Rights and the Decline of the Doctrine of De Facto Expropriation

On the coming into force of the Charter, Gérard La Forest, then a Justice of the New Brunswick Court of Appeal, wrote a short article discussing its likely impact on Canadian law.[2] In the piece, he emphasized that the Constitution's commitment to basic rights did not begin with the Charter. "Thus far," wrote Justice La Forest, "our basic rights have by and large been protected by our traditions of liberty and the political understandings that undergird the supremacy of Parliament and the legislatures."[3] He went on to stress the constitutional significance of constitutional protections for property rights that predated the Charter, including restrictions against arbitrary interference with property by the executive and the presumption against expropriation without compensation in the absence of clear statutory authorization.[4] Addressing the omission of property rights from the Charter, Justice La Forest anticipated that these older protections for property would continue, and indeed take on renewed significance:

> Like other constitutional principles, however, the precise content of a right intended to preserve individual freedom must be adjusted to conform to evolving social realities. This is particularly true in relation to property rights where the courts must not place themselves in a position of frustrating the work of Parliament and the legislatures which, of course, have the primary burden of adjusting economic power in the state by reallocating rights and resources. It may have been to permit these bodies more flexibility in performing this task that property rights were not expressly inserted in the *Charter*. This places an additional obligation on Parliament and the legislatures to avoid arbitrary action in this field. This duty the courts will continue to assist our legislative bodies to perform by interpreting statutes so as not to arbitrarily or unjustly interfere with the liberty and property of the individual. This has the further benefit of reminding them, of their continuing duty in this regard. The *Charter*, as it seems to me, reaffirms this judicial function by underlining in section 26 that "the guarantee in this Charter of certain rights and freedoms shall not be construed as denying the existence of any other rights or freedoms that exist in Canada."[5]

Unfortunately, Justice La Forest's expectations regarding the ongoing judicial commitment to secure property rights were not borne out by subsequent events. Indeed, it is as if courts took the omission of property rights from the Charter as a signal of the diminished importance of these rights in our constitutional order.[6] The judicial diminishment of protections for property rights over the past several decades is seen most clearly in two areas: (1) the law of de facto expropriation (also known as regulatory takings); and (2) judicial interpretation of section 53 of the Constitution Act, 1867, which requires that "bills for appropriating any part of the public revenue, or for imposing any tax or impost, shall originate in the House of Commons."[7]

As outlined in chapter 2, Canada's legal heritage includes a range of protections for property. These protections, while robust, are nevertheless aligned with Parliamentary supremacy. The executive branch of the state has no authority to interfere with property rights outside of emergencies, save for powers derived from a validly enacted statute. Moreover, courts have adopted presumptions against interfering with vested property rights, and against the uncompensated taking of property, except where the language of the statute clearly authorizes this result.[8] In the mid-twentieth century, with the rise of the regulatory state, Canadian courts were at the vanguard in adapting these traditional common law protections to address new forms of interference with property rights under regulatory regimes. In particular, courts came to recognize, under the doctrine of de facto expropriation, that the state could deprive an owner of the benefit of her property without actually taking title.

The landmark case of *Manitoba Fisheries Ltd v. The Queen* from 1978 firmly established the doctrine of de facto expropriation as part of Canadian law.[9] The case involved federal legislation that nationalized the freshwater fish export industry. By prohibiting parties other than a Crown corporation from exporting fish, the legislation effectively put the existing participants in the market, including the plaintiff in the case, out of business. The legislation in question did not expressly require payment of compensation to these existing businesses. Nevertheless, the Supreme Court unanimously held that the plaintiff was entitled to compensation from the federal Crown based on the value of the "goodwill" it had with existing participants in the market, including suppliers and customers who were now required by law to do business only with the government monopoly. The basis for the Crown's duty to pay compensation was the common law principle that "unless the words of the statute clearly so demand, a statute is not to be construed so as to take away the property of a subject without compensation."[10] The decision in *Manitoba Fisheries* clearly established that compensation could be required in cases where the government indirectly deprives a person of property, even where the government does not formally take title to tangible objects of property, and even in cases where the statute does not affirmatively require compensation.

For several decades after *Manitoba Fisheries*, de facto expropriation was an accepted part of Canadian law. For instance, in the Supreme Court's 1985 decision in *R v. Tener*, the Court required that compensation be paid to the owners of mineral rights that were rendered valueless by the establishment of a provincial park on the land that was subject to their mineral rights.[11] The *Tener* decision was also followed by lower court decisions from British Columbia involving mineral rights.[12] While de facto expropriation claims were relatively rare, they served an important function in preventing government bodies from effectively taking property in cases where the legislature had not deliberated on the matter and clearly authorized that outcome.

However, in a 2006 decision, *Canadian Pacific Railway v. Vancouver* (*CPR*), the Supreme Court abruptly reversed course.[13] The *CPR* case dealt with the Arbutus rail corridor, a stretch of extremely valuable land cutting through the west side of Vancouver. The *CPR* had long used the corridor for rail, but found it could no longer profitably be used for that purpose. The City of Vancouver wanted to preserve the land as an intact transportation corridor rather than see it developed. Instead of formally expropriating the land and paying its market value, the city instead zoned the land as a public thoroughfare for transportation. It was acknowledged that none of the uses permitted by this zoning designation, including cycling paths, transit, and rail, was economically viable.[14] The practical effect of the bylaw was to freeze the development of the land, requiring *CPR* to hold it intact for some as-yet-undetermined future transportation use. *CPR* brought an action seeking compensation, arguing that the bylaw effected a de facto expropriation.

In its decision rejecting *CPR*'s claim for compensation, the Supreme Court reformulated the test for de facto expropriation in two important ways. First, it required that an owner be deprived of all "reasonable" uses of the property in question before the requirement to pay compensation would be triggered. However, in its application of this requirement, the Court held that *CPR* had been left with "reasonable" uses of its land even though the Court acknowledged none of the permitted uses was profitable. As then Professor Russell Brown observed, it is difficult to see how uneconomic uses are "reasonable" uses, particularly for a corporation like *CPR*, which owes a fiduciary duty to shareholders.[15]

The second new requirement was even more significant, potentially narrowing the doctrine of de facto expropriation to the point of insignificance. The Court required that for compensation to be payable, the government must acquire a "beneficial interest" in the property. By beneficial interest, the Court appears to have had in mind a *property* interest rather than a mere collateral benefit or source of value. In the *CPR* case, the fact that residents of Vancouver used the corridor for cycling, walking, and even community gardens was insufficient to satisfy the beneficial interest requirement, since the city had not actually acquired a legal right to these activities. As Brown has argued, the "beneficial interest" requirement all but eliminates the distinction between a de facto expropriation and a formal, de jure expropriation.[16] If compensation is only required when the government formally acquires a property interest, then compensation is only required for de jure expropriations. That means that the category of de facto expropriation is effectively eliminated from Canadian law.

Several writers have strongly criticized the decision in CPR, including Brown, who regards it as "incoherent."[17] It has also been observed that as a result of the CPR decision, foreign investors in Canada benefit from stronger protections from de facto expropriation than Canadian citizens, due to provisions in foreign trade and investment agreements to which Canada is a party.[18] The practical result of the CPR decision has been noticeable. De facto expropriation claims are hardly brought anymore in Canadian courts.[19]

A proper recognition of the Constitution's commitment to secure property rights provides a compelling basis for reconsidering the holding in CPR. As noted by Justice La Forest, in insisting on a clear statutory authorization for any taking of property, courts exercise a constitutional function: "They are working along with the legislative branch to ensure the preservation of our fundamental political values. The legislature can, of course, by clear language overturn the court's ruling, but by insisting on such clarity the courts help to promote second thought and public debate, a debate that all recognize as an essential safeguard in a parliamentary democracy."[20]

The advent of the Charter, with its entrenched constitutional rights giving rise to judicial review of legislation, has obscured the significance of the courts' more subtle role in protecting property rights. The CPR decision is the end result of an increasing lack of judicial understanding of the constitutional role identified by Justice La Forest. In our system of government, the state cannot take property without compensation unless the legislature has expressly authorized that result. In *Manitoba Fisheries*, this requirement was enforced through a presumptive common law right to compensation in cases where the government takes property, whether directly through acquisition of title *or* indirectly through regulation. By contrast, the CPR decision allows governments to do indirectly through regulation what they cannot do directly. It reduces a fundamental constitutional protection for property owners to a matter of a formality – the state acquisition of a beneficial property interest – rather than substance.

In rehabilitating the doctrine of de facto expropriation, courts in common law jurisdictions may have something to learn from their counterparts in Quebec. The Quebec law in this area is distinctive because it is based on article 952 of the Civil Code of Quebec, which states: "No owner may be compelled to transfer his ownership except by expropriation according to law for public utility and in return for a just and prior indemnity."[21] In interpreting this provision, Quebec courts have developed the doctrine of "disguised expropriation," under which governments may be required to compensate owners in cases where regulation amounts to a complete negation of the rights of the owner.[22] Regulations or bylaws enacted through statutory delegation may also be declared null if they are found to amount to a disguised expropriation.[23] While disguised expropriations are evaluated based on all the circumstances of the case, the principal criterion in the jurisprudence is whether the property retains value. Regulations that leave an owner no profitable use are generally found to be disguised expropriations in Quebec.[24] For instance, zoning land for uses such as parkland, schools, and churches has been found to amount to disguised expropriation.[25] Moreover, there is no Quebec analogue to the CPR requirement that the government acquire a "beneficial interest."[26] This is a significant difference between the common law and the civil law that broadens the scope of protection available to Quebec property owners.

Had the facts in CPR arisen in Quebec, the bylaw in question likely would have been characterized as a disguised expropriation, given that it was accepted that none of the uses left to CPR was profitable.[27] While article 952 is unique to Quebec, the underlying principle that state action tantamount to expropriation requires compensation is consistent with the trajectory of the common law prior to CPR, and in keeping with Canada's constitutional traditions.

Realigning the Canadian common law approach to de facto expropriation with those constitutional traditions would require several doctrinal developments. First, the restrictive requirement that the owner be deprived of all "reasonable uses" should be reconsidered. Instead, a more open-ended requirement of substantial deprivation of ownership rights should be adopted. This change first serves to recognize there are other state actions besides use restrictions that can be tantamount to expropriation. These include physical intrusions and deprivations of exclusive possession.[28] However, use restrictions may also give rise to a de facto expropriation. There should be at least a strong presumption that depriving the owner of all profitable uses of the property, or depriving the owner of all or nearly all of the value of property, is a de facto expropriation.

Moreover, the CPR requirement that the state acquire a "beneficial interest" can safely be discarded. The purpose of the doctrine of de facto expropriation is to protect property owners from being deprived of their rights without compensation. The focus should be on the effect on the owner, not what is acquired by the state. It may be presumed that when a government body enacts a regulation affecting property rights, it does so in order to secure some kind of benefit for the government, the general public, or some other party. The specific nature of that benefit, including whether it amounts to a proprietary "beneficial interest," is irrelevant to the purposes of the doctrine of de facto expropriation.

This approach would still leave governments with a very wide margin of manoeuvre in enacting regulations in the public interest. Only a narrow set of highly intrusive regulations would meet the standard of substantially depriving an owner of the benefits of ownership. In those cases, requiring compensation is not only fair but arguably welfare-enhancing for society as a whole.[29] In any event, it would always remain possible for Parliament or a provincial legislature to clearly and affirmatively authorize an expropriation, de facto or de jure, without compensation. In this area of law, legislatures have the last word in reconciling the public interest with the rights of owners. The courts' role is a limited but vital one in protecting the security of property rights in a manner consistent with the ultimate authority of the legislative branch.

Section 53 and the Indirect Protection for Property under the Constitution Act, 1867

There is at least one other area in which courts in recent years have failed to give due regard to the constitutional commitment to secure property rights. Over the past several decades, the Constitution's procedural requirements for measures that impose taxes and other charges have been progressively weakened, opening the door to compulsory payments to government that have not been expressly authorized by the elected representatives of the people.

Section 53 of the Constitution Act, 1867, requires that "bills for appropriating any part of the public revenue, or for imposing any tax or impost, shall originate in the House of Commons." This provision also applies to the provinces by way of section 90, requiring provincial measures of this nature to originate with a bill in the legislative assembly.[30] As explained in chapter 2, this requirement is part of a range of procedural rules that serve to indirectly enhance the security of property interests. Among other requirements, fiscal measures must originate in the lower, elected house of Parliament (section 53) and must be recommended by the cabinet, thus eliminating the potential for such measures to be adopted by individual legislators' earmarks (section 54). These requirements make it less likely that measures interfering with the property rights of the citizenry will be adopted unless demonstrably justified. Section 53, in addition to helping secure democratic account-ability and responsible government through legislators' power of the purse, also reflects the Lockean ideal of protections for property that are overseen by the legislative branch.[31] According to Locke, whose ideas both informed and drew upon the constitutional settlement that followed the English revolutions of the seventeenth century, the consent of the elected representatives of the people is required for government interference with property rights, including by way of compulsory payments. Section 53 ratifies and constitutionalizes this Lockean element of our constitutional heritage.

In recent decades, the jurisprudence of the Supreme Court has undermined section 53 in two key ways. Firstly, the Court has recognized an ever-expanding category of "regulatory charges," which it has erroneously held to be exempt from the requirements of section 53. Since at least the 1978 *Agricultural Products Marketing Reference*, the Court has held that section 53 applies to taxes but not user fees or "regulatory charges."[32] A user fee is a fee for the use of government services or facilities. A regulatory charge is a compulsory payment with a sufficiently close nexus to a regulatory scheme. The permitted scope of regulatory charges has grown over time. The current test requires both the existence of a regulatory scheme and a connection between the charge in question and the regulatory scheme.[33] Connection to a regulatory scheme can be established in at least two ways: (1) the charge may help defray the costs of the regulatory scheme; or (2) the charge may be designed to alter incentives of parties subject to regulations.[34]

Regulatory charges designed to defray the costs of a regulatory scheme are limited by the costs of the scheme (subject to some margin for error on the part of the government).[35] Regulatory charges of this nature are not meant to generate surplus revenue for the state. As recently as 2008, the Supreme Court left open the question of whether regulatory charges designed to alter incentives were also limited by the cost of the regulatory regime.[36] However, in the *Greenhouse Gas Reference*, the Court decisively held that there is no such limit on the amount of regulatory charges. If the primary purpose of a charge is to alter incentives as part of a regulatory scheme, that is sufficient to render section 53 inapplicable, regardless of the amounts raised and regardless of whether the revenue generated is used to further the purposes of the regulatory scheme.[37]

With respect, the regulatory charge exception rests on a misinterpretation of section 53. The text and purpose of the provision both indicate that it is meant to apply to *any* compulsory payment exacted by the government acting in its sovereign capacity. While that would not include payments made to the government pursuant to a contract or other private law obligation, it would include any compulsory payments backed by the distinctive sovereign powers of the state, regardless of whether the payment would be characterized as a "tax" or a "regulatory charge" under the current test. Beginning with the text of section 53, it applies to both bills "appropriating any Part of the Public Revenue" and bills "imposing *any* Tax *or Impost*" (emphases added). The language used here and in section 54 is more capacious than other references to taxation in the Constitution Act, 1867, which do not mention imposts along with taxes. The reference to *any* tax *or impost* appears designed to capture the full spectrum of compulsory payments.

The accepted meaning of "tax" at the time of the enactment of the Constitution Act, 1867 reinforces this view. The 1865 edition of Webster's *American Dictionary of the English Language* defines a tax as "a charge, especially a pecuniary burden which is imposed by authority ... A levy of any kind made upon property for the support of a government."[38] The early Canadian case law is consistent with this broad understanding of the meaning of tax. That case law holds that a charge is a tax if it is: (1) enforceable by law; (2) imposed under the authority of the legislature; (3) levied by a public body; and (4) intended for a public purpose.[39]

Unlike the provisions in sections 91 and 92 and elsewhere, which refer only to "tax" or "taxation," sections 53 and 54 refer to "any tax or impost." Webster's 1865 edition defines "impost" as "that which is imposed or levied; a tax, tribute or duty; often a duty or tax laid by government on goods imported into a country."[40] Johnson's 1755 *Dictionary of the English Language* confirms the broad meaning of "impost," defining it as "[a] tax; a toll; custom paid."[41] The inclusion of "toll" is particularly telling, seemingly encompassing more than a strictly revenue-generating tax.

Both the use of the term "any" and the addition of the term "impost" indicate a legislative intent to adopt a broad understanding of what is encompassed by section 53. Moreover, sections 53 and 54 also apply to appropriations bills, indicating that the intent is to apply the requirement to all fiscal measures. Needless to say, there is nothing in the text of the Constitution Act, 1867 that indicates an intent to exempt compulsory payments with a regulatory purpose from the ambit of section 53.

The purposes of section 53 reinforce the position that it is meant to capture all compulsory payments exacted by the government acting in its sovereign capacity. As indicated above, section 53 serves two principal purposes. Firstly, it protects property rights by requiring that compulsory payments that interfere with those rights be consented to by the elected representatives of the people. In this respect, section 53 is part of a range of measures, including section 54, which together ensure that fiscal measures that could interfere with property rights receive proper scrutiny and are supported by each of the constituent components of Parliament or the provincial legislature. Notably, section 53 applies to measures that interfere either directly with property, as in the case of compulsory payments, or indirectly, as in the case of appropriations bills that could result in tax increases in the future. This first purpose of section 53 is based on a commitment to secure property rights through the Lockean mechanism of requiring that interference with those rights be approved by the legislative branch. Secondly, section 53 also serves the related purpose of securing democratic accountability and responsible government by requiring that governments receive funding for their activities only with the consent of the elected legislative chamber.

Neither of the purposes of section 53 is consistent with exempting regulatory charges from its ambit. The degree of interference with property rights brought about by a compulsory regulatory charge is no less significant than one brought about by a tax unrelated to a regulatory regime. Furthermore, exempting regulatory charges from section 53 undermines democratic accountability by allowing governments to fund their activities through mechanisms that are not subject to oversight by the legislative branch. The accountability problem with regulatory charges has been made particularly acute by the holding in the *Greenhouse Gas Reference* to the effect that there is no limit to the magnitude of incentive-altering regulatory charges, and that funds need not be put to a purpose connected to the regulatory regime. The constitutional requirement for the consent of the House of Commons for taxation measures originated in part in the attempts of English monarchs to fund their governments and require payments from subjects without parliamentary consent. The ever-enlarging category of regulatory charges threatens to recreate this problem in Canada. Once a government receives the delegated authority to enact a charge, it can use its authority to increase the magnitude of the charge, even quite substantially, without scrutiny from Parliament.

Courts have tended to assume that characterizing a charge as a tax for the purposes of section 53 automatically means that the charge is a tax for the purposes of the division of powers. This is significant, in part, because Parliament has jurisdiction over "the raising of Money by any Mode or System of Taxation," while provinces are limited to direct taxation.[42] If the scope of section 53 is taken to be coextensive with taxation for division of powers purposes, there is a valid concern that an expansive understanding of tax will enlarge federal authority at the expense of the provinces. This concern is reflected in the jurisprudence. For instance, in his dissent in the *Greenhouse Gas Reference*, Justice Brown agreed with the majority that the charge in question was not subject to section 53, in part, because "[i]t 'would afford the Dominion an easy passage into the Provincial domain' were every monetary measure to be regarded as a tax."[43]

Yet the text, context, and purpose of section 53 all distinguish it from section 91(3), and so there is no reason to expect that every measure covered by section 53 would necessarily be a tax under section 91(3). As discussed above, the language of section 53 is broader than section 91(3), referring to *any* tax *or impost*. Moreover, the contexts and purposes of sections 91(3) and 53 are very different. The references to taxation in sections 91 and 92 must necessarily be read within the context of the exhaustive scheme for the division of powers. The federal taxation power is limited by the exclusive heads of provincial power, including not just the provincial power over licence fees, but also powers over property and civil rights and matters of a local and private nature. An overly broad conception of the federal taxation power would permit inter-ferences in areas of provincial jurisdiction that would be inconsistent with the scheme of the division of powers. Furthermore, since provinces are denied the power to enact indirect taxes, the characterization of a provincial measure as a tax raises the prospect that it could be ultra vires if it is indirect rather than direct. The concept of a regulatory charge, as distinguished from a tax, can help save provincial measures that are closely connected to an otherwise valid provincial regulatory scheme from being struck down as indirect taxes.[44]

These important considerations have no bearing whatsoever on section 53. While a narrow understanding of the concept of a tax that exempts regulatory charges may be appropriate for the purposes of the division of powers, such an approach actually undermines section 53. The meaning of tax for the purposes of the division of powers should thus not be reflexively taken to define the scope of section 53. This approach is consistent with the text. Section 53 uses language that is different from the language used in referring to taxes in sections 91 and 92. Whereas sections 91 and 92 refer simply to modes of "taxation," sections 53 and 54 refer to both appropriations bills and bills imposing *any* tax *or impost*. There are thus persuasive reasons for distinguishing the concept of a tax in the division of powers context from the question of the scope of section 53. These questions should be disentangled.

Section 53 (and 54) should be held to apply even to measures that would be characterized as regulatory charges for the purposes of the division of powers.

The second manner in which the Court has diluted section 53 relates to the delegation of taxation authority by Parliament and provincial legislatures. In the 1998 case of *Eurig Estate*, the Court implicitly expressed the view that only the details and mechanism of taxation could be delegated, not the power to impose a tax itself.[45] The Court has since taken the more permissive position that the power to impose a tax can be delegated so long as the delegation occurs in statutory language that is "express and unambiguous."[46] This holding is based on another misinterpretation of section 53 that has further served to undermine its function.

The late Peter Hogg took the position that a delegation of the power to impose a tax, as opposed to powers limited to the details and mechanisms, was inconsistent with the text and purpose of section 53. With respect to the text, Hogg wrote: "While it is clearly established (and obviously necessary) that other legislative powers be subject to delegation, the taxing power is distinctive. It is distinctive for the legal reason that section 53 singles it out for the requirement that any bill must originate in the House of Commons."[47] The text of the Constitution prescribes a mandatory procedure for fiscal measures. The imposition of a tax by a statutory delegate is not contemplated by that procedure. Indeed, the very fact that there is a special constitutional requirement that fiscal measures originate in the House of Commons implies that such measures are subject to special restrictions beyond those that apply to other forms of legislation.

The purposes of section 53 reinforce the position that the power to impose a tax or regulatory charge should not be capable of delegation. Where taxation powers are delegated, the statutory delegate can impose or raise taxes and regulatory charges without the democratic accountability associated with a bill in the legislature. Moreover, delegated taxes or charges could involve substantial government interference with property rights beyond what would have been contemplated by the legislators passing the original delegation. Hogg summarized the case against delegation of section 53 fiscal powers in these terms:

> It must be remembered that the taxing power is the one
> upon which the rest of governance depends. As the King
> and Parliament both recognized in the 17th century, nothing
> important can be done without resources, and it is control of

the taxing power that provides the resources. Moreover, no other power has as direct and immediate an effect on citizens as the taxing power, and (for that reason) nothing government does is as unpopular as the imposition and collection of taxes. There is a huge incentive for governments to offload this power to a delegate, who can raise taxes quietly without any irritating fuss in the Parliament or Legislature, and who can shoulder the blame when the media do get wind of the action. The action of the government of Ontario in 1992 in tripling probate fees by order in council *after having publicly promised to stop raising taxes* perfectly illustrates the mischief of delegation in the case of the taxing power. The Court should have interpreted section 53 as prohibiting the delegation of this primary instrument of democratic governance.[48]

The details and mechanism of a tax or regulatory charge may be properly delegated, but the actual imposition of the tax must come about through primary legislation. In order to properly serve the objectives of securing the property rights of taxpayers and promoting democratic accountability, the act imposing the tax or regulatory charge must at least set out the property or activity that is subject to the tax and the rate of taxation. It may be appropriate to delegate some power to vary the rate of taxation, but the objectives of section 53 would seem to require a maximum rate to be set out in the primary legislation. Where the maximum rate of taxation has been approved by the elected chamber, either expressly or through a reasonably determinate formula, there will have been meaningful consent by the people's representatives to the range within which the delegate may fix the tax.

Property Rights in the Twenty-First Century

The rejuvenation of the doctrine of de facto expropriation and of the procedural requirements for fiscal measures contained in the Constitution Act, 1867 are two tangible ways Canadian law could be developed in order to more fully reflect the constitutional commitment to secure property rights. However, there are others. For instance, a renewed emphasis on canons of statutory interpretation that create a presumption against interference with vested property rights may be called for. That may have implications for administrative law.

Canadian administrative law currently allows for judicial review of measures that infringe property rights to be conducted on a deferential "reasonableness" standard, rather than a more demanding correctness standard. A commitment to secure property rights requires that government interference with those rights must be clearly authorized by legislation. Deferring to the legal interpretations of administrative bodies on these questions may enhance the flexibility of the administrative state, but it does so at the expense of certainty and predictability for property owners. The commitment to secure property rights does need to be reconciled with the ultimate authority of legislatures to enact statutes that regulate or limit property rights. In that sense, there is something to be said for the Supreme Court's current approach, which provides for deference to administrative decision-makers in cases where that is consistent with legislative intent, either express or implied.[49] That said, the Court may be too quick to find implied legislative intent to require deference on administrative decisions that significantly infringe property rights. Indeed, this approach may be at odds with the traditional interpretive canon requiring a strict reading of measures that interfere with vested rights.[50]

While there are a number of ways in which courts could more fully recognize the Constitution's commitment to secure property rights, a full judicial restoration of constitutional protections for property rights may be too much to hope for. Justice La Forest appears to have been wrong in his prediction that the older tradition of judicial protections for liberty, including property rights, would survive the entrenchment of the Charter. Instead, one effect of the Charter seems to have been to lower the esteem with which the judiciary regards these other, non-entrenched rights. A true restoration of the place of property rights in our constitutional order may in fact require action from legislators. One option would be a constitutional amendment that places property rights alongside the other rights protected in the Charter. In this respect, it is noteworthy that the Charter is currently a significant outlier among bills of rights around the world in not protecting property rights.[51] A constitutional amendment adding protection for property would correct this anomalous neglect for rights that are at the core of the liberal tradition.

A new Canadian property rights clause would not have to be modelled after the Fifth Amendment of the US Constitution, which requires due process for deprivations of property, as well as requiring that property may only be taken for public use with just compensation.[52] At the time the Charter was enacted, the US Bill of Rights was the principal model the drafters looked to. However, since 1982, many new human rights instruments have been adopted around the world. These provide potentially useful models, including with respect to property rights. For instance, the post-apartheid South African Constitution balances protections for property with measures that aim to correct historical injustices and ensure that the rights and benefits of property ownership are widely distributed in society.[53] As outlined in chapter 8, the accepted justifications for property today are broader than the primarily Lockean arguments that motivated the framers, and any future amendment to the Charter could seek to reflect this in the balance it strikes among competing values.

It is unlikely that the necessary consensus could be reached in the near term for a national constitutional amendment adding property rights to the Charter (though the prospects for a province-specific amendment using the bilateral amending formula are somewhat more promising).[54] Yet, even if a national constitutional amendment were politically feasible, judicial review of legislation for property rights infringements would have certain drawbacks.[55] Determining whether a given infringement of property rights is justified involves weighing a broad range of social and economic factors, as well as competing political interests. Property rights have never been absolute in Canadian law and a constitutional amendment would not change that. Instead, it would change who ultimately decides when an infringement is justified. Adding property rights to the Charter would shift responsibility from the legislature to the courts, which could potentially set a low bar for infringement or interpret the right in unpredictable ways.[56] Structural property rights protections backed up by legislators committed to protecting such rights may be preferable to property rights protections that depend on permissive forms of judicial review. Judicial review of property rights infringements is thus best seen as a possibly useful supplement, but not a replacement, for legislative vigilance and structural protections for property rights.

There are other steps legislators could take, short of amending the Charter, to enhance protections for property rights in Canadian law. One important step would be to amend the Canadian Bill of Rights.[57] The Bill of Rights is an ordinary federal statute that protects property, among other rights, requiring that property can only be taken away by "due process of law." Unfortunately, this right was given a very narrow reading by the Supreme Court in *Authorson v. Canada (Attorney General)*.[58] But Parliament could amend the Bill of Rights to replace "due process of law" with the more robust "principles of fundamental justice" standard that has been developed by the courts in the context of section 7 of the Charter. This move would ensure meaningful procedural and substantive protections against the unfair or arbitrary deprivation of property rights, though Parliament would retain the power to override these protections through subsequent legislation. Similar protections could be enacted at the provincial level.[59]

Parliament and provincial legislatures could also take other measures to strengthen protections. Sections 53 of the Constitution Act, 1867 could likely be amended unilaterally by Parliament (or by a provincial legislature, as it relates to that province) in order to clarify its application to regulatory charges and specify limits on delegated taxation.[60] Parliament and provincial legislatures could also enact legislation to overrule the unduly onerous CPR test for de facto expropriation, discussed above. For instance, legislation could provide that fair compensation is required whenever government action fundamentally deprives an owner of either the right to exclusive possession or the right to beneficial use of property. Parliament and provincial legislatures would retain the ultimate power to authorize exceptions to these requirements, but in the absence of an express exception, there would be a presumptive statutory entitlement to compensation whenever an owner is deprived of the fundamental features of the right of ownership. In an era when it has become easier for governments to seize or freeze assets, particularly digital assets and bank accounts, the need for stronger statutory safeguards for property rights may become an important issue in the years ahead.[61]

Local Autonomy and Subsidiarity: The Problem with "Flexible" Federalism

Besides the commitment to secure property rights, the Constitution is also committed to decentralized economic decision-making through local governance autonomy and subsidiarity with respect to economic policy. The principal manifestation of this commitment in the text of the Constitution is the division of powers between the provinces and the federal Parliament. Recent developments in the approach taken by the Supreme Court in division of powers cases, therefore, have significant implications for the economic vision of the Constitution.

Over the past several decades, the Supreme Court of Canada has transformed its approach to federalism. Moving away from what it now pejoratively labels the "watertight compartments" approach of the Privy Council, it has repeatedly endorsed a "flexible," "cooperative" approach to federalism. While often invoked together, flexible federalism and cooperative federalism are distinct concepts.[62] Flexible federalism aims to remove constraints on both orders of government, allowing each to pursue its conception of the public interest, even if this leads to overlapping jurisdiction. Cooperative federalism, by contrast, encourages intergovernmental agreements in pursuit of joint objectives, such as the joint federal-provincial scheme for agricultural products marketing that the Supreme Court endorsed in its landmark *Agricultural Products Marketing Reference*.[63] Encouraging intergovernmental cooperation, in cases where each order of government is operating within its jurisdiction and where each is free to withdraw at any time, is perfectly consistent with a commitment to local autonomy and subsidiarity.[64] By contrast, the move toward a "flexible" conception of the division of powers poses a serious threat to these values, albeit one whose effects are only starting to be felt.

The Supreme Court's move toward flexibility in recent years has affected its approach to several key doctrines. Two principal elements of this trend have been: (1) a greater openness to recognizing factual situations giving rise to a "double aspect," which can be validly addressed by both federal and provincial orders of government; and (2) greater openness to upholding measures that have ancillary features relating to matters under the jurisdiction of the other order of government.[65] Both the ready recognition of double aspects and a permissive approach to ancillary features have made provincial authority vulnerable to federal incursions. This is due to the fact that the doctrine of paramountcy renders valid provincial laws inoperative in cases where they conflict with valid federal laws. Approaches that increase the potential for jurisdictional overlap also expand the scope of federal paramountcy. The result is that provincial authority comes to exist at the sufferance of a federal Parliament that could oust the provincial law by enacting an inconsistent statute, or perhaps by simply indicating a legislative intent to "occupy the field" in regulating a matter.[66]

It must be admitted that these trends in the division of powers case law respond to a real challenge in the practice of Canadian federalism. There are genuine double aspects, for instance, and an overly rigid approach to ancillary features can be impractical, preventing minor incursions into the jurisdiction of the other order of government even when they are necessary to an otherwise valid legislative scheme. And yet, if the trend toward flexibility continues to be pursued without properly considering the implications for local autonomy and subsidiarity, it could fundamentally transform the division of powers, moving Canada toward a hierarchical model of federalism rather than one based on coordinate spheres of authority. The fact is that in our system of government, the provinces bear the brunt of any jurisdictional overlap.

The effect of a flexible approach to the division of powers is necessarily asymmetrical, since Parliament has the upper hand in the jurisdictional conflicts the approach engenders.[67] A limited degree of flexibility may enhance local autonomy in some ways by allowing provinces to enact measures that respond in pragmatic ways to local concerns even if they result in limited ancillary effects on areas of federal jurisdiction.[68] However, if the flexible approach to federalism is left unchecked, the overall result will be the diminution of provincial autonomy, as the exercise of provincial authority is subject to federal oversight.

The flexible approach to federalism favours the recognition of subjects of regulation with a double aspect.[69] A double aspect arises where a given factual situation may be regulated both as a matter under provincial jurisdiction and as a matter under federal jurisdiction. The example of driving offences is instructive.[70] Driving in an unsafe manner may be addressed both as a matter of road regulation, which falls under provincial jurisdiction, and as a criminal prohibition, a matter falling under federal jurisdiction. While the double aspect doctrine was originally recognized by the Privy Council in the late nineteenth century, the Supreme Court has been more eager to recognize double aspects than the Privy Council was, and this forms one part of the now-"dominant tide" of flexible federalism.[71]

While the potential for double aspects to erode provincial autonomy has long been recognized, until recently the doctrine had only minimal effects on provincial jurisdiction. That has changed with the Supreme Court's recent decision in the *Greenhouse Gas Reference*. By recognizing that carbon emissions have a double aspect, the Court upheld a federal law making provincial carbon pricing measures subject to federal standards.[72] In upholding a law subjecting provincial legislation to federal standards on the basis of the double aspect doctrine, the Court broke new ground.[73] As I will argue in the next chapter, there are strong justifications for recognizing federal jurisdiction over the interprovincial and international effects of carbon emissions. Yet this could have been achieved without allowing Parliament to direct the minutiae of provincial fiscal policies relating to carbon emissions. As emphasized in the dissenting opinions in the *Greenhouse Gas Reference*, the case opens the door for Parliament to establish minimum national standards in many other potential areas of jurisdictional overlap.

Justice Brown's dissenting opinion in the *Greenhouse Gas Reference* decries the "supervisory federalism" model that he says the majority endorses.[74] Parliament's "supervisory" jurisdiction over provincial climate policy is made possible by the recognition of a federal power to set minimum national standards for carbon pricing, combined with the application of the double aspect doctrine allowing for concurrent provincial jurisdiction. However, the potential for Parliament to require minimum standards for provincial laws has always been present in cases of jurisdictional overlap, given that federal laws have the upper hand due to the doctrine of paramountcy. Justice Brown is correct in asserting that supervisory federalism, in which provinces are induced to act as agents of federal policy, is inconsistent with the division of powers set out in the text of the Constitution Act, 1867.[75] However, the ultimate source of the problem is a flexible federalism that is prepared to readily recognize double aspects (and ancillary powers). Without jurisdictional overlap, "supervisory federalism" would not be possible.

Besides the double aspect doctrine, the other main source of jurisdictional overlap is the ancillary power doctrine. This doctrine deals with laws that are valid in their pith and substance but that have ancillary features relating to matters within the jurisdiction of the other order of government. For instance, the federal Competition Act is a valid law regulating competition, a matter falling under the general branch of the trade and commerce power.[76] However, the act contains a provision creating a civil cause of action for certain breaches of the act.[77] The creation of new civil causes of action is undoubtedly a matter falling under the provincial power over property and civil rights. The civil action in the Competition Act was upheld in its original form in *General Motors of Canada Ltd v. City National Leasing* (correctly, in my view).[78] It has long been recognized that laws primarily dealing with matters under the jurisdiction of the enacting legislature can have secondary features that extend into the jurisdiction of the other order of government. However, the appropriate approach to assessing such ancillary features has been controversial. Historically, courts developed two different approaches. In some cases, they took the position that features of an otherwise valid law need only have a "rational, functional" connection to the purposes of the law as a whole.[79] By contrast, in other cases, courts referred to an ancillary power doctrine that limited intrusions to those actually *necessary* to achieve the purposes of the impugned law.[80]

In the *General Motors* case, the Court attempted to reconcile this case law, holding that the standard for ancillary effects varies with the degree of the intrusion. For relatively minor encroachments, the standard is a rational, functional connection to the broader scheme. For more significant intrusions, a stricter test may apply, requiring that the measure be "truly necessary" to the broader scheme.[81] The *General*

Motors approach to ancillary powers is highly intuitive. It allows for a relatively permissive approach to minor encroachments that may assist in making a law practically effective while at the same time providing a meaningful check against measures that significantly intrude onto the jurisdiction of the other order of government. Providing a meaningful check against such incursions is particularly important for the provinces, since any resulting jurisdictional overlap is subject to the doctrine of federal paramountcy.

While *General Motors* has not been overturned, there are reasons to doubt the Supreme Court's continued acceptance of the stricter "necessity" standard for significant intrusions. For one thing, since *General Motors*, the Supreme Court has been reluctant to apply the necessity standard. In both *General Motors* itself and *Kirkbi v. Ritvik Holdings*, two cases involving the federal creation of new civil causes of action as part of broader legislative schemes, the Court applied the lower rationality standard rather than a standard of necessity.[82] Respect-fully, creating a new civil cause of action affects the domain of private law in a fundamental way. It is difficult to see how such a measure could be characterized as anything but a significant intrusion onto property and civil rights. That is not to say that such a measure could not be upheld as reasonably necessary to achieving a valid statutory purpose. However, the Court's characterization of these measures as being limited intrusions seems to indicate a certain lack of comfort with the stricter necessity standard that is connected to its commitment to flexible federalism.

The *General Motors* framework has also been criticized by scholars as being too uncertain and discretionary. According to Peter Hogg, it would be simpler to rely upon the rational connection standard for all intrusions – big or small.[83] His view was that a rational connection standard is sufficient to police the division of powers, particularly in an era in which jurisdictional overlap is openly accepted by the courts.

The holding in *R v. Comeau* provides further reason to doubt the Court's continued adherence to the *General Motors* approach.[84] While *Comeau* dealt with section 121, the Constitution's free trade clause, rather than the division of powers, it is fairly clear that the Court's approach to section 121 was intended to mirror a division of powers analysis. Indeed, one of the key themes in the *Comeau* hearing was the concern on the part of members of the Court that section 121 not be read so as to put further limits on provincial legislative power beyond those imposed by the division of powers. And so, the Court held that section 121 prohibits laws whose essence and purpose is to restrict interprovincial trade, a standard that mirrors the pith and substance approach to the division of powers.[85] The Court then went on to hold that section 121 does not prohibit measures that burden trade as an incidental feature of a larger, otherwise valid regulatory scheme. This aspect of the test obviously draws upon the division of powers case law on incidental or ancillary effects. However, in assessing the validity of such incidental burdens, the Court holds that a rational connection between the impugned measure and the broader scheme is sufficient to uphold the measure.[86] There is no mention whatsoever of a more stringent necessity standard for more significant burdens on interprovincial trade. The Court's test for section 121 thus draws inspiration from a particularly permissive version of the approach to ancillary powers in the division of powers cases. In taking this approach, the Court seems to be signalling its abandonment of the *General Motors* necessity standard for significant intrusions onto the jurisdiction of the other order of government.[87]

While the necessity standard for significant ancillary intrusions has been subject to criticism, my view is that it still has an important role to play in upholding a reasonable degree of exclusivity in the division of powers. Allowing significant intrusions into the jurisdiction of the other order of government on the basis of a mere rational connection provides a constitutional backdoor, allowing the division of powers to be effectively circumvented by passing particularly capacious laws. For instance, a stand-alone federal act regulating the means of extracting oil and gas would likely be ultra vires, being in pith and substance about natural resources in the province. Yet a far-reaching federal statute seeking to regulate the environmental and social impacts of designated projects could, in theory, regulate the means of extracting oil and gas, and much else besides, on the basis that the intrusions onto provincial jurisdiction bear a rational and functional connection to the statute's principal purposes, which arguably relate to areas of federal jurisdiction.[88]

George Vegh gives a different, but compelling example: "[I]f a province sought to keep the streets free of prostitution, a rational and functional way for it to do so would be to make prostitution a criminal offence."[89] Yet it simply cannot be correct that a provincial criminal prohibition of this nature should be upheld on the basis of a rational connection with a legislative scheme otherwise within provincial jurisdiction, such as one regulating roads. While the specific example of a criminal prohibition could be addressed by recourse to the interjurisdictional immunity (IJI) doctrine, the broader point is a valid one. Enacting broad regulatory schemes can allow for a constitutional backdoor. Requiring meaningful scrutiny for significant intrusions, through a necessity standard, addresses this problem in all cases of federal or provincial encroachment, even where 1J1 does not apply.

Those committed to a flexible conception of federalism may not view such a constitutional backdoor as a problem. If the main concern is to get the Constitution out of the way of policymaking from both orders of government, then perhaps a rational connection should be sufficient. One might argue, for instance, that the powers set out in sections 91 and 92 are only "exclusive" in the sense that each order of government may make laws that relate in pith and substance to the subjects in question, not that each order of government is restricted in its ability to intrude on the heads of power of the other order of government through rationally connected components of a broader scheme.[90]

However, I hope that the economic vision of the Constitution as set out in this book provides convincing reasons to uphold the principle of jurisdictional exclusivity, including with respect to ancillary powers. As I have argued, the exclusivity of the division of powers is a key feature of this economic vision. Sections 91 and 92 are not just positive grants of power over particular subjects; they are also negative denials of power to the other order of government. The Constitution's commitment to local autonomy and subsidiarity is reflected not only in the positive grant of power over local subjects, including property and civil rights, but also in the denial of federal jurisdiction over those subjects. A failure to effectively police federal intrusions raises the prospect that exercises of provincial jurisdiction will come to exist at the sufferance of the federal Parliament. As with the double aspect doctrine, a liberalized approach to ancillary powers creates the potential for the federal enactment of minimum federal standards for provincial legislation. This is inconsistent with a commitment to meaningful local autonomy under a coordinate system of federalism. It is also inconsistent with the principle of subsidiarity since federal intrusions based on a rational connection standard will not necessarily be limited to areas in which centralization is necessary for effective governance.

The threat to provincial autonomy posed by flexible federalism has remained mostly hypothetical up to now, with the major exception of the *Greenhouse Gas Reference*.[91] The absence of case law expanding federal jurisdiction in recent years has been due in part to the reluctance of Parliament to intrude in new ways on areas of provincial jurisdiction.[92] Yet that may be changing, as the federal government takes strong positions on a range of matters implicating provincial jurisdiction, including environmental policy and childcare.[93] The trend toward flexible federalism has set the stage for Canadian courts to recognize a significant expansion of federal authority through the double aspect and ancillary powers doctrines. However, the Constitution's commitment to local autonomy and subsidiarity, through the specific mechanism of exclusive provincial powers, provides grounds for caution.

Local Autonomy and Subsidiarity: The Case for Water-Resistant Compartments

There are three key ways the constitutional doctrine can be developed in order to better reflect the Constitution's commitment to local autonomy and subsidiarity. First, courts should exercise restraint in recognizing new factual situations giving rise to a double aspect. There are genuine double aspects, and courts should still be prepared to acknowledge them where they exist. However, an overly liberal approach risks the continued growth of jurisdictional overlap, creating the conditions in which supervisory, hierarchical federalism can take hold. Ultimately, the recognition of a double aspect is a qualitative matter of judgment. Perhaps the most that can be said is that courts should exercise restraint and only recognize a double aspect in cases where the federal and provincial characteristics of a factual situation are "roughly equal in importance," to use Hogg's formulation.[94] In all other cases, the appropriate course of action is to choose which features – federal or provincial – predominate, and recognize exclusive jurisdiction on that basis.[95]

Second, courts should build on the *General Motors* framework to apply meaningful scrutiny to ancillary measures within otherwise valid laws. The application of a rational connection standard for all ancillary federal intrusions poses a threat to provincial autonomy. On such a standard, new, far-reaching federal regulatory regimes could freely include measures within areas of provincial jurisdiction, as long as those measures support the regulatory scheme in some way as a matter of reason or logic.[96] Rational connection is simply too low of a bar for significant intrusions, demanding little in the way of actual justification for infringing the jurisdiction of the provinces.

The *General Motors* approach has been criticized for being too uncertain and discretionary. Yet there are ways to address this criticism. Rather than thinking of the significance of the jurisdictional intrusion as a matter of degree along a spectrum, as the Supreme Court arguably did in *General Motors*, it may be helpful to think more in terms of a binary distinction between minor and significant intrusions. For truly minor intrusions, a rationality standard is appropriate. However, for anything beyond a minor intrusion, courts should require that the intrusion be justified on a standard of reasonable necessity. Significant jurisdictional encroachments ought to be allowed only when they are reasonably necessary to achieve the objectives of the statute. This approach strikes a balance between the need to uphold the exclusivity of the division of powers, on the one hand, and the limited flexibility that may be required to achieve statutory objectives, on the other.

Providing meaningful limits to jurisdictional overlap under the double aspect and ancillary powers doctrines would go a long way toward upholding the principles of local autonomy and subsidiarity guaranteed by the exclusivity of provincial powers. However, even with these steps, provinces could remain vulnerable in one crucial respect. Starting in the latter decades of the twentieth century, Parliament has become accustomed to using its taxation and spending powers to influence provinces in exercising their own jurisdiction. This has mostly occurred through the use of conditional grants of funding. However, the legislation at issue in the *Greenhouse Gas Reference* demonstrated that conditional taxation (or regulatory charge) regimes, applicable only if a province does not toe the line, are also possible. In some cases, the conditional use of taxation and spending powers can be coercive, effectively forcing provinces to exercise their jurisdiction in line with federal priorities.[97] The potential misuse of federal fiscal powers to coerce state governments has been recognized through doctrines in US constitutional jurisprudence for some years.[98] Canadian courts have the tools they need to uphold local autonomy and subsidiarity in the face of federal fiscal coercion. The third key recommendation, therefore, is that courts use these tools to meaningfully scrutinize federal fiscal measures in areas of provincial jurisdiction.

Perhaps most significantly, federal fiscal measures attempting to direct provincial policy may be held to be ultra vires as colourable attempts to legislate areas of provincial jurisdiction. A federal tax or spending provision may be invalid if its true purpose is to govern matters under exclusive provincial jurisdiction.[99] Importantly, the fact that a given measure has a possible "double aspect" as both a fiscal measure and a measure directed at provincial heads of power should not be enough to uphold a measure if the *dominant* purpose is to regulate matters under provincial jurisdiction. Similarly, the fact that a federal fiscal measure aimed at provincial objectives is part of a larger fiscal or regulatory regime should not be enough to exempt it from meaningful scrutiny. The necessity standard for significant intrusions may help courts to resist federal fiscal coercion. Finally, the distinction between taxes and regulatory charges, while irrelevant for the purposes of section 53, has a role to play in the division of powers analysis. Federal regulatory charges, unlike federal taxes, must be linked to another head of federal power in order to be upheld.

Together, these recommendations are part of an approach to federalism based on what may be termed "water-resistant compartments." A renewed commitment to exclusivity is needed in order to support local autonomy and subsidiarity. However, the criticisms of the occasional excesses of the Privy Council's commitment to jurisdictional exclusivity are well taken. Watertight is not a fitting metaphor, since it implies that there should be no jurisdictional overlap whatsoever. While the text and purposes of the Constitution demand a strong commitment to exclusivity, the Constitution must also be interpreted in a manner that is pragmatic and suited to the evolving governance needs of a large and complex nation. I believe the approach outlined above is suited to reconciling these competing imperatives.

Indigenous Self-Government: Sovereignty and Property

The provisions of the Constitution Act, 1867 provided strong protections for the local governance autonomy of some of Canada's constitutive political communities, but not others. While the interests of Quebec, the Maritime provinces, and Ontario Grits concerned about local self-government were well represented in the vigorous negotiations leading to Confederation, those of Canada's Indigenous peoples were not. In the broad arc of Canada's history, the late nineteenth century was a low point for the recognition of the rights of self-governing Indigenous peoples, and the Constitution Act, 1867 does reflect that unfortunate aspect of its historical context.

Admittedly, there were provisions of the act that reflected an older legal tradition of respect for Indigenous autonomy. The conferral of exclusive jurisdiction over Indigenous relations on the federal Parliament, under section 91(24), was arguably based on a tradition of nation-to-nation treaty-making that predated Confederation. As I have argued, relations with Indigenous peoples were seen as interjurisdictional in character and better suited to the central government. The federal power over Indigenous relations may have also reflected the view that a more central government would be less likely to favour the local interests of settlers and more likely to deal with Indigenous people in an even-handed manner. Section 109, which sets the terms on which provinces take title to public land, also reflects an older tradition of more respectful engagement with Indigenous peoples. Under section 109, provincial title to Crown land is subject to prior interests, which even at the time of Confederation would have been understood to include Indigenous land rights.[100]

Yet, despite these provisions, the Constitution Act, 1867 fell far short of recognizing Indigenous nations as equal participants in Canada's federal structure. This became increasingly clear in the late nineteenth and twentieth centuries, as governments adopted models for Indigenous policy based on top-down control aimed at segregation and assimilation rather than engagement with self-governing constituent nations. The inclusion of protections for Aboriginal and treaty rights under section 35 of the Constitution Act, 1982 heralded a new era.[101] Judicially recognized Aboriginal rights under section 35 have mostly been limited to rights to culturally significant practices and Aboriginal title to land, rather than collective self-government by Indigenous nations.[102] Yet, at the same time, Indigenous peoples have been increasingly vocal in asserting an inherent right to self-government. In response, federal and provincial governments have been increasingly willing to recognize Indigenous self-government powers through modern treaties, self-government agreements, and sectoral self-government legislation dealing with matters such as land management and child services.[103] These developments have raised questions about the scope of Indigenous self-government and how to reconcile it with Crown sovereignty and the broader constitutional order set out in the Constitution Act, 1867.

There are three ways in which the economic vision of the Constitution can be adapted to accommodate demands for meaningful autonomy on the part of Indigenous nations and to reconcile that autonomy with Canada's broader constitutional order. First, the express provisions of the Constitution Act, 1867 that protect Indigenous autonomy should be given their full effect, consistent with the Constitution's commitment to local autonomy and subsidiarity. Second, the federal division of powers between Parliament and provincial legislatures can serve as a model for reconciling unity with Indigenous diversity. And third, Canadian law limiting Indigenous property rights can be developed in a manner that gives Indigenous owners a degree of local control comparable to what is enjoyed by non-Indigenous property owners.

The first step in reconciling Indigenous self-government with our constitutional order is to give full effect to the provisions of the Constitution that protect Indigenous autonomy. While it may seem odd to claim that the exclusive federal power over "Indians and lands reserved for the Indians" has an underlying purpose aligned with Indigenous autonomy, that is indeed the case. The provision reflects a view of Indigenous relations as being interjurisdictional in character, and, importantly, it withdraws jurisdiction over Indigenous relations from the provinces, which historically have given priority to the interests of local settlers over those of Indigenous people. As with other powers set out in sections 91 and 92, the federal power over Indigenous relations has both a positive and a negative component. Each of these can be developed in a manner consistent with Indigenous autonomy.

Firstly, the positive aspect of section 91(24) can be used by Parliament to affirmatively recognize Indigenous jurisdiction, including inherent self-government. This has already been happening for some time. Through modern treaties, self-government agreements, and legislation conferring jurisdiction over certain "sectors" of policymaking – such as land management – Parliament has begun to give robust effect to the claims of Indigenous nations as a self-governing third order of government. In its 2019 legislation dealing with child services, Parliament has gone further.[104] In contrast with prior self-government regimes, which required agreements between the government and an Indigenous nation before it could exercise its jurisdiction, this legislation recognizes "inherent" self-government. In other words, the self-government powers apply automatically, without the need for an agreement with the federal government. This is an important shift, particularly in light of the courts' hesitancy regarding the recognition of inherent Indigenous self-government powers in the absence of legislation or a Crown-Indigenous agreement. Positive use of Parliament's jurisdiction to enhance Indigenous self-government can help align Canada with the international movement toward Indigenous autonomy, including through rights recognized in the *United Nations Declaration on the Rights of Indigenous Peoples*.[105] It is to be hoped that in the future, Parliament's use of its section 91(24) power will be focused on recognizing self-government and providing for the interjurisdictional relations between Indigenous and non-Indigenous governments, rather than the top-down regulation of Indigenous people that was too often the focus in the nineteenth and twentieth centuries.

Parliament's section 91(24) power also has a negative aspect, denying jurisdiction to the provinces. This, too, serves a purpose related to Indigenous autonomy, and yet it has sadly been neglected in recent years. The exclusion of Indigenous lands and peoples from provincial jurisdiction promotes Indigenous autonomy by limiting the number of legislative bodies to which Indigenous governments are subject. It also ensures that jurisdiction over Indigenous nations is not exercised by a provincial legislature swayed by local interests that might view Indigenous governments as competitors for resources, residents, or a tax base. Restricting provincial regulation of Indigenous peoples and lands also helps to affirm Indigenous nations as equal partners in the federation, not subject to significant interference by other local orders of government.

However, the scope of provincial legislatures' ability to regulate Indigenous peoples and lands has grown in recent years, despite the existence of an expressly exclusive federal power in this area. The trend toward flexible federalism, through the double aspect doctrine and ancillary powers, has increased the scope for provincial laws to affect Indigenous interests. Moreover, in the *Tsilhqot'in* Aboriginal title decision, the Supreme Court of Canada overturned recent precedent regarding the application of interjurisdictional immunity (IJI) to Indigenous rights. Previous case law had held that Aboriginal and treaty rights were protected from provincial legislation by IJI. Essentially, provincial laws of general application could not be applied to limit such rights since these rights are at the "core" of the exclusive federal power over Indigenous peoples and lands. Needless to say, this served as an important form of protection for Indigenous interests. Nevertheless, the Supreme Court in *Tsilhqot'in* overturned its own 2006 decision on this point and held that IJI would no longer apply to Aboriginal and treaty rights.[106]

The Court's decision to abandon IJI for Aboriginal and treaty rights seemed to prioritize regulatory flexibility for provincial governments. The Court's position was that the balancing of interests provided by the test for infringements of section 35 rights provided an appropriate degree of protection for these rights. Indeed, the Court went so far as to call the application of IJI to Indigenous rights an "absurdity," in one of the most egregious instances in recent years in which the Court has failed to grasp the principles underlying the structural provisions of the Constitution.[107] While section 35 does provide protection for Indigenous rights, the Court's interpretation of section 35 also affirms governments' power to infringe those rights. With respect, section 35 is not an adequate replacement for the *jurisdictional* protections for Indigenous interests that are rooted in pre-Confederation legal traditions and set out explicitly in the text of the Constitution Act, 1867.

I hope that in the coming years, the Court will revisit its IJI holding in *Tsilhqot'in*, which has already been the subject of criticism.[108] Far from a formalist "absurdity," IJI, as applied to Indigenous rights, is an important component of the economic vision of the Constitution. Indeed, it is one of the principal ways in which the structural provisions of the Constitution make space for Indigenous self-government.

The second way in which the economic vision of the Constitution can assist in developing Indigenous self-government is by providing a model for reconciling unity with Indigenous diversity. As I have argued throughout this book, the federal division of powers reconciles local autonomy with economic integration in impressively thoughtful ways. It must be acknowledged that the circumstances of Indigenous groups vary dramatically, and the specifics of how to reconcile self-government with Canadian sovereignty and unity will also vary. The federal division of powers should not be adopted reflexively. Nevertheless, it does provide a useful and compelling guide to which subjects are of primarily local concern, and which subjects are likely to affect parties in other jurisdictions and are thus best left to the federal (rather than provincial or Indigenous) orders of government.

The federal division of powers has already been used as a model in a number of cases in which Indigenous self-government powers have been recognized. This is most obviously the case with respect to the territorial legislature and government of Nunavut. The creation of the Inuit-majority territory was one of the commitments in the Nunavut Land Claims Agreement, and since the creation of the territory it has functioned as a de facto Inuit government.[109] The jurisdiction of the territorial legislature mirrors that of provincial legislatures under the Constitution Act, 1867, providing robust control over local matters, including the broad category of "property and civil rights," without trenching on Parliament's heads of power.[110]

Provincial heads of power also seem to have influenced the jurisdiction of First Nations governments under other modern treaties and self-government agreements, though with more customization than occurred with respect to the territory of Nunavut. These agreements often provide for a broad range of jurisdiction over primarily local matters, such as lands, natural resources, environmental protection, public safety, roads and transportation, local or village governments, industrial relations, public works, health, education, social services, the solemnization of marriage, and child and family services.[111] However, the agreements generally do not extend Indigenous jurisdiction to any of the significant heads of federal economic power, though there are some limited exceptions related to distinctive Indigenous concerns, such as Indigenous control over fisheries.[112] The areas in which federal legislation provides for sectoral self-government also align with areas of provincial jurisdiction, including land management and child and family services.[113]

Scholars have previously identified federalism as a promising model for reconciling Indigenous self-government with the Canadian constitutional order.[114] Indeed, the federal division of powers presents a compelling model for federal self-government legislation, Crown-Indigenous agreements, and possibly judicially recognized self-government powers. By providing for presumptive local control over most economic questions, while reserving matters of genuine common concern for the federal Parliament, the Constitution's division of powers reflects a commitment to local autonomy and subsidiarity. This commitment can and should be extended to accommodate the self-government interests of Indigenous nations. Canada's Constitution initially failed to fully recognize the importance of local autonomy and subsidiarity in relation to Indigenous nations, even while it gave effect to those principles for other founding political communities. Yet the federal division of powers provides a model for how to complete the project of Confederation by recognizing the local autonomy of Indigenous nations within a united Canada.

The third way in which the economic vision of the Constitution can be extended to accommodate Indigenous self-government relates to property rights. Property rights in land are often overlooked in discussions of Indigenous self-government, yet they contribute in vital ways to Indigenous territorial autonomy, complementing the jurisdiction of Indigenous governments.[115] Collectively held property interests in land allow Indigenous communities to "set the agenda" for their resources according to their own values and priorities.[116] In addition to collectively held title, distinctive individual property interests held by members allow Indigenous communities to provide for uses such as housing, commerce, and farming, while ensuring those uses are aligned with the long-term interests of the community.[117] Importantly, the traditional laws, circumstances, and priorities of Indigenous communities vary significantly. That means that property institutions suited to one community will not necessarily be appropriate for another. Meaningful self-government for Indigenous nations requires that they have flexibility in adapting property institutions to local needs.[118]

Unfortunately, in recent years, the Supreme Court has developed the law of Aboriginal title in ways that limit the decision-making autonomy of Indigenous title holders. Firstly, the Court has held that Aboriginal title is subject to a special "inherent limit," which prevents the land from being put to uses inconsistent with an Indigenous group's relationship with the land. To put it bluntly, no one knows what this means. It is a unique restriction, applicable only to Indigenous property owners, which the Court invented out of whole cloth in its 1997 *Delgamuukw* decision.[119]

Secondly, while Aboriginal title has long been subject to restraints on alienation, the Court has extended these restraints in new and unpredictable ways.[120] For centuries, it has been clear that Aboriginal title itself can only be surrendered to the Crown, and cannot be transferred directly to private parties.[121] This restriction may serve a valid purpose in ensuring that an Indigenous community's land base serves as a locus for a distinctive self-governing community over the long run.[122] Yet, in *Tsilhqot'in*, the Court went further, holding that Aboriginal title "cannot be alienated except to the Crown *or encumbered in ways that would prevent future generations of the group from using and enjoying it.*"[123] The scope of the new limit on encumbrances is unclear, but it could conceivably restrict mortgages of leasehold or member possessory interests, or even the granting of such interests in the first place.[124] If so, the limit would severely restrict the decision-making autonomy of Aboriginal title holders, along with their ability to adapt their property systems to their own circumstances, values, and legal traditions.

While Aboriginal title is only one form of property in land held by Indigenous nations, the Supreme Court has gone decidedly in the wrong direction in imposing novel restrictions on use and expanding restrictions on transfer. It is to be hoped that the Court will reverse course in future decisions. The Constitution is committed to secure property rights and local autonomy, and both of these values are served by limiting the scope of uncertain and discretionary restrictions on Indigenous nations' title to land. Beyond the Aboriginal title context, policymakers and Indigenous leaders should continue to stress the importance of local control over rules of land tenure.[125] There are existing mechanisms for Indigenous communities to exert greater control over these rules, including by enacting a land code under the First Nations Land Management Act or enacting legislation under jurisdiction recognized through a modern treaty or self-government agreement.[126] These property-based tools should not be overlooked in the continuing movement to establish Indigenous self-government within Canada's constitutional order.

Conclusion

The economic vision of the Constitution is not just about economic union. Throughout this book, I have attempted to show that the centralizing elements of the economic vision are balanced by a strong commitment to local decision-making based on both secure property rights and local governance autonomy. Unfortunately, courts have begun to lose touch with the economic vision, including these decentralizing features. My hope is that the foregoing provides a blueprint for a renewal of the Constitution's commitment to secure property rights and local governance autonomy, including how these commitments can be extended in order to make Indigenous peoples full partners in Confederation. The question of how to reconcile these features with economic integration and free trade is the subject of the next and final chapter of the book.

Renewing the Economic Constitution

Economic Integration and Free Trade

In addition to its decentralizing commitments to secure property rights and local autonomy, the economic vision of the Constitution also includes important unifying features – namely, the constitutional commitments to economic integration and free internal trade. These centralizing features of the economic Constitution provided the historical impetus for Confederation. Moreover, since they relate to genuine issues of common concern, they provide an ongoing basis for our shared political life, despite Canadians' many differences and specific, local concerns.

Unfortunately, courts in recent years have lost touch with the economic vision underlying the Constitution, including with respect to economic integration and free trade. In this final chapter, I hope to identify the areas in which courts have failed to uphold the economic vision, and what a renewed understanding of the economic Constitution would mean for these issues. There are two broad dimensions of this topic that will be considered in turn: first, the commitment to positive integration, including the scope and definition of federal economic jurisdiction; and second, the commitment to free trade through negative integration, including limits on provincial, Indigenous, and local governments' powers to restrict trade and mobility. Each of these issues will be considered in turn, with the aim of completing the account of a renewed understanding of the economic Constitution that I began in the previous chapter.

Positive Economic Integration and
Water-Resistant Compartments

Positive economic integration refers to positive measures that aim to promote economic relations.[1] As I have argued in this book, one of the principal underlying objectives of many of the enumerated heads of federal power is to allow Parliament to take positive steps to promote economic integration. Parliament's enumerated powers provide it with broad authority in this regard. While Parliament has exercised its enumerated powers in many areas with the aim of promoting economic integration, there are still areas in which Parliament could go further than it has. However, future federal legislation aimed at promoting economic integration could involve federal intrusions into areas that have traditionally been under provincial control. This could give rise to new federalism disputes, making it all the more important to have a proper understanding of the scope of Parliament's economic powers.

For instance, there is room for Parliament to act in bringing a greater degree of harmonization to the rules governing interprovincial trucking, an industry that remains subject to a thicket of often inconsistent provincial laws.[2] Interprovincial trucking undoubtedly falls under Parliament's section 92(10)(a) power over interprovincial undertakings.[3] Indeed, the provincial role in regulating the industry is largely the result of a previous choice by Parliament to abdicate its responsibility in this area and delegate its authority to provincial governments.[4] Parliament would merely need to reassert its authority in order to bring greater harmonization to the trucking industry.

Another area in which Parliament could potentially go further is with respect to interprovincial direct-to-consumer liquor sales. Current federal legislation no longer prohibits liquor sales within Canada, though these sales remain subject to a range of restrictions imposed by the provinces.[5] Parliament could likely go further than it has under its interprovincial trade and commerce power, affirmatively mandating that interprovincial liquor sales be permitted subject only to federally imposed limits.[6]

However, moves of this nature would again raise the contentious question of how to assess the secondary effects of legislation from one order of government on the jurisdiction of the other order of government. If Parliament were to pass new legislation falling principally under federal heads of power relating to interprovincial trade, communication, and transportation, what would be the appropriate way to assess the legislation's intrusions into areas of provincial jurisdiction?

With respect to federal powers over transportation and communication, courts have generally allowed for some incidental regulation of intraprovincial components of interprovincial transportation and communications undertakings.[7] That is appropriate, given the need for integrated transportation and communications networks, and the difficulty in separating interprovincial and intraprovincial elements of such networks.

By contrast, however, courts have taken an unduly restrictive view of Parliament's power to regulate intraprovincial matters as a secondary feature of legislation aimed at interprovincial trade. Beginning with the Privy Council and extending into the Supreme Court's late-twentieth-century jurisprudence, courts largely took a categorical approach that effectively precluded any regulation of intraprovincial trade, even in cases where the legislation principally aimed at interprovincial trade.[8] This effectively neutralized the trade and commerce power as a means of positive economic integration since there are few measures that can address interprovincial trade while leaving intraprovincial trade entirely untouched.

The 1979 case of *Dominion Stores* exemplifies the pitfalls of an unduly restrictive approach to the secondary effects of federal laws in areas of provincial jurisdiction.[9] The case dealt with the Canada Agricultural Products Standards Act, which allowed the federal cabinet to establish grade names for various agricultural products, such as "Canada Extra Fancy" apples, and to set the standards that had to be met for those grade names.[10] The act made the use of the designated grade names mandatory in interprovincial and international trade of agricultural products covered by the act. The act notably did *not* make the use of the grade names mandatory in intraprovincial trade. However, under section 3(2) of the act, products that did use one of the grade names had to actually meet the standards for that grade name. This requirement did apply in intraprovincial trade. In other words, sellers engaged in transactions within a single province did not have to use the grade names, but if they did, the products had to meet the applicable standards. A majority of the Court found that even this largely voluntary extension of the scheme to intraprovincial transactions was too much. The Court held that the aspects of the act that applied to intraprovincial transactions were ultra vires. In so holding, the Court continued the categorical approach of the Privy Council that had precluded even incidental regulation of intraprovincial trade pursuant to the interprovincial and international branch of the trade and commerce power.

Dominion Stores is notable in that it involved a relatively minor intrusion into intraprovincial trade, and one that was clearly integral to the success of a legislative scheme directed primarily at interprovincial and international trade. The act sought to facilitate interjurisdictional trade in agricultural products by lowering information barriers to transactions. The basic idea was to ensure that a consumer or wholesaler buying BC apples in Nova Scotia would be able to quickly and easily ascertain what she was getting by reference to a uniform set of grade names. Such grade names are particularly useful for interprovincial and international trade. Buyers from another province or country are less likely to be familiar with particular producers, and so they may be more likely to rely on standardized signals of product quality. In order for such a scheme to succeed in lowering information barriers in interjurisdictional trade, it is not strictly necessary for those engaged in intraprovincial trade to adopt the same set of grade names. However, the use of grade names by products that do not actually comply with the requisite standards is another matter. The whole point of the scheme is that when you see a label like "Canada Extra Fancy," you know what you are getting. When products in intraprovincial trade use those same grade names but do not comply with the applicable standards, they cause confusion and degrade the informational value of the label. Accordingly, preventing the non-compliant use of the grade names was arguably necessary to the success of a federal scheme aimed primarily at facilitating trade across jurisdictional lines.

I would not be the first to suggest that *Dominion Stores* was wrongly decided.[11] The case shows how a strictly categorical approach to the division of powers can be impractical, and indeed can be inconsistent with the economic vision underlying the economic heads of power. It is difficult to effectively regulate interprovincial and international trade while leaving intraprovincial transactions completely unaffected. A pragmatic and purposive approach to the division of powers would allow for ancillary regulatory intrusions that are truly necessary to the success of an otherwise valid scheme. Such a statement would largely be accepted wisdom in other areas of federalism jurisprudence, but when it comes to the interprovincial trade and commerce power, the courts have unfortunately policed jurisdictional boundaries with such a strictness as to undermine much of its practical utility as a basis for positive economic integration.

While *Dominion Stores* is technically still good law, one may rightly doubt whether the current Supreme Court would take such a restrictive approach to the ancillary features of a federal law, even a law enacted under the interprovincial trade and commerce power. Indeed, in light of jurisprudential trends favouring a flexible approach to federalism, the more significant risk going forward may be that courts go too far in the opposite direction, allowing for levels of intrusion that tend to undermine local autonomy. What is needed is a principled approach that gives meaningful effect to the federal heads of power, while at the same time protecting provincial autonomy from unnecessary intrusions.

The most appropriate way forward is an approach based on the idea of water-resistant compartments that I developed in previous chapters. Essentially, ancillary jurisdictional intrusions should be allowed where they are reasonably necessary to achieve an objective within the jurisdiction of the enacting body. On this standard, the scheme in *Dominion Stores* would undoubtedly have been upheld. Preventing non-compliant use of grade names was necessary to the effectiveness of a scheme aimed at lowering information barriers in interprovincial and international trade. While ancillary intrusions would still be permitted in certain cases, governments would have to provide a robust justification based on a standard of reasonable necessity. This approach would avoid the problems associated with the more permissive standard requiring only a rational and functional connection, which I discussed in the previous chapter. Such an approach would too readily permit federal intrusions that could undermine local autonomy and the principle of subsidiarity. The water-resistant approach gives full effect to the enumerated heads of power, preventing them from being hemmed in by strict and impractical policing of jurisdictional boundaries, which has been the fate of the trade and commerce power for most of its history. At the same time, it gives due consideration to the important objectives reflected in the principle of jurisdictional exclusivity, including the commitment to local autonomy and subsidiarity.

Enumerated Federal Powers and Positive Integration

Dominion Stores notwithstanding, the most significant impediments to positive integration in recent decades have been political rather than legal. Successive federal governments have been largely unwilling to use the constitutional tools at their disposal to reduce trade barriers and actively promote economic integration, with a few notable exceptions.[12] There are a number of specific areas in which Parliament could take positive legislative action to reduce trade barriers, including interprovincial trucking and liquor sales, discussed above, as well as interprovincial pipelines and electrical transmission lines.

With respect to interprovincial pipelines, the policy challenge for economic integration lies largely with hostile or indifferent provincial and local governments. Regulations from these orders of government can frustrate the plans of project proponents by adding to cost and uncertainty, even in cases where a pipeline has been federally approved. Parliament could help address this problem by seeking to "occupy the field," indicating an intent to comprehensively regulate these pipelines to the exclusion of provincial and local laws.[13] There is no doubt that interprovincial pipelines are under federal jurisdiction as interprovincial undertakings.[14] The benefit of a legislative attempt to occupy the field is that it should render inoperative any provincial or local laws regulating such pipelines (including those that may have an ulterior motive to discourage the building of pipelines). In theory, the doctrine of interjurisdictional immunity should make such legislation unnecessary, but in light of the courts' recent skepticism toward that doctrine, a federal attempt to occupy the field may help reduce legal uncertainty surrounding the regulatory regime applicable to interprovincial pipelines.

While pipelines have been among the more controversial federalism issues in recent years, disputes over electrical transmission lines may become more common in the future. As Canada's economy shifts away from fossil fuels, demand for electricity, including electricity from remote sources like hydro dams, is likely to increase. Up to this point, Canada's electrical grid has been largely segmented into distinct provincial grids, with relatively little interprovincial transmission.[15] Allowing for more interprovincial transmission, for instance from large producers of hydroelectricity in British Columbia and Quebec to other provinces, may help Canada achieve its goals in reducing carbon emissions.[16] Unfortunately, new electrical transmission lines are often no less controversial than pipelines, sparking opposition from communities along a proposed route.[17] As with interprovincial pipelines, there may be a role for Parliament in comprehensively regulating these undertakings in order to streamline the regulatory burden faced by proponents and make it less likely that they can be held up by provincial and local laws that do not reflect the national interest.

Federal legislation addressing pipelines and transmission lines could also seek to establish clearer frameworks and timelines for Indigenous consultation. While Indigenous consent is the appropriate ideal for resource development projects with primarily local effects, other approaches may be needed for linear projects that affect dozens or hundreds of distinct communities.[18] Reaching unanimity among affected communities for these kinds of projects is often an impractical, and indeed, impossible objective. Moreover, different Indigenous communities along a route may have competing constitutionally protected rights. While opponents of a project may argue that there will be negative environmental impacts affecting their Aboriginal rights and title, supportive Indigenous communities also have constitutionally protected rights at stake, including rights to derive economic benefits from their lands and resources.[19] An approach to consultation that stymies Indigenous communities' ability to draw economic benefits from development, including through impact-benefit agreements with project proponents, ultimately fails to acknowledge the significance of the economic dimensions of Indigenous rights, including Aboriginal title.[20]

It is ultimately the role of Parliament and the federal government to determine whether an interjurisdictional pipeline or transmission line is in the national interest, with due consideration to local concerns. Legislation providing an appropriate framework for Indigenous consultation on linear projects would undoubtedly be within federal jurisdiction. By prioritizing national interest considerations with respect to interjurisdictional linear projects, such an approach would be consistent with the economic vision of the Constitution.

Beyond these specific industries, there may also be a way for Parliament to legislate so as to reduce trade barriers more generally. Federal efforts to reduce trade barriers in recent years have mostly been focused on executive agreements with provincial and territorial governments, including the recent Canadian Free Trade Agreement (CFTA).[21] This approach is attractive to the federal government because it is consensual, allowing the government to move incrementally on the issue of internal trade while avoiding political and legal disputes with the provinces. However, the results have been disappointing.[22] The CFTA contains hundreds of pages of exceptions to the general principle of free trade, inserted at the behest of individual provinces.[23]

A bolder alternative approach would be for Parliament to unilaterally enact legislation affirmatively requiring free interprovincial trade in goods and services, subject only to restrictions that do not discriminate based on province of origin unless that is necessary to achieve an important objective. Such legislation would relate in pith and substance to interprovincial trade and would thus fall under Parliament's section 91(2) power over trade and commerce. Inconsistent provincial laws, that is, laws discriminating against goods or services based on province of origin in an unjustified manner, would be rendered inoperative. Such legislation would affect a wide range of matters under provincial jurisdiction, including provincial economic regulations. If the

Supreme Court were to adopt the restrictive *Dominion Stores* approach to the trade and commerce power, those effects on areas of provincial jurisdiction would likely be constitutionally fatal to the legislation. However, assuming the Supreme Court could be persuaded to allow such effects as are necessary to achieve a federal objective relating to interprovincial trade, the legislation could be upheld.

Unilateral federal action to reduce trade barriers in this way would require bold and decisive shifts on two fronts – firstly from the federal Parliament, in choosing to take action over possible objections from the provinces, and secondly from the Supreme Court, in giving full effect to the federal power over trade and commerce. Boldness on both of these fronts simultaneously seems unlikely in the near future. Federal legislation of this nature would be disruptive to the established practices of Canadian federalism, in which trade barriers erected by provinces have been tolerated for so long. Nevertheless, despite being disruptive, such positive action by Parliament would be perfectly consistent with the economic vision of the Constitution. The Constitution unambiguously favours economic integration, and it gives Parliament positive powers to lower trade barriers and encourage integration, including the power over interprovincial trade. Positive action by Parliament to reduce barriers to trade should be welcomed, as long as it is directed primarily at interprovincial trade and its effects on areas of provincial jurisdiction are necessary to achieve its objectives.

General Federal Powers and the Economic Constitution

In addition to helping explain the scope of its specifically enumerated powers, the economic vision of the Constitution can also help shed light on debates over the scope of Parliament's more general economic powers, namely the peace, order and good government (POGG) power, and the "general" trade and commerce power. Parliament's residual power is grounded in the power to make laws for the peace, order, and good government of Canada, set out in the preamble to section 91.[24] In addition, section 91 also contains another, quasi-residual economic power. The general branch of the trade and commerce power, while not technically a residual power, functions very much like one in practice. That power recognizes federal jurisdiction over matters that transcend particular industries, transactions or local markets and relate to "trade as a whole."[25] Since this federal power is framed at such a high level of abstraction, it has provided the basis for federal jurisdiction over a diverse range of matters, including trademarks, competition law, and systemic risk in capital markets.[26] The general trade and commerce power is quasi-residual, in that it draws into its ambit particular matters that are not part of specifically enumerated powers and that meet certain general criteria.

Parliament's general economic powers have been a recurring source of tension in Canadian constitutional law, including in the recent *Greenhouse Gas Reference*.[27] In that case, the Court upheld a relatively far-reaching federal regime establishing minimum national standards for carbon pricing based on the "national concern" branch of POGG.[28] Another relatively recent dispute involved a proposal on the part of the federal government to create a national securities regulator pursuant to its authority under the general trade and commerce power. The Court unanimously held the proposed act to be unconstitutional, though it did recognize a federal power over systemic risk in capital markets and a related power over data collection in those markets.[29] Cases involving the scope of Parliament's general economic powers tend to be contentious because they raise fundamental questions about the nature of the federation, including whether economic jurisdiction should be centralized or decentralized. These cases also raise difficult questions of interpretation, including how much authority courts should be able to recognize based on general and open-ended federal powers.

A proper understanding of the economic vision of the Constitution may shed some light on how to approach cases involving general economic powers going forward, though it is unlikely to make these cases any less contentious. There are two key propositions about Parliament's general powers that can be derived from the economic vision of the Constitution expounded in this book: (1) the scope of the general economic powers should be informed by the principles underlying Parliament's specifically enumerated powers; and (2) the scope of these powers must be strictly limited to those necessary to give effect to the principles underlying Parliament's jurisdiction. This latter requirement serves to reconcile Parliament's general powers with the Constitution's commitment to local autonomy and subsidiarity, as well as the balance reflected in the specifically enumerated powers.

The established tests for the national concern branch of POGG and the general trade and commerce power already reflect the principles underlying Parliament's specifically enumerated powers to a significant degree. As discussed in previous chapters, Parliament's enumerated powers relate to: interjurisdictional economic relations, the infrastructure of exchange, national fiscal policy, non-rivalrous national goods (e.g., intellectual property and census data), and economic activity with direct extraprovincial effects (e.g., fisheries). The dominant justifications for these categories of federal power are essentially twofold. Firstly, they include subjects in which a decision in one locality has significant effects on other localities. On such matters, a centralized authority is better placed to account for all of the relevant policy considerations. And secondly, federal powers include subjects on which national policy coordination is a paramount consideration, for instance due to the nature of the subject or the need for standardization.

These two justifications are represented in the tests for both the national concern branch of POGG and the general trade and commerce power. The Court in the *Greenhouse Gas Reference* appropriately recognized the extraprovincial or international nature or effects of a matter as a key consideration in the recognition of a matter under POGG.[30] Moreover, the POGG national concern test also includes a requirement of provincial inability to deal with the matter, which is an indication of the need for national policy coordination.[31] The test for the recognition of a matter under the general trade and commerce power also emphasizes provincial inability and extraprovincial effects.[32] In addition, the test includes a requirement that the matter relate to "trade as a whole," rather than particular industries, transactions, or local markets.[33] This is best understood as a conceptual requirement that explains why a given matter requires national policy coordination. Because the matter is qualitatively distinct from local matters and transcends particular industries, transactions, or local markets, it must be addressed at the national level or not at all.

Canadian courts have already incorporated the principles underlying federal economic jurisdiction into their approach to both the national concern branch of POGG and the general trade and commerce power. Indeed, these principles are at the heart of both tests. Yet the Court has been less consistent in actually *limiting* the scope of residual powers to those necessary to give effect to the principles underlying federal jurisdiction. In this regard, the *Securities Reference* and the *Greenhouse Gas Reference* provide an interesting contrast. In the *Securities Reference*, the Supreme Court rejected the argument that comprehensive federal securities regulation could be grounded in the general trade and commerce power, instead holding that federal jurisdiction was limited to much more specific matters – namely, systemic risk and related data collection.[34] Much of securities regulation amounts to the regulation of a particular industry, as well as particular transactions and markets – meaning that it appropriately falls largely under provincial jurisdiction.

In the *Securities Reference*, only the specific phenomena that transcend those areas were found to fall under federal jurisdiction.

In the *Greenhouse Gas Reference*, the majority quite properly found that the greenhouse gas emissions involve significant extraprovincial effects, and that there is a provincial inability to adequately address the issue.[35] In the absence of federal action, there is no way to ensure that provinces would properly account for the external effects of their emissions on other provinces and countries. The extraprovincial aspects of the problem of carbon emissions fall squarely within the principles that underpin federal economic jurisdiction more broadly. It is a matter defined by extraprovincial effects and requiring national (and international) coordination. However, the specific legislation that was upheld in the case goes well beyond addressing the extraprovincial effects requiring national policy coordination. Unlike in the *Securities Reference*, the majority decision in the *Greenhouse Gas Reference* does not confine federal jurisdiction just to the specific matters that transcend local competence.

The Court in the *Greenhouse Gas Reference* recognized that establishing minimum national standards for price stringency to reduce greenhouse gas emissions is a matter falling under the federal POGG power.[36] The Court was justified in coming to this conclusion, in light of the extraprovincial dimensions of the problem of carbon emissions and the need for national policy coordination. Yet there is a very straightforward and targeted way Parliament could have chosen to implement such minimum national pricing standards: it could have imposed a uniform national carbon tax or a minimum carbon price, with possible deductions permitted for taxes and prices imposed by provincial legislation. Instead, Parliament did something quite different. It established two distinct regimes, a fuel charge directed at consumers and a pricing regime based on emissions intensity for large emitters.[37] Under both regimes, it delegated sweeping authority to the federal cabinet to determine the content of the federal pricing regime and to assess whether the federal pricing regime would apply in a given province.

In determining whether to apply the federal regime in a province, the primary, but not sole, factor to be considered is the stringency of provincial pricing mechanisms.[38] The fact that price stringency is not the only relevant factor introduces a significant element of discretion into the decision-making process. Indeed, the cabinet has already deemed certain provincial regimes to be compliant despite the fact that they result in lower effective prices than those required in other provinces.[39] With respect to the regime for large emitters, the act allows for more or less stringent pricing standards to be set by industry, based on factors other than the need for minimum standards of price stringency to reduce emissions.[40] The current regulations establish pricing standards that vary across sectors of the economy.[41]

In allowing the cabinet to consider factors other than price stringency in determining whether to apply the federal regime in a province, and in allowing broad discretion to determine the content of the pricing regimes, including on an industry-by-industry basis, the act goes well beyond addressing the extraprovincial effects of carbon emissions. It apparently allows the federal cabinet to pick winners and losers based on factors unrelated to carbon emissions. In that sense, as Justices Brown and Rowe point out in their respective dissents, the act allows cabinet to engage in federal industrial policy within areas of provincial jurisdiction.[42]

In my view, Justice Côté's cogent dissent in the *Greenhouse Gas Reference* gets it right in holding that establishing minimum national standards for price stringency to reduce greenhouse gas emissions is a matter falling under federal jurisdiction, but this particular Act cannot be characterized in those terms.[43] The discretion afforded to the governor in council is simply too broad. It permits policymaking in areas of provincial jurisdiction that are not necessary to achieve objectives relating to establishing minimum standards for carbon price stringency. The Court ought to have required a more narrowly tailored approach, focused on the specific matters that transcend provincial competence, as it did in the *Securities Reference*.

In future cases involving the national concern branch of POGG and the general trade and commerce power, two sets of considerations should be born in mind. Firstly, section 91 includes broad, open-ended grants of authority, including the POGG and trade and commerce powers, which permit the recognition of federal jurisdiction over unenumerated subjects that reflect the general principles underlying federal jurisdiction. Whether one is a textualist or a living constitutionalist, one ought to acknowledge the open-textured nature of federal jurisdiction and the possibility for new subjects to be recognized, in keeping with the general principles underlying the Constitution. Secondly, and just as importantly, however, the recognition of federal authority under these heads of powers must be strictly limited to legislative action necessary to give effect to those principles. The alternative would be to undermine the careful balance reflected in the specifically enumerated powers, as well as the constitutional commitment to local autonomy and subsidiarity.[44]

Negative Integration and Free Trade: Section 121, the Division of Powers, and a Way Forward after Comeau

In addition to the positive integration provided for through federal economic powers, the Constitution also provides for negative integration, restricting the ability of provinces and local governments to create barriers to trade. Unfortunately, judicial decisions in two closely related areas have tended to undermine negative integration in recent years. The first is the broad trend toward a permissive approach to laws that have secondary features relating to matters within the exclusive jurisdiction of the other order of government. This approach opens the door to increased provincial regulation of economic matters that are supposed to be under the exclusive jurisdiction of Parliament, including matters dealing with interjurisdictional economic relations and the infrastructure of exchange. The principle of jurisdictional exclusivity is crucial to how the Constitution achieves negative economic integration. Jurisprudential trends away from that principle therefore have implications for the constitutional guards against barriers to trade. The second area in which judicial decisions have undermined negative integration is in the interpretation of section 121, the Constitution's stand-alone free trade provision, in the *Comeau* case.[45] This second area is closely related to the first, since the permissive approach to trade barriers that the Court took in *Comeau* was designed to mirror a flexible federalism analysis.

In order to properly understand the history of negative integration under the Constitution, it is important to consider section 121 together with the division of powers, and in particular, courts' approach to provincial measures that affect interprovincial trade. It is true that early decisions limited the scope of section 121 to a prohibition against interprovincial tariffs, a relatively narrow (and mistaken) interpretation of a broadly worded provision.[46] Yet this limited reading of section 121 came at a time when the division of powers acted as a meaningful source of negative integration. Until recent decades, provincial measures that limited interprovincial trade were given serious scrutiny and were regularly struck down on the basis that they related not to intraprovincial objectives, but rather to interprovincial trade, a subject under exclusive federal jurisdiction.[47]

The history of regimes governing the distribution of alcohol provides an instructive case study on how constitutional restrictions against provincially enacted trade barriers have changed over time. In the aftermath of Prohibition, provinces sought to establish government monopolies on the distribution of liquor. In order for provincial liquor boards to operate as monopolies, there had to be a restriction on liquor imported by anyone other than the liquor board. Otherwise, parties could circumvent the liquor board by buying from outside the province. Yet it was understood at the time, on the basis of existing case law, that provinces could not prohibit the importation of goods from another province. Such a measure would relate in pith and substance to interprovincial trade and thus would be ultra vires the provincial legislature.[48] And so Parliament and the provinces established a cooperative scheme. The provinces established liquor monopolies. These were then reinforced by the federal Importation of Intoxicating Liquors Act (IILA), which until recently prohibited the importation of liquor into a province by anyone except the provincial liquor monopoly.[49]

Similar cooperative schemes were also later required to establish marketing monopolies for agricultural products, with federal legislation addressing the interprovincial dimensions of the scheme, including restrictions on the sale of agricultural products in interprovincial markets.[50] If provinces could have restricted interprovincial trade as an ancillary feature of liquor distribution or agricultural marketing regimes, on the basis of a mere rational connection to provincial objectives, the federal portions of these cooperative schemes would have been unnecessary. Yet at the time, it was understood that the restrictions on interprovincial trade necessary to uphold such regimes were within the exclusive jurisdiction of Parliament. The division of powers reinforced negative economic integration by denying provinces the power to restrict such trade. Only Parliament, representing interests from across the country, had the power to enact restrictions of this nature.

It is in this context that the Comeau decision should be assessed. The statutory provision at issue in Comeau prohibited the possession of all but small quantities of liquor not purchased from the New Brunswick Liquor Control Board.[51] An obvious effect of this prohibition is to limit the importation of liquor into the province from any source other than the Liquor Control Board. In a previous era, such a provision very likely would have been struck down as ultra vires the provincial legislature, at least if it was not supported by the federal component of an interlocking federal-provincial scheme. Yet the emergence of flexible conceptions of federalism has cast that view very much into doubt, a point reinforced by the Comeau decision.

As I have previously argued, the Court in Comeau sought to align section 121 with the Court's division of powers jurisprudence.[52] The Court quite properly moved away from an understanding of section 121 that was limited to a bar against tariffs, recognizing that non-tariff measures could similarly restrict trade contrary to the text and purpose of the provision. At the same time, the Court apparently sought to avoid placing any meaningful restraints on provincial legislatures beyond those already imposed by the division of powers. Unfortunately, the Court aligned section 121 with a version of the division of powers analysis infused with contemporary ideas about flexible federalism.[53] Under the Court's approach, a measure that restricts trade across a provincial boundary may still be upheld if it is rationally connected to a larger regulatory regime that is otherwise within provincial jurisdiction.[54] The decision in *Comeau* strongly implies that not only is this the test for section 121, but it is also the approach to take in determining whether a provincial measure infringes the exclusive federal jurisdiction over interprovincial trade.

If that is the case, then the federal IILA was superfluous.[55] Recall that it was enacted in order to reinforce provincial liquor monopolies on the understanding that the provinces themselves could not prohibit interprovincial liquor transactions. Yet if provinces can simply bar out-of-province liquor as an incidental feature of their liquor control statutes, without needing an assist from Parliament, then there is no need for the federal portion of the cooperative scheme governing liquor distribution. Moreover, the federal components of other cooperative schemes would also appear to be largely or entirely superfluous, including with respect to agricultural marketing boards. If provinces can restrict imports and exports as a rational and functional part of a scheme directed primarily at agricultural transactions within the province, then it appears provinces should have the power to enact agricultural products marketing regimes on their own, despite twentieth-century case law to the contrary.[56] This provocative suggestion should serve to underscore just how far down the road of flexible federalism the courts seem to have gone, and what that means for the Constitution's commitment to negative economic integration. If provinces can restrict trade pursuant to regulatory regimes in areas where they have traditionally needed the support of federal legislation, they can also do it in other areas, enacting new kinds of trade barriers that fail to account for the national interest.

The principle of jurisdictional exclusivity in division of powers cases protects economic integration and free trade. Indeed, as I have argued, this is a crucial design feature of the economic constitution. The grant of power over interprovincial trade to Parliament is significant; but equally significant is the *denial* of such power to the provinces, which are more likely to enact restrictions based on parochial considerations at odds with the national interest. If the Court had continued to hew more closely to a classical conception of federalism in its division of powers case law, then the decision in *Comeau* regarding the interpretation of section 121 would have been much less significant. Provincial trade barriers permitted under section 121 would still have been meaningfully restricted by the division of powers. Instead, it appears that flexible federalism is the dominant idea driving both the Court's approach to the division of powers and its approach to section 121. Despite the strong indications stemming from the text, purpose, and legislative history of section 121, that it was indeed meant to ensure free trade in goods among the provinces, the Court was simply unwilling to countenance an approach to section 121 that was perceived to be at odds with the "dominant tide" of flexible federalism.[57]

While the Court's approach to the division of powers may help explain the disappointing result in the *Comeau* case, a renewed understanding of the importance of jurisdictional exclusivity could also provide a promising way forward after *Comeau*. The essential idea animating the approach in *Comeau* is that section 121 should go no further than the division of powers in limiting provincial action relating to interprovincial trade. This would be an appropriate approach to take if the Court's federalism jurisprudence recognized the significance of the principle of jurisdictional exclusivity to the Constitution's economic framework. Accordingly, if there were to be a renewed appreciation for exclusivity in the division of powers in future cases, that would serve to address the same concerns raised by the permissive approach to trade barriers in *Comeau*.

As I have argued throughout this book, both the text of the Constitution and its underlying purposes require that due weight be given to the exclusive nature of the powers allocated in sections 91 and 92, including the federal power over trade and commerce. Experience and logic suggest that strict adherence to exclusivity – a true "watertight compartments" approach – is impractical, and as likely to frustrate the purposes underlying the division of powers as give effect to them. It is difficult to effectively regulate intraprovincial trade without having some effect on interprovincial trade, and vice versa. Yet it does not follow that we should abandon the exclusivity principle and allow significant ancillary regulation on the basis of a mere rational connection with valid statutory objectives. Instead, what I have labelled the water-resistant compartments approach offers the best way forward, balancing the Constitution's commitment to exclusivity with the need for a pragmatic and purposive interpretation of the heads of power allocated to Parliament and provincial legislatures.

With respect to provincially enacted barriers to interprovincial trade, this approach would have three components. First, provincial legislatures may not enact measures that relate in pith and substance to interprovincial trade, including laws whose primary purpose is to restrict trade or favour local industries over those in other provinces. Second, there should be a restrained approach to the recognition of policy areas with a "double aspect," including those involving the federal trade and commerce power. And third, provincial measures that significantly restrict interprovincial trade as part of a broader legislative scheme within provincial jurisdiction should only be upheld if they are reasonably necessary to achieving the provincial objective. Importantly, for this approach to provide meaningful scrutiny, the provincial objective used for the analysis would have to be the true policy objective of the measure and not merely the means adopted. For instance, in *Comeau*, the Supreme Court erroneously described the objective of the law as being "to enable public supervision of the production, movement, sale, and use of alcohol within New Brunswick."[58] Respectfully, those are the *means* adopted by the legislation, not the ultimate objective, which may have been to generate revenue or promote public health. It is circular to assess the necessity (or rational connection) of the means adopted by a legislative scheme in order to achieve those same means.[59]

This proposed approach would not categorically rule out provincially enacted trade barriers. It would merely require provincial governments to provide a reasoned justification for them, one that gives due weight to both the Constitution's grant of jurisdiction to the provinces over most matters relating to intraprovincial trade, and its equally significant denial of provincial jurisdiction over interprovincial trade.

Section 121 and the division of powers should be read together, with the clear commitment to free internal trade set out in the former reinforcing the significance of the exclusive federal power over interprovincial trade contained in the latter.[60] The approach to the division of powers set out above would be fully aligned with section 121 and would give effect to the purpose underlying it. While it is unlikely the Court will revisit the approach to section 121 in the near future, the division of powers provides a more promising route to renewing the Constitution's commitment to negative economic integration. If the Court can be convinced to take jurisdictional exclusivity seriously, that will help reinforce the negative economic integration provided for under the Constitution. In light of the close link between the Court's section 121 jurisprudence and the division of powers, a shift away from flexible federalism may eventually motivate a reconsideration of the test for section 121 laid down in *Comeau*. Accordingly, those committed to free trade under the Constitution would likely do well to focus their attention on the division of powers. Jurisdictional exclusivity is not just an esoteric and formalistic anachronism. Rather, it is a key mechanism through which the Constitution achieves its purposes, including those relating to its underlying economic vision.

Some might suggest that it would be better to leave economic integration to negotiations among political leaders, rather than address these issues through judicially developed constitutional law. Unfortunately, the structure of federalism makes that approach unlikely to succeed. There is a collective action problem built into any federal system of government, in which local governments prioritize their own interests over those of the nation as a whole. This could include not just overt acts of protectionism, but also regulations that have a disproportionate effect on parties in other jurisdictions. While local governments are empowered to enact a range of economic policies in pursuit of local interests and values, they cannot reliably be counted upon to consider the effects of their policies on outsiders. Free trade may sound appealing in principle. However, local governments will inevitably seek to make exceptions in order to serve local interests, and the cumulative effect of these exceptions can ultimately frustrate the aspiration toward free trade.

That is exactly what has happened with federal-provincial executive agreements seeking lower interprovincial trade barriers, such as the Canadian Free Trade Agreement (CFTA).[61] The general principles agreed to in the CFTA are sound, committing parties to free internal trade subject to stringent requirements to justify trade barriers.[62] However, these general principles are subject to hundreds of pages of exceptions. Moreover, the problem of locally enacted trade barriers is likely to become harder to address through agreement over time because the number of relevant parties is likely to grow. The CFTA does not include Indigenous governments. As Indigenous governments take on greater jurisdiction, there will be dozens of additional parties that would have to come together and agree on an approach to trade barriers. If the collective action problem posed by internal trade is difficult with ten provinces and three territories, the addition of Indigenous governments with significant jurisdiction will make it insurmountable.

Yet the Constitution points to potential solutions. Generally speaking, Indigenous jurisdiction ought to be developed in a manner consistent with the model provided by the division of powers. Areas of exclusive economic federal jurisdiction ought to be preserved, not just vis-à-vis the provinces, but also Indigenous governments. Moreover, section 121 ought to be held to apply to Indigenous governments as well as the provinces. This would be consistent with both the text of the provision, which does not limit the ambit of section 121 to provincial legislatures, as well as its purpose in promoting economic integration.

Barriers to trade are a problem inherent in the constitutional structure of a federation. Our Constitution addresses this problem in thoughtful ways, through the exclusive economic jurisdiction of Parliament and stand-alone constitutional provisions like section 121. In other words, trade barriers are a constitutional problem with a clear, well-established constitutional solution.

Interjurisdictional Immunity and the Economic Constitution

So far, I have focused primarily on section 121 and the principles governing the validity of provincial legislation. However, there are other important sources of negative integration under the Constitution, including in particular the doctrine of interjurisdictional immunity (IJI). IJI protects the core of certain federal powers from being impaired by otherwise valid provincial legislation, rendering provincial laws inapplicable in these areas. IJI has been a significant doctrinal tool in promoting economic integration, preventing activities and undertakings within federal jurisdiction from being bogged down by locally enacted laws pursuing local objectives. IJI has notably been applied in relation to cellular transmission towers, aerodromes, interprovincial pipelines, international bus lines, and the management and operations of an interprovincial telephone company, in each case rendering provincial laws inapplicable to the federal matter in question.[63]

IJI promotes economic integration by helping to give effect to the exclusive nature of federal jurisdiction over subjects of key significance to an integrated national economy, including especially interprovincial trade, transportation, and communications. The cumulative effect of even well-meaning local laws in these areas could be to deter economic activity of benefit to the country. As I have argued throughout this book, the federal Parliament is best placed to account for interests across different regions and provide the regulatory coordination required in these areas.

Unfortunately, the Supreme Court has had a conflicted relationship with IJI in recent years, leading to uncertainty regarding how the doctrine would be applied in the future. In *Canadian Western Bank*, a decision strongly influenced by the prevailing orthodoxy of flexible federalism, the Court signalled a retreat from IJI, stating that in the future it should largely be reserved to areas already covered by precedent.[64] The Court in *Canadian Western Bank* seemed to treat IJI as an embarrassing doctrinal holdover from a less-enlightened time of watertight compartments, which was difficult to justify in the era of flexible federalism.

In *Canadian Western Bank* itself, the Court declined to apply IJI so as to render provincial insurance licensing requirements inapplicable to chartered banks, a reasonable enough outcome given that insurance has not traditionally been a core function of banks. However, in a somewhat puzzling decision released at the same time as *Canadian Western Bank*, the Court declined to apply IJI to land-use decisions in the Port of Vancouver, which overlaps with eight different BC municipalities.[65] The Vancouver Port Authority has the power to regulate land use at the port, pursuant to legislation enacted under the federal power over navigation and shipping. At issue for the Court was whether municipal zoning requirements could also apply to activities at the port. The Court found that they could (though they were rendered inoperative by federal paramountcy in this case). As Peter Hogg observed: "If ever there was a case for interjurisdictional immunity, this was it. How could the Vancouver Port Authority (or any other Port Authority for that matter) develop and implement coherent land-use policies for the port if the port was also blanketed by a patchwork of municipal land-use regimes?"[66] Indeed, it would seem that the use of land within a port is of fairly central significance to navigation and shipping. Moreover, municipal land-use policies might easily fail to account for economic interests that rely on the port in other parts of the country.

There have also been other recent cases in which the Court has declined to apply IJI, reiterating its commitment to flexible federalism.[67] The *Tsilhqot'in* Aboriginal title decision, discussed in the previous chapter, is a particularly strong manifestation of the Court's recent IJI skepticism.[68] That decision overturned a very recent precedent in coming to the conclusion that IJI does not apply to Aboriginal and treaty rights.[69]

Fortunately, the Court recovered some of its enthusiasm for IJI in other recent decisions in which the economic implications of local interference with federal undertakings were obvious. In *Quebec v. COPA*, the Court held that provincial land-use laws could not prohibit the use of land as an aerodrome, since that would impair the core of the federal power over aeronautics.[70] Similarly, in *Rogers Communications v. Châteauguay*, the Court held that municipal zoning laws could not apply to prevent the construction of cellular antennas, as this would impair the core of the federal power over radiocommunications.[71] In both of these areas, the application of local laws had the potential to undermine integrated national transportation or communications networks. The location of an airfield or a cell tower is not just a local matter, since it has implications for transportation and communications by parties from outside the area in question. From the perspective of economic integration, these were clear cases in which the application of IJI promoted economic integration.

While it is encouraging that the Court remains willing to apply IJI in cases where the justification is compelling, the uncertainty around the doctrine has had some undesirable effects. One of the virtues of IJI is the clear signal it can send regarding the applicability of provincial laws. The doctrine tends to establish bright lines around matters that provincial and local authorities cannot touch. By contrast, analyzing the validity of legislation depends on the characterization of the law's pith and substance, a process that can be difficult to predict. Moving away from IJI means more legal uncertainty, since more turns on this less predictable validity analysis.

Jurisdictional uncertainty can itself create barriers to trade and economic integration. For instance, it is an established point in Canadian law that interprovincial pipelines are under exclusive federal jurisdiction. Nevertheless, the British Columbia government proposed amendments to its Environmental Management Act with the implicit aim of stopping the Trans Mountain Pipeline expansion. In particular, it proposed to enact restrictions on the possession of heavy oil in the province, which was the principal product to be carried by the expanded pipeline.[72] While BC argued that the legislation related to areas of provincial jurisdiction over public lands, property and civil rights, and matters of a local and private nature, it was clear to many observers that the true purpose of the law was to regulate an interprovincial pipeline.

Unfortunately, there was just enough ambiguity in the analysis relating to the validity of the legislation to make British Columbia's jurisdictional claims plausible. Indeed, they were supported by at least one legal scholar.[73] While there was past case law from the Supreme Court indicating that interprovincial pipelines are protected by IJI, the Court's recent signals regarding IJI cast doubt on the continued relevance of that jurisprudence. In an already challenging regulatory environment, British Columbia's constitutionally dubious bitumen law added to the legal uncertainty, causing private-sector investors to pull out of the Trans Mountain Pipeline expansion.[74] Even though the BC Court of Appeal ultimately held the law to be unconstitutional since it related in pith and substance to an interprovincial undertaking, the uncertainty created in the interim was significant and might have killed the pipeline if not for the federal government's decision to buy it.[75]

A clearer and more robust doctrine of IJI would have helped to mitigate the uncertainty created by the provincial attempt to block the pipeline. If it had been clear that the Supreme Court would continue to uphold its own precedents applying IJI to interprovincial pipelines, then there never would have been any doubt as to the unconstitutional nature of the BC law. In this respect, it is somewhat regrettable that neither the British Columbia Court of Appeal nor the Supreme Court of Canada addressed IJI in their decisions in this case.[76] It would have been helpful to have a court expressly reaffirm the application of IJI to interprovincial undertakings.[77]

The Supreme Court's recent ambivalence regarding IJI stems in part from the difficulty in articulating a justification for the ongoing application of the doctrine. The economic vision of the Constitution outlined in this book helps to supply such a justification, at least with respect to Parliament's heads of economic power. IJI serves to reinforce negative integration through the principle of jurisdictional exclusivity. It should be applied to aspects of federal heads of power in which the cumulative effect of local enactments might otherwise frustrate the goal of economic integration. The recent decisions in COPA and *Châteauguay* respecting aerodromes and telecommunications equipment exemplify this function of IJI, which is similar in some respects to the "dormant Commerce Clause" in US constitutional jurisprudence.[78] At the very least, adopting a coherent justification for IJI would allow the Court to establish some clarity in an area of law that has been beset by its own inconsistency regarding the continued place of the doctrine.

Mobility Rights and the Charter

While the principal focus of this book has been on the structural provisions of the Constitution rather than the Charter, there is one Charter right that deserves consideration in assessing what a renewed understanding of the economic Constitution could mean. Section 6 of the Charter protects mobility rights, including, under section 6(2)(b), the right "to pursue the gaining of a livelihood in any province."[79] That right is subject to qualification, including, under section 6(3)(a), "any laws or practices of general application in force in a province other than those that discriminate among persons primarily on the basis of province of present or previous residence."[80] In a sense, these provisions serve as an analogue to section 121 of the Constitution Act, 1867. While that provision protects free trade in goods, section 6 of the Charter ensures a free and integrated national labour market, subject to non-discriminatory laws of general application.

While section 6 is framed in terms of individual rights, and as part of the Charter it serves a human rights purpose, it also serves to promote economic union. The Supreme Court was, at one time, prepared to acknowledge the relationship between section 6 and the Constitution's commitment to economic union. Justice La Forest's majority opinion in *Black v. Law Society of Alberta* places section 6 in the broader context of economic union under the Constitution, while at the same time emphasizing that the provision is framed in terms of individual rights.[81] Unfortunately, in *Canadian Egg Marketing Agency v. Richardson*, less than a decade after *Black*, a majority of the Court rejected this framing, holding that section 6 "guarantees the mobility of persons, not as a feature of the economic unity of the country, but in order to further a human rights purpose."[82] Respectfully, there is no inconsistency between the human rights purpose of the provision and considerations relating to the economic union. As Justice McLachlin's dissent in *Richardson* cogently argues, section 6 both promotes economic union *and* protects a range of individual mobility rights, including the right to pursue a livelihood anywhere in Canada.[83]

Contextual factors support a reading of section 6 that recognizes its place in promoting economic union. Part of the historical motivation to include mobility rights in the Charter was to promote economic union.[84] Moreover, the provision has to be considered in its larger constitutional context, including the Constitution's long-standing commitment to economic integration and free trade. The economic purpose of the provision can also be reasonably deduced from its text. A guarantee of mobility to pursue the gaining of a livelihood in any province does protect an important individual interest, but it also has the obvious, and surely intended, effect of promoting the integration of national labour markets.

Unfortunately, the problems with the *Richardson* decision do not end with the majority's understanding of the purposes served by section 6. The case dealt with the system of quotas for the sale of eggs in interprovincial markets. Because quotas were allocated based on historical production patterns, there were no quotas allocated to the territories. This meant that residents of the territories could not sell eggs in interprovincial markets. Territorial egg producers challenged the regime on the basis that it prevented them from pursuing a livelihood in the province or territory of their choice. The majority in *Richardson* held that this restriction did impair the egg producers' right to pursue the gaining of a livelihood in the province or territory of their choice, but that it did not discriminate *primarily* on the basis of residence. Instead, the regulations were based primarily on historical production, which had the secondary effect of shutting territorial producers out of the market.[85] On this basis, the majority held that the restriction was consistent with section 6(3)(a).

Justice McLachlin's dissent took a less permissive approach, holding that the exception in section 6(3)(a) applies only where the discrimination is incidental to some larger purpose.[86] Since the effect of the law in question was to shut territorial providers out of the national market, for no reason other than the historical happenstance relating to past production, Justice McLachlin would have held that this restriction was inconsistent with section 6.

The majority and the dissent's differing understanding of the purposes of section 6 inform their divergent approaches to the application of the provision. Justice McLachlin's more demanding approach to justifying restrictions is clearly more consistent with its purpose in promoting economic union. Yet there is no obvious tension between her preferred approach and the human rights purpose of the provision. Individual human rights interests were clearly engaged in the case. As Michael Trebilcock pointed out, some of the parties affiliated with the egg producers in *Richardson* had close personal connections to the Northwest Territories. Indeed, one of the respondents was wholly owned by the Dene nation. In Trebilcock's words, "[t]hese individuals are effectively forbidden by the regulatory scheme from ever making a livelihood in the production of eggs, unless they choose to move from their ancestral home to a province where they can acquire a quota."[87] The law's impact on the parties' fundamental right of mobility was significant, and it served no higher purpose since the exclusion of the territories from the quota scheme was essentially arbitrary.

It is true that the text of section 6 exempts measures that do not discriminate "primarily" based on residency. Yet this need not amount to a licence to allow obvious and severe indirect discrimination of the kind experienced by territorial egg producers, so long as a facially neutral principle like historical production patterns is put forward. Justice McLachlin's approach, requiring that a discriminatory measure be incidental to a larger purpose, is consistent with the text. Moreover, it is also aligned with both the human rights and economic purposes of the provision.

In the context of section 6 of the Charter, a renewed understanding of the economic vision of the Constitution would begin with Justice La Forest's majority opinion in *Black* and Justice McLachlin's dissent in *Richardson*. Section 6 leaves broad discretion to Parliament and provincial legislatures to set economic policy, including in a manner that disadvantages residents of other provinces, as long as it is in service of a legitimate objective. Providing a meaningful check against discriminatory measures that are *not* incidental to a larger purpose is important in upholding not just the human rights objectives of the provision, but also the Constitution's commitment to economic integration.

Conclusion

First and foremost, my aim in this book has been to dispel the perception that the Canadian Constitution is somehow neutral on economic questions. On the contrary, the structural provisions of the Constitution reflect a sophisticated economic vision, balancing four principal commitments: secure property rights, local autonomy and subsidiarity, economic integration, and free internal trade. The essential claims of this book have been as follows. Firstly, the text of the Constitution, as read in its original historical and legal context, does indeed reflect these commitments. Secondly, these constitutional commitments have remained important features of our constitutional order as it developed over time, and, despite significant changes in our society, they remain relevant today. Thirdly, legal discourse in this country, as reflected principally in recent jurisprudence of the Supreme Court, has begun to lose touch with these commitments. And finally, a renewed understanding of the economic vision of the Constitution is both possible and desirable, and can inform contemporary constitutional issues and debates.

The economic vision of the Constitution involves a thoughtful balance between commitments to decentralized decision-making and centralization. Decentralization, through both secure property rights and local government, is necessary for effective decision-making in a large and diverse country. At the same time, though, decentralization creates the potential for decision failures in certain areas, particularly those in which measures in one locality affect interests in others, or where national coordination is needed for effective policymaking. The Constitution generally provides for centralization on these subjects, helping to solve problems of political economy that are ultimately grounded in enduring features of human nature. This basic constitutional structure provides a framework not only for economic prosperity, but also for peace and security through cooperation on matters of common concern.

The economic vision of the Constitution may be obscured by the fact that the structural provisions of the Constitution sometimes pursue objectives indirectly. For instance, property rights are protected by limits on executive power, by presumptions about legislative intent, and by constitutional provisions setting out procedures with checks and balances for measures that affect property. Rather than a constitutionally entrenched right to property enforced by judges, the Constitution instead structures government authority in a way that aims to protect property while leaving the legislature as the ultimate arbiter of property and the common good.

Similarly, the constitutional commitments to local autonomy and subsidiarity, economic integration, and free trade are all promoted, somewhat indirectly, through the exclusive nature of the jurisdiction allocated to Parliament and provincial legislatures. Jurisdictional exclusivity protects local governance autonomy and subsidiarity by ensuring there is a broad sphere of decision-making on local matters in which provincial legislatures are not subject to the supervening authority of Parliament. By the same token, Parliament's exclusive economic powers allow it to coordinate policy on matters of national concern without interference from provincial laws prioritizing local interests. Jurisdictional exclusivity is particularly important to the Constitution's commitment to free trade. The Constitution not only grants authority to Parliament over areas like interjurisdictional economic relations. It also *denies* authority over these matters to provincial and local governments, · partly on the basis that these governments are more likely to be swayed by local interests favouring protectionism.

The Constitution's unambiguous textual commitment to exclusive spheres of jurisdiction has come under attack in recent years from those who favour a flexible approach to federalism and regard exclusivity as a kind of constitutional anachronism. Part of my hope in this book is to show that there are still compelling justifications for jurisdictional exclusivity. While the aspiration toward truly "watertight" compartments was misplaced, a strong commitment to exclusivity that limits jurisdictional overlap to cases where it is meaningfully justified is in keeping with both the text and purposes of the Constitution.

The basic structure of our Constitution was established in 1867, and of course, much has changed since that time. Yet the Constitution provides compelling solutions to the persistent challenges of a shared life in a large, diverse, and complex economy and society. Importantly, the economic vision of the Constitution can be extended to encompass not only political communities that did not exist in their current form at Confederation, such as Alberta and Saskatchewan, but also Indigenous communities that were unjustly marginalized at that time. In its balance between centralization on matters of common concern and decentralization on matters of local difference, the Constitution provides a model for Canada's future relations with Indigenous nations. This model is not to be adopted reflexively, without special attention to the distinctiveness of particular Indigenous nations. Yet, from the Nisga'a Nation to Nunavut, Canada's federal model has already begun to be extended as a framework for Indigenous self-government within a united Canada.

Canadian modesty sometimes prevents us from celebrating the genius of our constitutional order. It has provided the basis for one of the most secure, peaceful, and prosperous societies in human history. Of course, Canada's history contains chapters in which we did not fully live up to our constitutional ideals. Yet those ideals, including the economic vision of the Constitution, can nevertheless point us to a better path forward. That economic vision is not merely an artifact of our legal and political heritage. Rather, it remains a central feature in a living constitutional order and a platform for future cooperation and coordination in a large, diverse, and complex federation.

Key Constitutional Provisions

Constitution Act, 1867

Preamble

An Act for the Union of Canada, Nova Scotia, and New Brunswick, and the Government thereof; and for Purposes connected therewith

WHEREAS the Provinces of Canada, Nova Scotia, and New Brunswick have expressed their Desire to be federally united into One Dominion under the Crown of the United Kingdom of Great Britain and Ireland, with a Constitution similar in Principle to that of the United Kingdom:

And whereas such a Union would conduce to the Welfare of the Provinces and promote the Interests of the British Empire:

And whereas on the Establishment of the Union by Authority of Parliament it is expedient, not only that the Constitution of the Legislative Authority in the Dominion be provided for, but also that the Nature of the Executive Government therein be declared:

And whereas it is expedient that Provision be made for the eventual Admission into the Union of other Parts of British North America:

...

Declaration of Union

3. It shall be lawful for the Queen, by and with the Advice of Her Majesty's Most Honourable Privy Council, to declare by Proclamation that, on and after a Day therein appointed, not being more than Six Months after the passing of this Act, the Provinces of Canada, Nova

Scotia, and New Brunswick shall form and be One Dominion under the Name of Canada; and on and after that Day those Three Provinces shall form and be One Dominion under that Name accordingly.

...

Declaration of Executive Power in the Queen

9. The Executive Government and Authority of and over Canada is hereby declared to continue and be vested in the Queen.

...

Appropriation and Tax Bills

53. Bills for appropriating any Part of the Public Revenue, or for imposing any Tax or Impost, shall originate in the House of Commons.

Recommendation of Money Votes

54. It shall not be lawful for the House of Commons to adopt or pass any Vote, Resolution, Address, or Bill for the Appropriation of any Part of the Public Revenue, or of any Tax or Impost, to any Purpose that has not been first recommended to that House by Message of the Governor General in the Session in which such Vote, Resolution, Address, or Bill is proposed.

Royal Assent to Bills, etc.

55. Where a Bill passed by the Houses of the Parliament is presented to the Governor General for the Queen's Assent, he shall declare, according to his Discretion, but subject to the Provisions of this Act and to Her Majesty's Instructions, either that he assents thereto in the Queen's Name, or that he withholds the Queen's Assent, or that he reserves the Bill for the Signification of the Queen's Pleasure.

Disallowance by Order in Council of Act assented to by Governor General

56. Where the Governor General assents to a Bill in the Queen's Name, he shall by the first convenient Opportunity send an authentic Copy of the Act to One of Her Majesty's Principal Secretaries of State, and if the Queen in Council within Two Years after Receipt thereof by the Secretary of State thinks fit to disallow the Act, such Disallowance (with a Certificate of the Secretary of State of the Day on which the Act was received by him) being signified by the Governor General, by Speech or Message to each of the Houses of the Parliament or by Proclamation, shall annul the Act from and after the Day of such Signification.

Signification of Queen's Pleasure on Bill reserved

57. A Bill reserved for the Signification of the Queen's Pleasure shall not have any Force unless and until, within Two Years from the Day on which it was presented to the Governor General for the Queen's Assent, the Governor General signifies, by Speech or Message to each of the Houses of the Parliament or by Proclamation, that it has received the Assent of the Queen in Council.

An Entry of every such Speech, Message, or Proclamation shall be made in the Journal of each House, and a Duplicate thereof duly attested shall be delivered to the proper Officer to be kept among the Records of Canada.

...

Application to Legislatures of Provisions respecting Money Votes, etc.

90. The following Provisions of this Act respecting the Parliament of Canada, namely, – the Provisions relating to Appropriation and Tax Bills, the Recommendation of Money Votes, the Assent to Bills, the Disallowance of Acts, and the Signification of Pleasure on Bills reserved, – shall extend and apply to the Legislatures of the several Provinces as if those Provisions were here re-enacted and made applicable in Terms to the respective Provinces and the Legislatures thereof, with the Substitution of the Lieutenant Governor of the Province for the Governor General, of the Governor General for the Queen and for a Secretary of State, of One Year for Two Years, and of the Province for Canada.

VI. Distribution of Legislative Powers: Powers of the Parliament

Legislative Authority of Parliament of Canada

91. It shall be lawful for the Queen, by and with the Advice and Consent of the Senate and House of Commons, to make Laws for the Peace, Order, and good Government of Canada, in relation to all Matters not coming within the Classes of Subjects by this Act assigned exclusively to the Legislatures of the Provinces; and for greater Certainty, but not so as to restrict the Generality of the foregoing Terms of this Section, it is hereby declared that (notwithstanding anything in this Act) the exclusive Legislative Authority of the Parliament of Canada extends to all Matters coming within the Classes of Subjects next hereinafter enumerated; that is to say,

1A. The Public Debt and Property.
2. The Regulation of Trade and Commerce.
2A. Unemployment insurance.
3. The raising of Money by any Mode or System of Taxation.
4. The borrowing of Money on the Public Credit.
5. Postal Service.
6. The Census and Statistics.
7. Militia, Military and Naval Service, and Defence.
8. The fixing of and providing for the Salaries and Allowances of Civil and other Officers of the Government of Canada.
9. Beacons, Buoys, Lighthouses, and Sable Island.
10. Navigation and Shipping.
11. Quarantine and the Establishment and Maintenance of Marine Hospitals.
12. Sea Coast and Inland Fisheries.
13. Ferries between a Province and any British or Foreign Country or between Two Provinces.
14. Currency and Coinage.
15. Banking, Incorporation of Banks, and the Issue of Paper Money.
16. Savings Banks.
17. Weights and Measures.
18. Bills of Exchange and Promissory Notes.
19. Interest.
20. Legal Tender.
21. Bankruptcy and Insolvency.
22. Patents of Invention and Discovery.
23. Copyrights.

24. Indians, and Lands reserved for the Indians.
25. Naturalization and Aliens.
26. Marriage and Divorce.
27. The Criminal Law, except the Constitution of Courts of Criminal Jurisdiction, but including the Procedure in Criminal Matters.
28. The Establishment, Maintenance, and Management of Penitentiaries.
29. Such Classes of Subjects as are expressly excepted in the Enumeration of the Classes of Subjects by this Act assigned exclusively to the Legislatures of the Provinces.

And any Matter coming within any of the Classes of Subjects enumerated in this Section shall not be deemed to come within the Class of Matters of a local or private Nature comprised in the Enumeration of the Classes of Subjects by this Act assigned exclusively to the Legislatures of the Provinces.

Subjects of Exclusive Provincial Legislation

92. In each Province the Legislature may exclusively make Laws in relation to Matters coming within the Classes of Subjects next hereinafter enumerated; that is to say,

1. Repealed.
2. Direct Taxation within the Province in order to the raising of a Revenue for Provincial Purposes.
3. The borrowing of Money on the sole Credit of the Province.
4. The Establishment and Tenure of Provincial Offices and the Appointment and Payment of Provincial Officers.
5. The Management and Sale of the Public Lands belonging to the Province and of the Timber and Wood thereon.
6. The Establishment, Maintenance, and Management of Public and Reformatory Prisons in and for the Province.
7. The Establishment, Maintenance, and Management of Hospitals, Asylums, Charities, and Eleemosynary Institutions in and for the Province, other than Marine Hospitals.
8. Municipal Institutions in the Province.
9. Shop, Saloon, Tavern, Auctioneer, and other Licences in order to the raising of a Revenue for Provincial, Local, or Municipal Purposes.

10. Local Works and Undertakings other than such as are of the following Classes:
    a) Lines of Steam or other Ships, Railways, Canals, Telegraphs, and other Works and Undertakings connecting the Province with any other or others of the Provinces, or extending beyond the Limits of the Province:
    b) Lines of Steam Ships between the Province and any British or Foreign Country:
    c) Such Works as, although wholly situate within the Province, are before or after their Execution declared by the Parliament of Canada to be for the general Advantage of Canada or for the Advantage of Two or more of the Provinces.
11. The Incorporation of Companies with Provincial Objects.
12. The Solemnization of Marriage in the Province.
13. Property and Civil Rights in the Province.
14. The Administration of Justice in the Province, including the Constitution, Maintenance, and Organization of Provincial Courts, both of Civil and of Criminal Jurisdiction, and including Procedure in Civil Matters in those Courts.
15. The Imposition of Punishment by Fine, Penalty, or Imprisonment for enforcing any Law of the Province made in relation to any Matter coming within any of the Classes of Subjects enumerated in this Section.
16. Generally all Matters of a merely local or private Nature in the Province. Non-Renewable Natural Resources, Forestry Resources and Electrical Energy

Laws respecting non-renewable natural resources, forestry resources and electrical energy

92A (1) In each province, the legislature may exclusively make laws in relation to
  (a) exploration for non-renewable natural resources in the province;
  (b) development, conservation and management of non-renewable natural resources and forestry resources in the province, including laws in relation to the rate of primary production therefrom; and
  (c) development, conservation and management of sites and facilities in the province for the generation and production of electrical energy.

Export from provinces of resources

(2) In each province, the legislature may make laws in relation to the export from the province to another part of Canada of the primary production from non-renewable natural resources and forestry resources in the province and the production from facilities in the province for the generation of electrical energy, but such laws may not authorize or provide for discrimination in prices or in supplies exported to another part of Canada.

Authority of Parliament

(3) Nothing in subsection (2) derogates from the authority of Parliament to enact laws in relation to the matters referred to in that subsection and, where such a law of Parliament and a law of a province conflict, the law of Parliament prevails to the extent of the conflict.

Taxation of resources

(4) In each province, the legislature may make laws in relation to the raising of money by any mode or system of taxation in respect of
- (a) non-renewable natural resources and forestry resources in the province and the primary production therefrom, and
- (b) sites and facilities in the province for the generation of electrical energy and the production therefrom,

whether or not such production is exported in whole or in part from the province, but such laws may not authorize or provide for taxation that differentiates between production exported to another part of Canada and production not exported from the province.

Primary production

(5) The expression primary production has the meaning assigned by the Sixth Schedule.

Existing powers or rights

(6) Nothing in subsections (1) to (5) derogates from any powers or rights that a legislature or government of a province had immediately before the coming into force of this section.

...

Uniformity of Laws in Ontario, Nova Scotia, and New Brunswick

Legislation for Uniformity of Laws in Three Provinces

94. Notwithstanding anything in this Act, the Parliament of Canada may make Provision for the Uniformity of all or any of the Laws relative to Property and Civil Rights in Ontario, Nova Scotia, and New Brunswick, and of the Procedure of all or any of the Courts in those Three Provinces, and from and after the passing of any Act in that Behalf the Power of the Parliament of Canada to make Laws in relation to any Matter comprised in any such Act shall, notwithstanding anything in this Act, be unrestricted; but any Act of the Parliament of Canada making Provision for such Uniformity shall not have effect in any Province unless and until it is adopted and enacted as Law by the Legislature thereof.

Old Age Pensions

Legislation respecting old age pensions and supplementary benefits

94A. The Parliament of Canada may make laws in relation to old age pensions and supplementary benefits, including survivors' and disability benefits irrespective of age, but no such law shall affect the operation of any law present or future of a provincial legislature in relation to any such matter.(52)

Agriculture and Immigration

Concurrent Powers of Legislation respecting Agriculture, etc.

95. In each Province the Legislature may make Laws in relation to Agriculture in the Province, and to Immigration into the Province; and it is hereby declared that the Parliament of Canada may from Time to Time make Laws in relation to Agriculture in all or any of the Provinces, and to Immigration into all or any of the Provinces; and any Law of the Legislature of a Province relative to Agriculture or to Immigration shall have effect in and for the Province as long and as far only as it is not repugnant to any Act of the Parliament of Canada.

...

Property in Lands, Mines, etc.

109. All Lands, Mines, Minerals, and Royalties belonging to the several Provinces of Canada, Nova Scotia, and New Brunswick at the Union, and all Sums then due or payable for such Lands, Mines, Minerals, or Royalties, shall belong to the several Provinces of Ontario, Quebec, Nova Scotia, and New Brunswick in which the same are situate or arise, subject to any Trusts existing in respect thereof, and to any Interest other than that of the Province in the same.

...

Canadian Manufactures, etc.

121. All Articles of the Growth, Produce, or Manufacture of any one of the Provinces shall, from and after the Union, be admitted free into each of the other Provinces.

Constitution Act, 1982

PART I: *Canadian Charter of Rights and Freedoms*
Whereas Canada is founded upon principles that recognize the supremacy of God and the rule of law:

...

Mobility Rights

Mobility of citizens

6(1) Every citizen of Canada has the right to enter, remain in and leave Canada.

Rights to move and gain livelihood

(2) Every citizen of Canada and every person who has the status of a permanent resident of Canada has the right
   (a) to move to and take up residence in any province; and
   (b) to pursue the gaining of a livelihood in any province.

Limitation

(3) The rights specified in subsection (2) are subject to
  (a) any laws or practices of general application in force in a province other than those that discriminate among persons primarily on the basis of province of present or previous residence; and
  (b) any laws providing for reasonable residency requirements as a qualification for the receipt of publicly provided social services.

Affirmative action programs

(4) Subsections (2) and (3) do not preclude any law, program or activity that has as its object the amelioration in a province of conditions of individuals in that province who are socially or economically disadvantaged if the rate of employment in that province is below the rate of employment in Canada.

Legal Rights

Life, liberty and security of person

7 Everyone has the right to life, liberty and security of the person and the right not to be deprived thereof except in accordance with the principles of fundamental justice.

...

PART II: Rights of the Aboriginal Peoples of Canada
Recognition of existing aboriginal and treaty rights

35(1) The existing aboriginal and treaty rights of the aboriginal peoples of Canada are hereby recognized and affirmed.

Definition of aboriginal peoples of Canada

(2) In this Act, aboriginal peoples of Canada includes the Indian, Inuit and Métis peoples of Canada.

Land claims agreements

(3) For greater certainty, in subsection (1) treaty rights includes rights that now exist by way of land claims agreements or may be so acquired.

Aboriginal and treaty rights are guaranteed equally to both sexes

(4) Notwithstanding any other provision of this Act, the aboriginal and treaty rights referred to in subsection (1) are guaranteed equally to male and female persons.

...

PART III: Equalization and Regional Disparities

Commitment to promote equal opportunities

36(1) Without altering the legislative authority of Parliament or of the provincial legislatures, or the rights of any of them with respect to the exercise of their legislative authority, Parliament and the legislatures, together with the government of Canada and the provincial governments, are committed to

  (a) promoting equal opportunities for the well-being of Canadians;

  (b) furthering economic development to reduce disparity in opportunities; and

  (c) providing essential public services of reasonable quality to all Canadians.

Commitment respecting public services

(2) Parliament and the government of Canada are committed to the principle of making equalization payments to ensure that provincial governments have sufficient revenues to provide reasonably comparable levels of public services at reasonably comparable levels of taxation.

....

Order of Her Majesty in Council admitting British Columbia into the Union (16 May 1871)

11. The Government of the Dominion undertake to secure the commencement simultaneously, within two years from the date of the Union, of the construction of a railway from the Pacific towards the Rocky Mountains, and from such point as may be selected, east of the Rocky Mountains, towards the Pacific, to connect the seaboard of British Columbia with the railway system of Canada; and further, to secure the completion of such railway within ten years from the date of the Union.

Order of Her Majesty in Council admitting Prince Edward Island into the Union (26 June 1873)

That the Dominion Government shall assume and defray all the charges for the following services, viz.:--

....

Efficient Steam Service for the conveyance of mails and passengers, to be established and maintained between the Island and the mainland of the Dominion, Winter and Summer, thus placing the Island in continuous communication with the Intercolonial Railway and the railway system of the Dominion;

...

That a fixed crossing joining the Island to the mainland may be substituted for the steam service referred to in this Schedule; [clause inserted through a bilateral amendment in 1993]

...

Notes

Chapter One

1 *Tear Down These Walls: Dismantling Canada's Internal Trade Barriers* (Senate Standing Committee on Banking, Trade, and Commerce, June 2016); Brian Lee Crowley, Robert Know, and John Robson, *Citizen of One, Citizen of The Whole: How Ottawa Can Strengthen our Nation by Eliminating Provincial Trade Barriers With a Charter of Economic Rights* (Ottawa: Macdonald-Laurier Institute, 21 June 2010), online, https://www.macdonaldlaurier.ca/citizenofone/; Trevor Tombe and Lukas Albrecht, "Internal Trade, Productivity and Interconnected Industries: A Quantitative Analysis," *Canadian Journal of Economics* 49, no. 1 (2016). Ryan Manucha and Trevor Tombe, *Liberalizing Internal Trade through Mutual Recognition: A Legal and Economic Analysis* (Ottawa: Macdonald-Laurier Institute, 20 September 2022), online, https://macdonaldlaurier.ca/wp-content/uploads/2022/09/20220911_Interprovincial_trade_Manuch_Tombe_PAPER_FWeb.pdf.

2 Canadian Free Trade Agreement - Consolidated Version, 2017, arts 600–705 (entry into force 1 July 2017) [CFTA]; Canadian Free Trade Agreement Implementation Act, SC 2017, c. 33.

3 *Tear Down These Walls*, 4; Jane Cordy and Diane Bellemare, "Interprovincial Trade Barriers are a National Embarrassment: Senators Cordy, Bellemare," *SenCA Plus*, 17 January 2019, online, https://sencanada.ca/en/sencaplus/opinion/interprovincial-trade-barriers-are-a-national-embarrassment-senators-cordy-bellemare/.

4 Justine Hunter and Kelly Cryderman, "Alberta, B.C. Pipeline Dispute Escalates as Wine Ban Heads to Trade Tribunal," *Globe and Mail*, 19 February 2018, online, https://www.theglobeandmail.com/news/british-columbia/bc-launches-challenge-against-albertas-wine-ban/article38020662/; Catharine Tunney, "Arrests, Travel Disruptions as Wet'suwet'en Solidarity Protests Spread Across Canada," *CBC News*, 25 February 2020, online, https://www.cbc.ca/news/politics/blockades-continue-hamilton-bc-1.5474916.

5   Ian A. Blue, *Free Trade within Canada: Say Goodbye to Gold Seal* (Ottawa:
    Macdonald-Laurier Institute, May 2011), online, https://perma.cc/J43Y-D9Z5;
    Andrew Coyne, "Supreme Court Beer Ruling Ties the Constitution in Knots,
    and the Economy With it," *National Post*, 20 April 2018, online, https://
    nationalpost.com/opinion/andrew-coyne-supreme-court-beer-decision-ties-
    the-constitution-in-knots-and-the-economy-with-it; Emmett Macfarlane,
    "In its 'free-the-beer' Ruling, the Supreme Court Reveals its Contradictions,"
    Maclean's, 19 April 2018, online, https://perma.cc/49JN-QYF2; Dwight
    Newman, *Pipelines and the Canadian Constitution: Canadian Dreams and
    Canadian Nightmares* (Ottawa: Macdonald-Laurier Institute, April 2018),
    online, https://macdonaldlaurier.ca/files/pdf/MLICommentary_April2018_
    Newman_FWeb.pdf.

6   *R v. Comeau*, 2016 NBPC 3 [*Comeau* (NBPC)], rev'd by *R v. Comeau*, 2018 SCC
    15 [*Comeau* (SCC)].

7   *Comeau* (NBPC), at paras 6–10.

8   Constitution Act, 1867 (UK), 30 & 31 Vict, c 3, s 121, reprinted in RSC 1985,
    Appendix II, No. 5.

9   *Comeau* (NBPC), at paras 189, 193.

10 Ibid., at paras 91–101.

11 *Tear Down These Walls*, 51.

12 Ibid.

13 See Malcolm Lavoie, "Beer Case Gives Supreme Court a Chance to
    Correct Past Mistakes," *Toronto Star*, 5 May 2017, online, https://perma.cc/
    TGP7-D6Y4; Malcolm Lavoie, "Supreme Court's 'free-the-beer' Decision
    Privileges One Part of the Constitution Over Another," *CBC News*, 19 April
    2018, online, https://perma.cc/H6P9-AAFE; Bruce Pardy, "Amazingly, the
    Constitution Always Says Exactly What Our Supreme Court Thinks it
    Should," *Financial Post*, 13 July 2018, online, https://perma.cc/7G7P-GEE3;
    Malcolm Lavoie, "R. v Comeau and Section 121 of the Constitution Act,
    1867: Freeing the Beer and Fortifying the Economic Union," *Dalhousie Law
    Journal* 40, no. 1 (2017); Bruce Pardy, *Protecting Government from Free Trade*
    (Vancouver: Fraser Institute, 2018), online, https://www.fraserinstitute.org/
    sites/default/files/protecting-government-from-free-trade.pdf; Malaika Bacon-
    Dussault, "L'importation interprovinciale des boissons alcoolisées à des fins
    personnelles: R c. Comeau et la confirmation de règles de droit de la période
    de la prohibition," *McGill Law Journal* 64, no.1 (2018); Coyne, "Supreme
    Court Beer Ruling"; Macfarlane, "'free-the-beer' Ruling"; *Tear Down These
    Walls*; Asher Honickman, "Comeau Is a Casualty of Confused Doctrine,"
    Advocates for the Rule of Law, 24 April 2018, online, http://www.ruleoflaw.
    ca/comeau-is-a-casualty-of-confused-doctrine/; Leonid Sirota, "Unmaking
    History," *Double Aspect Blog*, 20 April 2018, online, https://doubleaspect.
    blog/2018/04/20/unmaking-history/; Michael Marschal, "R. v. Comeau: Good

Law, Bad Application," *Saskatchewan Law Review*, 2 February 2019, online, https://sasklawreview.ca/comment/r-v-comeau-good-law-bad-application.php; Jorge Alvarez, Ivo Kznar, and Trevor Tombe, "Internal Trade in Canada: Case for Liberalization," IMF Working Paper No. 19/158 (2019), 28.

14 Agreement on Internal Trade, 1 July 1995, www.cfta-alec.ca/agreement-on-internal-trade/; Agreement on Internal Trade Implementation Act, SC 1996, C 17; Michael P. Leidy, "The Canadian Agreement on Internal Trade: Developments and Prospects," IMF Working Paper No. 98/51 (1998).

15 CFTA.

16 *R v. Comeau*, [2016] NBJ No 232 (CA); *R v. Comeau*, [2017] SCCA No. 25.

17 A case law search did not reveal any previous case that had gone directly from an inferior court to the Supreme Court of Canada without a decision on the merits by a superior trial or appellate court.

18 Multi-day hearings are relatively rare at the Supreme Court of Canada. Recent cases with multi-day hearings have included: *Reference re Senate Reform*, 2014 SCC 32; *Reference re Securities Act*, 2011 SCC 66.

19 See Ian Blue, "Long Overdue: A Reappraisal of Section 121 of the Constitution Act, 1867," *Dalhousie Law Journal* 33, no. 2 (2010); Blue, *Free Trade within Canada*; but see Kerri Froc and Michael Marin, "The Supreme Court's Strange Brew: History, Federalism and Anti-Originalism in Comeau," *University of New Brunswick Law Journal* 70 (2019).

20 *Comeau* (SCC), (Transcript of Hearing, Day 1 at 49).

21 Ibid., at para 83.

22 Lavoie, "Supreme Court's 'free-the-beer' Decision."

23 *Comeau* (SCC), at paras 113–4.

24 See *Canadian Western Bank v. Alberta*, 2007 SCC 22 at paras 36–7; *Canada (Attorney General) v. PHS Community Services Society*, 2011 SCC 44 at paras 62–3. While "flexible" and "cooperative" federalism are often used interchangeably, these terms refer to distinct concepts. See Julien Boudreault, "Flexible and Cooperative Federalism: Distinguishing the Two Approaches in the Interpretation and Application of the Division of Powers," *National Journal of Constitutional Law* 40, no. 1 (2020). See also Kate Glover, "Structural Cooperative Federalism," *Supreme Court Law Review*, 2nd ed., 76 (2016): 47–53.

25 Blue, *Free Trade within Canada*; Donald Creighton, *British North America at Confederation: A Study Prepared for the Royal Commission on Dominion-Provincial Relations* (Ottawa: J.O. Patenaude, 1939), 40; Andrew Smith, "The Historical Origins of Section 121 of the Constitution Act, 1867: A Study of Confederation's Political, Social and Economic Context," *Canadian Business Law Journal* 61, no. 1 (2018–19); Province of Canada, Legislative Assembly, *Parliamentary Debates on the Subject of the Confederation of the British North America Provinces*, 8th Leg, 3rd Sess, (6 February 1865), 28–9 (John A. MacDonald); Province of Canada, Legislative Assembly, *Parliamentary*

Debates on the Subject of the Confederation of the British North America Provinces, 8th Leg, 3rd Sess (7 February 1865), 55 (George-Étienne Cartier); A.T. Galt, *Speech on the Proposed Union of the British North American Provinces, Delivered at Sherbrooke, C.E.* (Montreal: Longmoore & Co, 1864), 10, cited in Smith, "The Historical Origins of Section 121."

26 The cause of reducing internal trade barriers is supported by an overwhelming majority of Canadians from across the political spectrum. See Sean Simpson, "Nine in Ten Canadians Support Fewer Trade Restrictions Between Provinces," *Ipsos*, 29 March 2018, online, https://perma.cc/56RU-REAN. This may help explain why governments of every stripe profess their commitment to reducing trade barriers, even as they work to maintain many of them on behalf of local interests in behind-the-scenes negotiations.

27 Previous Canadian scholarship on federalism has tended to emphasize diverse local preferences more than locally held knowledge. Yet as I argue in this book, both are important justifications for decentralization. See Katherine E. Swinton, *The Supreme Court and Canadian Federalism: The Laskin-Dickson Years* (Toronto: Carswell, 1990), 132–7; but see Richard Simeon, "Criteria for Choice in Federal Systems," *Queen's Law Journal* 8 (1982): 147 (listing the difficulty in acquiring information about local needs as a possible argument against centralization).

28 Lavoie, "Supreme Court's 'free-the-beer' Decision"; Donald Regan, "The Supreme Court and State Protectionism: Making Sense of the Dormant Commerce Clause," *Michigan Law Review* 84 (1986); Amelia Simpson, "Grounding the High Court's Modern Section 92 Jurisprudence: The Case for Improper Purpose as the Touchstone," *Federal Law Review* 33, no. 3 (2005); Peter W. Hogg and Wade Wright, *Constitutional Law of Canada*, 5th ed. Supp. (Scarborough, ON: Carswell, 2007), Part II, 20.2; Kathleen M. Sullivan and Noah Feldman, *Constitutional Law*, 18th ed. (St Paul: Foundation Press, 2013), 221–2; John Hart Ely, *Democracy and Distrust: A Theory of Judicial Review* (Cambridge, MA: Harvard University Press, 1980), 83–4.

29 Larissa Katz, "Property's Sovereignty," *Theoretical Inquiries in Law* 18, no. 2 (2017): 302–3.

30 Dwight Newman, "Changing Division of Powers Doctrine and the Emergent Principle of Subsidiarity," *Saskatchewan Law Review* 74, no. 1 (2011); *Cambridge Dictionary*, s.v. "subsidiarity," online, https://dictionary.cambridge.org/dictionary/english/subsidiarity, accessed 1 June 2021.

31 See Swinton, *The Supreme Court and Canadian Federalism*, 132–7; A.E. Safarian, *Canadian Federalism and Economic Integration* (Ottawa: Information Canada, 1974), 6–9.

32 Structural protections of this nature are found in the constitutions of the United States, Australia, and the European Union, among many other countries and supranational governance regimes. See Lavoie, "R. v Comeau and Section 121": 207–13.

33 Michael J. Trebilcock, "The Supreme Court and Strengthening the
    Conditions for Effective Competition in the Canadian Economy," *Canadian
    Bar Review* 80, no. 1–2 (2001): 553–4.

34 See, e.g., David Ricardo, *On the Principles of Political Economy and Taxation*,
    3rd ed. (London, UK: John Murray, 1821), 139; *Comeau* (NBPC), at paras 92,
    95–6, citing a speech by George Brown on 12 September 1864, a speech
    by John A. Macdonald on 7 February 1865, and a speech by Alexander
    Galt on 12 September 1867. The speeches, originally cited in Blue, "Long
    Overdue," may be found in Edward Whalen, *The Union of the British Provinces:
    A Brief Account of the Several Conferences Held in the Maritime Provinces and
    in Canada, in September and October 1864, on the Proposed Confederation of
    the Provinces, Together with a Report of the Speeches, delivered by the Delegates
    from the Provinces, on Important Public Occasions* (Charlottetown: GT Haszard,
    1865); Simpson, "Nine in Ten Canadians."

35 See, e.g., Asher Honickman and Ben Woodfinden, "Canada needs a New
    National Policy," *National Post*, 26 May 2020, online, https://perma.cc/ST2F-
    A9FB; John Gilmour, "Canada's Supply Chain Vulnerabilities and the Links
    to National Interests," *UOttawa Security, Economics and Technologies Blog*, 5
    June 2020, online, https://perma.cc/A26Y-892L; Lizzie O'Leary, "The Modern
    Supply Chain Is Snapping," *The Atlantic* (19 March 2020), online, https://
    perma.cc/55SX-8LQW.

36 The *Oxford English Dictionary* definition of "water-resistant" includes the
    following: "resistant to the adverse or damaging effects of water; not readily
    damaged, penetrated, or removed by water," s.v. "water-resistant," accessed
    1 June 2021.

37 George Vegh, "The Characterization of Barriers to Interprovincial Trade
    under the Canadian Constitution," *Osgoode Hall Law Journal* 34, no. 2 (1996).

38 *Black v. Law Society of Alberta*, [1989] 1 SCR 591 at 608–10, 58 DLR (4th) 317;
    Canadian Egg Marketing Agency v. Richardson (1997), [1998] 3 SCR 157 at paras
    60–7, Iacobucci and Bastarache JJ, 122–7, McLachlin J, dissenting, 166 DLR
    (4th) 1.

39 On fit and justification as criteria for legal theory, see Ronald Dworkin,
    "Hard Cases," *Harvard Law Review* 88, no. 6 (1975): 1097–101.

40 Ibid. Implicit in this approach is a commitment to some version of legal
    formalism – i.e., the view that the law has its own standards for assessing
    legality, separate from politics or morality. While the law may draw
    upon underlying principles or purposes, it is not directly reducible to
    unconstrained moral or political choices made by a judge or anyone else.
    In other words, the law is a partially autonomous domain. Though the law
    may not supply a uniquely correct answer in all cases, there are still better
    and worse ways to approach legal questions. Moreover, there are standards
    for evaluating those approaches that are distinctively legal in nature. This
    is true of the judicial interpretation of the Constitution no less than other

areas of law. Despite the far-reaching claims of some legal realists, this book proceeds on the premise that the question of how to approach the structural provisions of the Constitution is not simply a political question. See generally Ernest J. Weinrib, "The Jurisprudence of Legal Formalism," *Harvard Journal of Law & Public Policy* 16 (1993). For contrasting realist positions, see Patrick J. Monahan, "At Doctrine's Twilight: The Structure of Canadian Federalism," *University of Toronto Law Journal* 34, no. 1 (1984); Paul Weiler, "The Supreme Court of Canada and Canadian Federalism," in *Law and Social Change* (Toronto: Osgoode Hall Law School, 1973).

41 Ruth Sullivan, *Sullivan on the Construction of Statutes*, 6th ed. (Markham: LexisNexis Canada), §2.6; Eric M. Adams, "Canadian Constitutional Interpretation," in Cameron Hutchison, *The Fundamentals of Statutory Interpretation* (Toronto: LexisNexis Canada, 2018): 143–6; *Comeau* (scc), at para 5.

42 Herbert L.A. Hart, "Positivism and the Separation of Law and Morals," *Harvard Law Review* 71, no. 4 (1958): 607.

43 *Comeau* scc, at para 52; *R v. Big M Drug Mart Ltd*, [1985] 1 scr 295 at 344, 18 dlr (4th) 321.

44 This statement does not necessarily foreclose the possibility that an enacting body as a whole could have a collective intent that is not fully reducible to the aggregate of the intentions of individual members. See generally Richard Ekins, *The Nature of Legislative Intent* (Oxford: Oxford University Press, 2012).

45 Friedrich A. Hayek, *The Road to Serfdom* (New York, NY: Routledge, 2001), 75–7; Friedrich A. Hayek, *The Constitution of Liberty*, 2nd ed. (New York, NY: Routledge, 2006), 180–4; A.V. Dicey, *Introduction to the Study of the Law of the Constitution*, 8th ed. (London, UK: Macmillan, 1915), 107–22; Joseph Raz, "The Rule of Law and its Virtue," in *The Authority of Law: Essays on Law and Morality* (Oxford: Clarendon Press, 1979), 213–20.

46 See Keith E. Whittington, "Originalism: A Critical Introduction," *Fordham Law Review* 82, no. 2 (2013): 379–82.

47 Ibid., 382; Sullivan, *Construction of Statutes*, §9.28–9.32.

48 Whittington, "Originalism," 382.

Chapter Two

1 Canadian Charter of Rights and Freedoms, Part I of the Constitution Act, 1982, being Schedule B to the Canada Act 1982 (uk), 1982, c 11.

2 Beverley McLachlin, "Coming of Age: Canadian Nationhood and the Charter of Rights" (speech delivered at the Association of Canadian Studies Conference titled Canadian Rights and Freedoms: 20 Years Under the Charter, Ottawa, on, 17 April 2002), online, https://www.scc-csc.ca/judges-juges/spe-dis/bm-2002-04-17-eng.aspx.

3 Dwight Newman and Lorelle Binnion, "The Exclusion of Property Rights from the Charter: Correcting the Historical Record," *Alberta Law Review* 52, no. 3 (2015): 543, citing Gregory S. Alexander, *The Global Debate over Constitutional Property: Lessons for American Takings Jurisprudence* (Chicago: University of Chicago Press, 2006), 41; and Jeremy Webber and Kristy Gover, "Proprietary constitutionalism," in *Routledge Handbook of Constitutional Law*, ed. Mark Tushnet, Thomas Fleiner and Cheryl Saunders (London: Routledge, 2013), 364, nn 7–12.

4 Constitution Act, 1867 (UK), 30 & 31 Vict, c 3, reprinted in RSC 1985, Appendix II, No 5.

5 Ibid., ss 91 Preamble, 91(2), 91(9).

6 Ibid., ss 92(9), 92(13).

7 A hypothetical saloon on Sable Island would arguably have a double aspect, meaning it would be subject to both provincial legislation governing saloons, as well as any federal laws pertaining to the island. Federal laws would prevail in the event of any inconsistency under the doctrine of paramountcy.

8 Constitution Act, 1867, ss 21–36, 37–52, 53–7.

9 As discussed later, a compelling answer is provided in Janet Ajzenstat, *The Canadian Founding: John Locke and Parliament* (Montreal: McGill-Queen's University Press, 2007), 59–60.

10 Constitution Act, 1867, s 92(2). See also Gérard V. La Forest, *The Allocation of Taxing Power Under the Canadian Constitution*, 2nd ed. (Toronto: Canadian Tax Foundation, 1981), 56–7.

1 Constitution Act, 1867, s 91(13).

2 Ibid., Preamble.

3 La Forest, *Allocation of Taxing Power*, 78–9.

4 A.B. McCullough, *Money and Exchange in Canada to 1900* (Toronto: Dundurn Press, 1984), 114, 156–7, 181; On the surprising original meaning of the term "dollar" in the US Constitution, see Lawrence B. Solum, "Surprising Originalism: The Regula Lecture," *ConLawNow* 9, no. 1 (2018): 243–5.

5 See George Vegh, "The Characterization of Barriers to Interprovincial Trade under the Canadian Constitution," *Osgoode Hall Law Journal* 34, no. 2 (1996).

6 See La Forest *Allocation of Taxing Power*, 92.

7 Constitution Act, 1867, s 121; Ian Blue, "Long Overdue: A Reappraisal of Section 121 of the Constitution Act, 1867," *Dalhousie Law Journal* 33, no. 2 (2010); Malcolm Lavoie, "R. v Comeau and Section 121 of the Constitution Act, 1867: Freeing the Beer and Fortifying the Economic Union," *Dalhousie Law Journal* 40, no. 1 (2017).

   See Douglass C. North and Barry R. Weingast, "Constitutions and Commitment: The Evolution of Institutions Governing Public Choice in

Seventeenth-Century England," *Journal of Economic History* 49, no. 4 (1989). See also A.V. Dicey, *An Introduction to the Study of the Law of the Constitution*, 10th ed. (London, UK: MacMillan, 1959), 110. Dicey's first of three meanings of the rule of law is that "no man is punishable or can be made to lawfully suffer in body *or goods except for a distinct breach of law established in the ordinary Courts of the land*." Emphasis added.

19 Magna Carta (UK) 1215, 17 John, cl 39, online, avalon.law.yale.edu/medieval/ magframe.asp, cited in Paul A. Warchuk, "Rethinking Compensation for Expropriation," *University of British Columbia Law Review* 48, no. 2 (2015): 660.

20 Warchuk, "Compensation for Expropriation," 660–2.

21 *The King's Prerogative in Saltpetre* (1606), 12 Co Rep 12 at 12, 77 ER 1294, cited in Warchuk, "Compensation for Expropriation," 661.

22 See *R v. Hampden* (1637), 3 St Tr 825, *Re Petition of Right*, [1915] 3 KB 629, 1915 WL 18715 cited in Warchuk, "Compensation for Expropriation," 661–2.

23 *Entick v. Carrington* (1765), 19 St Tr 1029.

24 Ibid.

25 Joseph Chitty, *A Treatise on the Law of the Prerogatives of the Crown; and the Relative Duties and Rights of the Subject* (London, UK: Joseph Butterworth & Son, 1820), 49–50.

26 Ibid., 49.

27 Ibid., 50.

28 *Sir Francis Barrington's Case* (1610), 8 Co Rep 136b at 138, 77 ER 681; *Mayor of Yarmouth v. Simmons* (1878), 10 Ch D 518 at 527; *Western Counties v. Windsor and Annapolis* (1882), 7 AC 178 at 188; *Attorney-General v. Horner* (1884), 14 QBD 245 (CA), esp. per Brett MR at 256–7; *London and North-Western Railway Co v. Evans*, [1893] 1 Ch 16 (CA) per Bowen LJ at 28; *Attorney-General v. De Keyser's Royal Hotel*, [1920] UKHL 1, [1920] AC 508 per Lord Atkinson at 542, Lord Parmoor at 576, 579; *Colonial Sugar Refining Co v. Melbourne Harbour Trust Commissioners* (1927), 38 CLR 547 (PC) at 559. For a discussion of courts' development of these principles, see Tom Allen, "A Constitutional Right to Property," in *Common Law Constitutional Rights*, ed. Mark Elliot and Kristy Hughes (London, UK: Hart Publishing, 2020).

29 Kent McNeil, "Aboriginal Title as a Constitutionally Protected Property Right," in *Beyond the Nass Valley: National Implications of the Supreme Court's Delgamuukw Decision*, ed. Owen Lippert (Vancouver, BC: The Fraser Institute, 2000), 57.

30 Ibid.

31 Bill of Rights 1689 (UK), 1 Will & Mar, sess 2, c 2.

32 The text of the Bill of Rights provides that "levying money for or to the use of the Crown by pretence of prerogative, without grant of Parliament,

for longer time, or in other manner than the same is or shall be granted, is illegal[.]" Ibid.

33 See Peter Laslett, "The English Revolution and Locke's 'Two Treatises of Government,'" *Cambridge Historical Journal* 12, no. 1 (1956): 40–55.

34 Ibid; John Locke, *Two Treatises of Government*, ed. Peter Laslett (Cambridge, UK: Cambridge University Press, 1960).

35 The work continues to resonate today. In Jeremy Waldron, *The Right to Private Property* (Oxford: Clarendon Press, 1988), Waldron takes Locke's theory as one of two exemplars of arguments for a natural right to property (before ultimately rejecting Locke's approach). See also Robert Nozick, *Anarchy, State, and Utopia* (Oxford: Blackwell, 1974) and Randy E. Barnett, *Our Republican Constitution: Securing the Liberty and Sovereignty of We the People* (New York, NY: Broadside Books, 2016).

36 Locke, *Two Treatises*, 350–1.

37 Ibid., 360–2.

38 Michael P. Zuckert, *Natural Rights and the New Republicanism* (Princeton, NJ: Princeton University Press, 1994), 16, 18; Donald L. Doernberg, "'We the People': John Locke, Collective Constitutional Rights and Standing to Challenge Government Action," *California Law Review* 73, no. 1 (1985): 57–9.

39 *Entick v. Carrington*.

40 Ajzenstat, *The Canadian Founding*, 52.

41 Ibid., 3–21.

42 Ibid., 50.

43 Ibid., 3–110.

44 Janet Ajzenstat, Paul Romney, Ian Gentles, and William D. Gairdner, eds, *Canada's Founding Debates* (Toronto: University of Toronto Press, 2003). See page 58 per Robert Pinsent, Newfoundland House of Assembly, 11 February 1869; 154–5 per Hugh Hoyles, Newfoundland House of Assembly, 11 February 1869; 174 per Charles Tupper, Nova Scotia House of Assembly, 10 April 1866; 247 per Judge John Black, Convention at Fort Gary, English and French Delegates in Council, 1 February 1870; 290 per John Sanborn, Canadian Legislative Council, 9 February 1865; 335 per George-Étienne Cartier, Canadian Legislative Assembly, 7 February 1865. See also editors' comments on 229; Ajzenstat, *The Canadian Founding*, 50 per F.B.T. Carter, Newfoundland House of Assembly, 23 February 1969.

5 Ajzenstat, *The Canadian Founding*, 77 per Charles Tupper, Nova Scotia House of Assembly, 10 April 1866, originally cited in Ajzenstat et al., *Canada's Founding Debates*, 174.

6 Ajzenstat et al., *Canada's Founding Debates*, 174.

7 Ibid., 247.

8 Ibid., 290–1.

49 Ajzenstat, *The Canadian Founding*, 51–2.
50 Ibid., 51–2, citing Dicey, *Law of the Constitution*, ch. 4.
51 CCLC. On the expectation that rights would be protected by the common law and civil law traditions, see Donald V. Smiley, *Canada in Question: Federalism in the Eighties*, 3rd ed. (Toronto: McGraw-Hill Ryerson, 1980), 42 cited in Ajzenstat, *The Canadian Founding*, 54.
52 The Legislative Assembly of the Province of Canada passed the resolutions in favour of Confederation on 11 March 1865. Donald Creighton, *The Road to Confederation: The Emergence of Canada, 1863–67*, rev. ed. (Don Mills, ON: Oxford University Press, 2012), 256.
53 Art 406 CCLC.
54 Art 407 CCLC.
55 See *City of Montreal v. Hogan* (1900), 31 SCR 1, requiring statutory authorization for the taking of property and decrying the "tyrannical" conduct of the municipality in taking possession without such authorization.
56 Constitution Act, 1867, Preamble.
57 Robert Marleau and Camille Montpetit, *House of Commons Procedure and Practice* (Ottawa: House of Commons, 2000), 12–15.
58 Ajzenstat, *The Canadian Founding*, 59–60.
59 Ibid.
60 Constitution Act, 1867, s 53; Ajzenstat, *The Canadian Founding*.
61 Constitution Act, 1867, s 54; Ajzenstat, *The Canadian Founding*, 60.
62 Ajzenstat, *The Canadian Founding*, 60.
63 Constitution Act, 1867, s 90.
64 Janet Ajzenstat, *The Once and Future Canadian Democracy: An Essay in Political Thought* (Montreal: McGill-Queen's University Press, 2003), 65.
65 Constitution Act, 1867, s 23.
66 Ajzenstat et al., *Canada's Founding Debates*, 91 per Joseph Armand, Canadian Legislative Council, 15 February 1865; 107 per William Annand, Nova Scotia House of Assembly, 12 April 1865.
67 Constitution Act, 1867, ss 56–7, 90.
68 Ajzenstat et al., *Canada's Founding Debates*, 290–1, per E.P. Taché (responding to John Sanborn), Canadian Legislative Council, 9 February 1865.
69 A number of pre-Confederation cases deal with the statutory powers of railways to infringe on private property rights, subject to compensation. See *Sommerville v. Great Western Railway*, [1854] 11 UCQB 304; *Great Western Railway v. Chauvin*, [1854] 1 PR 28; *Day v. Grand Truck Railway*, [1855] 5 UCCP 420.
70 Dicey, *Law of the Constitution*, 10.
71 Steven Shavell, *Foundations of Economic Analysis of Law* (Cambridge, MA: Harvard University Press, 2004), 124–5.

72 Tony Honoré, "Ownership," in *Making Law Bind: Essays Legal and Philosophical* (Oxford: Clarendon Press, 1987), 171.

73 On post-Confederation understandings of the role of the legislature in mediating claims of property rights and the public interest, see R.C.B. Risk and R.C. Vipond, "Rights Talk in Canada in the Late Nineteenth Century: 'The Good Sense and Right Feeling of the People'," in R.C.B. Risk, *A History of Canadian Legal Thought: Collected Essays* (Toronto: University of Toronto Press, 2006).

74 Gérard V. La Forest, "The Canadian Charter of Rights and Freedoms: An Overview," *Canadian Bar Review* 61, no. 1 (1983).

Chapter Three

1 "Folk dancing and raw seal herald Canada's new territory," *Birmingham Post*, 2 April 1999.

2 Ibid.

3 Ibid.

4 Frank Tester and Peter Kulchyski, *Tammarniit (Mistakes): Inuit Relocation in the Eastern Arctic, 1939–63* (Vancouver: UBC Press, 1994); Alan Rudolph Marcus, *Relocating Eden: The Image and Politics of Inuit Exile in the Canadian Arctic* (Lebanon, NH: Darthmouth Press, 2014).

5 "Folk dancing and raw seal herald Canada's new territory."

6 Agreement between the Inuit of The Nunavut Settlement Area and Her Majesty the Queen in Right of Canada, 25 May 1993, online (PDF), Government of Nunavut, https://publications.gc.ca/collections/Collection/R32-134-1993E.pdf, art 4. Implemented by Nunavut Act, SC 1993, c 28.

7 Nunavut Agreement, art 19; *1996–1997 Annual Report on the Implementation of the Nunavut Land Claims Agreement*, 1997, online (PDF), Government of Canada, https://perma.cc/3WTF-XM92.

8 André Légaré, "The Reconstruction of Inuit Collective Identity: From Cultural to Civic," in *Aboriginal Policy Research: Moving Forward, Making a Difference*, ed. Jerry P. White, Susan Wingert, and Dan Beavon (Toronto: Thompson Education Publications, 2007), 103, 107; Janet Mancini Billson, "Inuit Dreams, Inuit Realities: Shattering the Bonds of Dependency," *American Review of Canadian Studies* 31, no. 1–2 (2001). The territory remains eighty-four per cent Inuit. Statistics Canada, "Nunavut [Territory] and Canada [Country]," Census Profile, 2016 Census, online, https://www12.statcan.gc.ca/census-recensement/2016/dp-pd/prof/details/Page.cfm?Lang=E&Geo1=PR&Code1=62&Geo2=&Code2=&SearchText=Nunavut&SearchType=Begins&SearchPR=01&B1=All&GeoLevel=PR&GeoCode=62&type=0, last modified 9 August 2019.

9   See Malcolm Lavoie, "Models of Indigenous Territorial Control in Common Law Countries: A Functional Comparison," in *Research Handbook on the International Law of Indigenous Rights*, ed. Dwight Newman (Cheltenham, UK: Edward Elgar, 2022), 226.

10 Nunavut Act, SC 1993, c 28, s 23.

11 Ibid., s 23(1).

12 Robert K. Vischer, "Subsidiarity as a Principle of Governance: Beyond Devolution," *Indiana Law Review* 35, no. 103 (2001): 108–26.

13 Dwight Newman, "Changing Division of Powers Doctrine and the Emergent Principle of Subsidiarity," *Saskatchewan Law Review* 74, no. 1 (2011); *Cambridge Dictionary*, s.v. "subsidiarity," online, https://dictionary.cambridge. org/dictionary/english/subsidiarity, accessed 1 June 2021.

14 Ernest J. Weinrib, *The Idea of Private Law*, rev. ed. (New York: Oxford University Press, 2013), 8–11.

15 Constitution Act, 1867 (UK), 30 & 31 Vict, c 3, s 92(13), reprinted in RSC 1985, Appendix II, No 5.

16 W.R. Lederman, "Unity and Diversity in Canadian Federalism: Ideals and Methods of Moderation," *Canadian Bar Review* 53 (1975): 601–4.

17 Royal Proclamation, 1763 (UK), reprinted in RSC 1985, Appendix II, No 1.

18 Ibid.

19 John E.C. Brierley and Roderick A. Macdonald, eds, *Quebec Civil Law: An Introduction to Quebec Private Law* (Toronto: Emond Publishing, 1993), 15; André Morel, "La réaction des Canadiens devant l'administration de la justice de 1764 à 1774: une forme de résistance passive," *Revue du Barreau*, 26 (1960); P.E. Lamarche, "French Civil Law under British Rule," *Canadian Law Times* 31, no. 6 (1911): 436; Ghislain Otis, "The Impact of the Royal Proclamation of 1763 on Quebec: Then and Now," (paper presented at Land Claims Agreements Coalition Creating Canada Symposium Canadian Museum of Civilization, Gatineau, QC, 7 October 2013), 4, SSRN, online, https://papers.ssrn.com/sol3/papers.cfm?abstract_id=2423785.

20 See Malcolm Lavoie and Moira Lavoie, "Indigenous Institutions and the Rule of Indigenous Law," *Supreme Court Law Review*, 2nd ed., 101 (2021).

21 Truth and Reconciliation Commission of Canada, *Canada's Residential Schools: The Final Report of the Truth and Reconciliation Commission of Canada, Volume 1: The History, Part 1 Origins to 1939* (Montreal: McGill-Queen's University Press, 2015).

22 Quebec Act, 1774 (UK), 14 Geo III, c 83, reprinted in RSC 1985, Appendix II, No 2.

23 Ibid., s 8.

24 Craig Forcese, Adam Dodek, Philip Bryden, Richard Haigh, Mary Liston, and Constance MacIntosh, *Public Law: Cases, Commentary, and Analysis*, 4th ed. (Toronto: Emond Publishing, 2020), 82.

25 Quebec Act, 1774, Part XI.

26 Forcese et al., *Public Law*, 82.

27 Ibid.

28 The first three books of the French civil code reflect these divisions. *Code civil des Français, Édition originale et seule officielle*, (Paris: de l'Imprimerie de la République, 1804); See also Preliminary Provision CCQ.

29 Property and Civil Rights Act, SUC 1792, C 1, S 1.

30 Ibid., S 3.

31 Paul Romney, "Upper Canada (Ontario): The Administration of Justice, 1784–1850," *Manitoba Law Journal* 23 (1995): 184–6,

32 The Union Act, 1840 (UK), 3 & 4 Vict, c 35.

33 Ibid.; *Property and Civil Rights Act*, SUC 1792, C 1.

34 Act Respecting the Civil Code of Lower Canada, 29 Vict c 41 (1865).

35 Ibid., Preamble to the Act; see also Act Respecting the Codification of the Laws of Lower Canada Relative to Civil Matters and Procedure, Preamble, Consolidated Statutes for Lower Canada, c 2.

36 The fact that there was a separate book dealing with "Commercial Law" within the Civil Code may lead one to believe that the framers saw a distinction between "commerce", on the one hand, and "property and civil rights", on the other. The subjects dealt with in the Civil Code's book on Commercial Law are mostly topics that were expressly assigned to Parliament through section 91 of the Constitution Act, 1867, such as shipping and bills of exchange. The only major exception is insurance contracts, which are part of the book on Commercial Law but were not expressly assigned to Parliament in s 91. The question of whether insurance contracts are under the federal power over trade and commerce or the provincial power over property and civil rights was the subject of the seminal federalism case of *Citizens' Insurance Company of Canada v. Parsons*, [1881] UKPC 49, 7 AC 96 (JCPC).

37 Brierley and Macdonald, *Quebec Civil Law*, 99–100; Preliminary Provision CCQ.

38 Brierley and Macdonald, *Quebec Civil Law*, 101–2.

39 Constitution Act, 1867, s 92(16).

40 *Reference re Assisted Human Reproduction Act*, 2010 SCC 61 at para 183, LeBel and Deschamps JJ; Peter W. Hogg, "Subsidiarity and the Division of Powers in Canada," *National Journal of Constitutional Law* (1993): 3.

41 Janet Ajzenstat, Paul Romney, Ian Gentles, and William D. Gairdner, eds, *Canada's Founding Debates* (Toronto: University of Toronto Press 2003), 296–7 per Étienne-Paschal Taché, Legislative Council, 20 February 1865, per John A. Macdonald, Legislative Assembly of the Province of Canada, 6 February 1865; Asher Honickman, "Watertight Compartments: Getting Back to the Constitutional Division of Powers," *Alberta Law Review* 55, no. 1 (2017): 227–34.

42 Jean Leclair, "The Supreme Court of Canada's Understanding of Federalism: Efficiency at the Expense of Diversity," *Queen's Law Journal* 28, no. 2 (2003): 418; *Bell Canada v. Quebec (Commission de la Santé et de la Sécurité du Travail)*, [1988] 1 SCR 749 at 766, 51 DLR (4th) 161.

43 Peter Hogg and Wade Wright, *Constitutional Law of Canada*, 5th ed. (Toronto: Thomas Reuters Canada, 2007), chapter 16.

44 Ibid., chapter 16.1.

45 Ibid.

46 Leclair, "Supreme Court of Canada's Understanding of Federalism," 766.

47 Kathleen M. Sullivan and Noah Feldman, *Constitutional Law*, 18th ed. (New York: Foundation Press, 2013), 136.

48 *US v. Lopez*, 514 US 549 (1995) (striking down a federal prohibition on having a firearm in a school zone as being insufficiently connected to interstate commerce); *US v. Morrison*, 529 US 598 (2000) (striking down a federal civil action for gender-based violence as being insufficiently connected to interstate commerce); *National Federation of Independent Business v. Sebelius*, 567 US 519 (2012) (five of nine judges held that a federal individual mandate to purchase health insurance could not be grounded in the Commerce Clause, though the mandate was upheld on other grounds).

49 Hogg and Wright, *Constitutional Law*, chapter 20.2(b), (the authors refer to the "bad old days" of the Privy Council's "watertight compartments"); Honickman, "Watertight Compartments," 226; *Ontario (Attorney General) v. OPSEU*, [1987] 2 SCR 2 at 18, 41 DLR (4th) 1; *Reference re Assisted Human Reproduction Act* at para 139.

50 Honickman, "Watertight Compartments," 227–35.

51 Constitution Act, 1867, s 92.

52 Ibid., s 91.

53 Ibid.

54 Ibid., s 95.

55 Ibid.

56 Honickman, "Watertight Compartments," 234–5.

57 Ajzenstat et al., *Canada's Founding Debates*, 283 per John A. Macdonald, Legislative Assembly of the Province of Canada, 6 February 1865.

58 See *Provincial Secretary of Prince Edward Island v. Egan*, [1941] SCR 396 at 402, 3 DLR 305 (Duff CJC); *Smith v. The Queen* [1960] SCR 776 at 784, 25 DLR (2d) 225.

59 Hogg and Wright, *Constitutional Law*, chapter 15.9(c).

60 Ibid., chapter 15.5(c).

61 Ibid.; *O'Grady v. Sparling*, [1960] SCR 804, 25 DLR (2d) 145; *Mann v. The Queen*, [1966] SCR 238, 56 DLR (2d) 1.

62 Hogg and Wright, *Constitutional Law*, chapter 16.1.

63 Ibid., chapter 20.2(b).

64 Honickman, "Watertight Compartments."

65 The *Oxford English Dictionary* definition of "water-resistant" includes the following: "resistant to the adverse or damaging effects of water; not readily damaged, penetrated, or removed by water," s.v. "water-resistant, adj," accessed 23 July 2021.

66 Honickman, "Watertight Compartments," 233; Paul Romney, "Why Lord Watson Was Right," in *Canadian Constitutionalism, 1791–1991*, ed. Janet Ajzenstat (Ottawa: Canadian Study of Parliament, 1992).

67 John T. Saywell, *The Lawmakers: Judicial Power and the Shaping of Canadian Federalism* (Toronto: University of Toronto Press, 2002), 9.

68 Province of Canada, Legislative Assembly of the Province of Canada (21 February 1865), 388 (Hector-Louis Langevin).

69 Act Respecting the Civil Code of Lower Canada.

70 Ajzenstat et al., *Canada's Founding Debates*, 279–80 per John A. Macdonald, Legislative Assembly of the Province of Canada, 6 February 1865.

71 Donald Creighton, *The Road to Confederation: The Emergence of Canada 1863–1867*, rev. ed. (Don Mills, ON: Oxford University Press, 2012), 60.

72 Ajzenstat et al., *Canada's Founding Debates*, 279 per John A. Macdonald, Legislative Assembly of the Province of Canada, 6 February 1865.

73 Ibid., 283.

74 Ibid., 288 per George Brown, Legislative Assembly of the Province of Canada, 8 February 1865; Honickman, "Watertight Compartments," 228.

75 Ajzenstat et al., *Canada's Founding Debates*, 291 per Louis Auguste Olivier, Legislative Council of the Province of Canada, 13 February 1865.

76 Ibid., 291 per Louis Auguste Olivier, Legislative Council of the Province of Canada, 13 February 1865.

77 Ibid., 292.

78 Ibid., 296–7 per Étienne-Paschal Taché, Legislative Council of the Province of Canada, 20 February 1865.

79 Ibid., 283 per John A. Macdonald, Legislative Assembly of the Province of Canada, 6 February 1865.

80 Honickman, "Watertight Compartments," 228–34.

81 Ibid.

82 Ibid., 229.

83 Ibid., 228–9; Romney, "Why Lord Watson Was Right," citing Andrée Desilets, *Hector-Louis Langevin, un père de la Confédération canadienne (1826–1906)* (Montreal: Presses de' l'Université Laval 1969), 164–7.

84 See Ajzenstat et al., *Canada's Founding Debates*, 282 per John A. Macdonald, Legislative Assembly of the Province of Canada, 6 February 1865. Constitution Act, 1867, ss 56, 57, 90.

    Ajzenstat et al., *Canada's Founding Debates*, 291 per John Sanborn, Canadian Legislative Council, 9 February 1865; see also Paul Romney, *Getting It Wrong:*

How Canadians Forgot Their Past and Imperilled Confederation (Toronto: University of Toronto Press, 1999), 95–7.

87 Romney, *Getting It Wrong*, 97.

88 The last time the federal government exercised its disallowance power was in 1941. See Gérard V. La Forest, *Disallowance and Reservation of Provincial Legislation* (Ottawa: Department of Justice, 1955), 82; Richard Albert, "Constitutional Amendment by Constitutional Desuetude," *American Journal of Comparative Law* 62, no. 3 (2014).

89 Indeed, in the early post-Confederation federalism cases, provinces repeatedly, though unsuccessfully, advanced the argument that the existence of the disallowance power rendered judicial review of provincial legislation superfluous. Saywell, *The Lawmakers*, 17–19.

90 Ibid., 83–101.

91 Ibid.

92 Donald G. Creighton, *British North America at Confederation: A Study Prepared for the Royal Commission on Dominion-Provincial Relations* (Ottawa: J.O. Patenaude, 1939); Frank R. Scott, "The Development of Canadian Federalism," in *Papers and Proceedings of the Canadian Political Science Association* (1931); Frank R. Scott, "The Special Nature of Canadian Federalism," *Canadian Journal of Economics and Political Science* 13, no. 1 (1947); Frank R. Scott, "Centralization and Decentralization in Canadian Federalism," *Canadian Bar Review* 29, no. 10 (951); Frank R. Scott, *Canada Today: A Study of Her National Interests and National Policy* (London: Oxford University Press, 1938); William Francis O'Connor, *Report Pursuant to Resolution of the Senate to the Honourable the Speaker by the Parliamentary Counsel Relating to the Enactment of the British North America Act, 1867, any lack of consonance between its terms and judicial construction of them and cognate matters* (Ottawa: King's Printer, 1939).

93 Peter W. Hogg and Wade K. Wright, "Canadian Federalism, the Privy Council and the Supreme Court: Reflections on the Debate about Canadian Federalism," *University of British Colombia Law Review* 38, no. 2 (2005): 330–9.

94 Creighton, *British North America at Confederation*, 50.

95 Ibid.

96 Brian J. Young, *The Politics of Codification: The Lower Canadian Civil Code of 1866* (Montreal: McGill-Queen's University Press, 1994), 4; Paul A. Crépeau, "Civil Code Revision in Quebec," *Louisiana Law Review* 34, no. 5 (1973–74): 931.

97 Donald Wright, "Introduction," in Creighton, *The Road to Confederation*, xv, citing Romney, *Getting It Wrong*; Brian Hodgins, "Disagreements at the Commencement: Divergent Ontario Views of Federalism, 1867–1781," in *Oliver Mowat's Ontario: Papers*, ed. Donald Swainson (Toronto: Macmillan,

1972), 21; Alan Cairns, "The Judicial Committee and Its Critics," *Canadian Journal of Political Science* 4, no. 3 (1971): 334–8 (arguing that the decentralized interpretation of the division of powers given by the Privy Council was not necessarily inconsistent with the text or the intent of the framers); Robert Vipond, *Liberty and Community: Canadian Federalism and the Failure of the Constitution* (Albany: SUNY Press, 1991). See also Gerald Peter Browne, *The Judicial Committee and the British North America Act: An Analysis of the Interpretative Scheme for the Distribution of Legislative Powers* (Toronto: University of Toronto Press, 1967).

98 Constitution Act, 1867, s 92.

99 Ibid., s 109.

100 The Alberta Natural Resource Act, SA 1930, c 21; Manitoba Natural Resources Agreement, SM 1930, c 30; The Saskatchewan Natural Resources Act, SS 1930, c 87; Constitution Act, 1982, being Schedule B to the Canada Act, 1982 (UK), 1982, c 11, s 92A.

101 Ajzenstat et al., *Canada's Founding Debates*, 290–1 per Étienne-Paschal Taché, James Currie, John Ross, John Sanborn, Canadian Legislative Council, 9 February 1865.

102 Ibid., Editor's note, 290–1.

103 Saywell, *The Lawmakers*, 9–14.

104 Nunavut Act, SC 1993, c 28, s 23(1)(l).

Chapter Four

1 As at least one skeptical legislator pointed out at the time that property rights and local government could remain secure under separate colonial governments. Janet Ajzenstat, Paul Romney, Ian Gentles, and William D. Gairdner, eds, *Canada's Founding Debates*, (Toronto: University of Toronto Press, 2003), 154–5 per Thomas Talbot, Newfoundland House of Assembly, 9 February 1869.

2 Michael J. Trebilcock, "The Supreme Court and Strengthening the Conditions for Effective Competition in the Canadian Economy," *Canadian Bar Review* 80, no. 1–2 (2001): 553–4.

3 Ibid., 553–71.

4 Malcolm Lavoie, "R. v. Comeau and Section 121 of the Constitution Act, 1867: Freeing the Beer and Fortifying the Economic Union," *Dalhousie Law Journal* 40, no. 1 (2017): 197, citing *R v. Comeau*, 2016 NBPC 3 at paras 81, 89, rev'd 2018 SCC 15; Andrew Smith, "The Historical Origins of Section 121 of the Constitution Act, 1867: A Study of Confederation's Political, Social and Economic Context," *Canadian Business Law Journal* 61, no. 1 (2018–2019).

5 Smith, "The Historical Origins of Section 121."

6 Ibid.
7 Donald Creighton, *The Road to Confederation: The Emergence of Canada, 1863–1867*, rev. ed. (Don Mills, ON: Oxford University Press, 2012), 24–31; Smith, "The Historical Origins of Section 121."
8 Creighton, *The Road to Confederation*, 181.
9 Smith, "The Historical Origins of Section 121."
10 Donald Creighton, *British North America at Confederation: A Study Prepared for the Royal Commission on Dominion-Provincial Relations* (Ottawa: J.O. Patenaude, 1939), 40.
11 Donald Wright, "Introduction," in *The Road to Confederation*, ed. Donald Creighton, xv, citing Paul Romney, *Getting it Wrong: How Canadians Forgot Their Past and Imperilled Confederation* (Toronto: University of Toronto Press, 1999); Brian Hodgins, "Disagreements at the Commencement: Divergent Ontario Views of Federalism, 1867–1781," in *Oliver Mowat's Ontario: Papers*, ed. Donald Swainson (Toronto: Macmillan of Canada, 1972), 21; Alan C. Cairns, "The Judicial Committee and Its Critics," *Canadian Journal of Political Science* 4, no. 3 (1971); Robert Vipond, *Liberty and Community: Canadian Federalism and the Failure of the Constitution* (Albany: SUNY Press, 1991). See also Gerald Peter Browne, *The Judicial Committee and the British North America Act: An Analysis of the Interpretative Scheme for the Distribution of Legislative Powers* (Toronto: University of Toronto Press, 1967); *R v. Comeau*, NBPC at paras 81–2, 89–101; Smith, "The Historical Origins of Section 121"; Ian Blue, "Long Overdue: A Reappraisal of Section 121 of the Constitution Act, 1867," *Dalhousie Law Journal* 33, no. 2 (2010).
12 Province of Canada, Legislative Assembly, *Parliamentary Debates on the Subject of the Confederation of the British North America Provinces*, 8th Leg, 3rd Sess (6 February 1865), 28–9 (John A. MacDonald).
13 A.T. Galt, *Speech on the Proposed Union of the British North American Provinces, Delivered at Sherbrooke, C.E.* (Montreal: Longmoore & Co, 1864), 10, cited in Smith, "The Historical Origins of Section 121."
14 Ibid.
15 Ajzenstat et al., *Canada's Founding Debates*, 132 per Peter Mitchell, Legislative Council of New Brunswick, 16 April 1866.
16 Province of Canada, Legislative Assembly, *Parliamentary Debates on the Subject of the Confederation of the British North America Provinces*, 8th Leg, 3rd Sess (7 February 1865), 55 (George-Étienne Cartier).
17 Creighton, *British North America at Confederation*, 40, 45.
18 Province of Canada, Legislative Assembly, *Parliamentary Debates*, 60 (George-Étienne Cartier).
19 Trebilcock, "Effective Competition in the Canadian Economy," 567–9, 574–5.
20 Smith, "The Historical Origins of Section 121."
21 UK, HL Deb (19 February 1867) vol 185, col 557–82 (Lord Carnarvon) cited by Smith, ibid.

22 Janet Ajzenstat, "Popular Sovereignty in the Confederation Debates," in *The Canadian Founding: John Locke and Parliament*, ed. Janet Ajzenstat (Montreal: McGill-Queen's University Press, 2007), 147.

23 Ajzenstat et al., *Canada's Founding Debates*, 281 per John A. Macdonald, Legislative Assembly of the Province of Canada, 6 February 1865.

24 Ibid., 281–4.

25 US Const., art I, § 8.

26 See *The Federalist Nos. 41, 42, 43* (James Madison).

27 John Stuart Mill, *Considerations on Representative Government* (London: Parker, Son, and Bourn, 1861), ch. 17.

28 Ibid.

29 Dwight G. Newman, "Federalism, Subsidiarity, and Carbon Taxes" *Saskatchewan Law Review* 82, no. 2 (2019): 192; Ajzenstat, *The Canadian Founding*, 7.

30 See John Hart Ely, *Democracy and Distrust: A Theory of Judicial Review* (Cambridge, MA: Harvard University Press, 1980), 83–4.

31 Donald H. Regan, "The Supreme Court and State Protectionism: Making Sense of the Dormant Commerce Clause," *Michigan Law Review* 84 (1986): 1112–6.

32 Creighton, *British North America at Confederation*, 46.

33 Ibid., 307–8.

34 See Alexander Smith, *The Commerce Power in Canada and the United States* (Toronto: Butterworths, 1963), 30–44. The early cases of the Supreme Court of Canada took a relatively expansive view of the scope of federal trade and commerce power with respect to trade within the province. This trend was reversed by the decision of the Privy Council in *Citizens Insurance Co of Canada v. Parsons*, [1881] UKPC 49 (BAILII), [1881] 7 AC 96 [*Parsons* cited to BAILII]. The early Supreme Court cases include *Severn v. The Queen*, 1878 CarswellOnt 240, 2 SCR 70 (striking down provincial legislation providing for the licensing of liquor wholesalers selling liquor within the province as an encroachment on the federal trade and commerce power); *City of Fredericton v. The Queen*, 1880 CarswellNB 116, 3 SCR 505 (upholding federal legislation that prohibited the sale of liquor in municipalities that opted into the legislation, on the basis of the trade and commerce power).

35 Peter W. Hogg and Wade Wright, *Constitutional Law of Canada*, 5th ed. Supp. (Scarborough, ON: Carswell, 2007), Part II, 20.

36 See Creighton, *British North America at Confederation*; Frank R. Scott, "The Development of Canadian Federalism," *Papers and Proceedings of the Canadian Political Science Association* 3 (1931); Frank R. Scott, "The Special Nature of Canadian Federalism," *Canadian Journal of Economics and Political Science* 13, no. 1 (1947); Frank R. Scott, "Centralization and Decentralization in Canadian Federalism," *Canadian Bar Review* 29, no. 10 (1951); Frank R. Scott, *Canada Today: A Study of Her National Interests and National Policy* (London:

Oxford University Press, 1938); William Francis O'Connor, *Report Pursuant to Resolution of the Senate to the Honourable the Speaker by the Parliamentary Counsel Relating to the Enactment of the British North America Act, 1867, any lack of consonance between its terms and judicial construction of them and cognate matters* (Ottawa: King's Printer, 1939).

37 *Parsons,* 10–12.

38 Ibid., 11.

39 John George Lambton (Earl of Durham), *Report on the Affairs of British North America* (Durham Report) (Montreal: Robert Stanton 1839), 107.

40 Creighton, *British North America at Confederation,* 54.

41 Ibid.

42 Charles M. Andrews, *The Colonial Period in American History,* 4 vols (New Haven: Yale University Press, 1934), 4:348–50.

43 Creighton, *British North America at Confederation,* 54.

44 *Dominion Stores v. The Queen* (1979), [1980] 1 SCR 844, 106 DLR (3d) [*Dominion Stores* cited to SCR]; *Murphy v. CPR,* [1958] SCR 626, 15 DLR (2d) 145; *Caloil Inc v. Attorney General of Canada,* [1971] SCR 543, 20 DLR (3d) 472; *Reference re Agricultural Products Marketing Act,* [1978] 2 SCR 1198, 84 DLR (3d).

45 See e.g., *The King v. Eastern Terminal Elevator,* [1925] SCR 434, 3 DLR 1.

46 *Dominion Stores,* 865–6.

47 Ibid.

48 Hogg and Wright, *Constitutional Law,* Part II, 20.2(b).

49 Constitution Act, 1867 (UK), s 92(10)(a)-(c), 30 & 31 Vict, c 3, reprinted in RSC 1985, Appendix II, No 5.

50 *Campbell-Bennett v. Comstock Midwestern Ltd.,* [1954] SCR 207, 3 DLR 481; *Saskatchewan Power Corporation et al. v. TransCanada Pipelines Ltd.,* [1979] 1 SCR 297, 88 DLR (3d) 289; *Hewson v. Ontario Power Co,* 1905 CarswellOnt 740, 36 SCR 596; *Reference re Environmental Act,* 2019 BCCA 181, leave to appeal to SCC refused, 45253 (16 January 2020); Dwight Newman, *Pipelines and the Constitution: Canadian Dreams and Canadian Nightmares* (Ottawa: Macdonald-Laurier Institute, April 2018), online (PDF), https://macdonaldlaurier.ca/files/pdf/MLICommentary_April2018_Newman_FWeb.pdf.

51 Constitution Act, 1867, s 91(13).

52 Hogg and Wright, *Constitutional Law,* § 22:10.

53 Constitution Act, 1867, s 91(11).

54 Ibid., ss 91(25), 95.

55 Ibid., ss 91(5), (10).

56 Hogg and Wright, *Constitutional Law,* Part II, 22.16, 22.17; *Capital Cities Comm v. CRTC,* [1978] 2 SCR 141, 81 DLR (3d) 609.

57 This was a fact recognized many decades previously in the American *Federalist Papers,* with which the framers of the Constitution Act, 1867 were familiar. See *The Federalist No. 42* (James Madison); Ajzenstat, "Popular Sovereignty in the Confederation Debates," 147.

58 Constitution Act, 1867, ss 91(9), 91(10); Harold St John, "Sable Island, with a Catalogue of its Vascular Plants," *Proceedings of the Boston Society of Natural History* 36, no. 1 (1921): 17.

59 *Reference re the Regulation and Control of Aeronautics in Canada*, [1932] AC 54 (PC) [*Aeronautics Reference*]; *Johannesson v. Municipality of West St. Paul* (1951), [1952] 1 SCR 292, [1951] 4 DLR 609.

60 Hogg and Wright, *Constitutional Law*, Part II, 17.3(b).

61 *Aeronautics Reference*, at 73.

62 Constitution Act, 1867, s 91(24).

63 Canada, *Report of the Royal Commission on Aboriginal Peoples*, 5 vols (Ottawa: Supply and Services Canada, 1996), 1:166–73.

64 Joshua Ben David Nichols, *A Reconciliation without Recollection? An Investigation of the Foundations of Aboriginal Law in Canada* (Toronto: University of Toronto Press, 2020), 116–30.

65 Truth and Reconciliation Commission of Canada, *Canada's Residential Schools: The Final Report of the Truth and Reconciliation Commission of Canada, Volume 1: The History, Part 1 Origins to 1939* (Montreal: McGill-Queen's University Press, 2015), 106–10.

66 *Report of the Royal Commission on Aboriginal Peoples*, 1:133.

67 Stuart Banner, *How the Indians Lost Their Land: Law and Power on the Frontier* (Cambridge, MA: Harvard University Press, 2005), 85–111.

68 Ibid. See also Malcolm Lavoie, "Why Restrain Alienation of Indigenous Lands?" *University of British Columbia Law Review* 49, no. 3 (2016): 1029–30; Kent McNeil, "Self-Government and the Inalienability of Aboriginal Title," *McGill Law Journal* 47, no. 3 (2002).

69 Banner, *How the Indians Lost Their Land*, 85–111.

70 Ibid., 85–95.

71 Ibid., 93.

72 The Royal Proclamation, 1763, reprinted in RSC 1985, Appendix, II, No 1.

73 Peter H. Russell, *Canada's Odyssey: A Country Based on Incomplete Conquests* (Toronto: Toronto University Press, 2007), 46–7.

74 Ibid., 48–50; *Report of the Royal Commission on Aboriginal Peoples*, 1:240–1.

75 An Act respecting the Management of Indian Lands and Property, SC 1860, c 151, s 4; Nichols, *A Reconciliation without Recollection?* 124.

76 Nichols, *A Reconciliation without Recollection?* 124–5. Nichols identifies this as a potential explanation, though he also sees a potential basis in the ideological justifications for the British Empire as a federation of self-governing Anglo-Saxon states.

77 See, e.g., Treaty No. 6 between Her Majesty the Queen and the Plain and Wood Cree Indians and other Tribes of Indians at Fort Carlton, Fort Pitt and Battle River with Adhesions, 9 September 1876, online, Government of Canada, https://www.rcaanc-cirnac.gc.ca/eng/1100100028710/158129256942.

78 On the federal government's failure to live up to promises relating to assistance in the transition to agriculture, see Sarah Carter, *Lost Harvests: Prairie Indian Reserve Farmers and Government Policy*, 2nd ed. (Montreal: McGill-Queen's University Press, 2019).

79 US Const., art I, § 8, cl 3.

80 Banner, *How the Indians Lost Their Land*, 118–21; *The Federalist No. 3* (John Jay).

81 Banner, *How the Indians Lost Their Land*, 85–111.

82 James Hopkins, *Bridging the Gap: Taxation and First Nations Governance* (National Centre for First Nations Governance 2008), 5–6, online (PDF), https://fngovernance.org/wp-content/uploads/2020/09/hopkins.pdf; Government of Canada, *Specific Claim Settlements Involving Land*, online, https://www.rcaanc-cirnac.gc.ca/eng/1100100030342/1539691869154#chp4, last modified 15 September 2010.

83 On this older vision of Indigenous relations and how it relates to section 91(24), see Nichols, *A Reconciliation without Recollection?* 187–9. See also Alan C. Cairns, *Citizens Plus: Aboriginal Peoples and the Canadian State* (Vancouver: University of British Columbia Press, 2000), 204–5.

84 Gérard V. La Forest, *The Allocation of Taxing Power Under the Canadian Constitution*, 2nd ed. (Toronto: Canadian Tax Foundation, 1981), 78–9.

85 See Don Fullerton and Gilbert E. Metcalf, "Tax Incidence," in *Handbook of Public Economics*, ed. Alan J. Auerbach and Martin Feldstein, 4 vols (Amsterdam: Elsevier, 2002), 4:1787–872.

86 Hogg and Wright, *Constitutional Law*, Part II, 31.3, citing *Atlantic Smoke Shops v. Conlon* 1943 CarswellNB 16, [1943] AC 550 at 568.

87 Ibid.

88 Ibid., Part II, 31.3, citing *British Columbia (Attorney General) v. McDonald Murphy Lumber Co* 1930 CarswellBC 35, [1930] AC 357; *Canadian Industrial Gas & Oil Ltd. v. Saskatchewan* 1977 CarswellSask 109, [1978] 2 SCR 545.

89 Constitution Act, 1867, s 121.

90 Ibid., s 94

91 Ibid., s 145.

92 Order of Her Majesty in Council admitting British Columbia into the Union, dated the 16th day of May, 1871 (British Columbia Terms of Union) reprinted in RSC 1985, Appendix II, No. 10; Order of Her Majesty in Council admitting Prince Edward Island into the Union, dated the 26th day of June, 1873 (Prince Edward Island Terms of Union) reprinted in RSC 1985, Appendix II, No. 12. Both are enumerated in the Schedule to the Constitution Act, 1982 as forming part of the Constitution of Canada. See also Constitution Act, 1982, s 52(2), being Schedule B to the Canada Act 1982 (UK), 1982, c 11.

93 British Columbia Terms of Union, s 11.

94 Prince Edward Island Terms of Union, paragraph beginning with "Effective Steam Service."

95 British North America Act, 1949, 12–13 Geo. VI c 22 (UK) (Newfoundland Act) (which is also identified as forming part of the Constitution of Canada – Constitution Act, 1982, Schedule, Item 21).

Chapter Five

1 Constitution Act, 1867 (UK), 30 & 31 Vict, c 3, ss 91(14)–91(20), reprinted in RSC 1985, Appendix II, No 5.

2 N. Gregory Mankiw, *Principles of Macroeconomics*, 4th ed. (Mason, OH: Thomson South-Western, 2007), 347–8.

3 Michael McLeay, Amar Radia, and Ryland Thomas, "Money Creation in the Modern Economy," *Bank of England Quarterly Bulletin* 54, no.1 (2014): 16–17, online, https://www.bankofengland.co.uk/-/media/boe/files/quarterly-bulletin/2014/money-creation-in-the-modern-economy.pdf?la=en&hash=9A8788FD44A62D8BB927123544205CE476E01654.

4 Benjamin M. Friedman, "Money Supply," in *The New Palgrave Dictionary of Economics*, ed. Steven N. Durlauf and Lawrence E. Blume (London: Palgrave Macmillan, 2008).

5 Elizabeth Renuart and Diane E. Thompson, "The Truth, The Whole Truth, and Nothing but the Truth: Fulfilling the Promise of Truth in Lending," *Yale Journal on Regulation* 25, no. 2 (2008): 207–17.

6 Interest Act, RSC 1985, c I-15, ss 3–4.

7 UK, HL Deb (19 February 1867), vol 185, col 557–82 (Lord Carnarvon) cited in Andrew Smith, "The Historical Origins of Section 121 of the Constitution Act, 1867: A Study of Confederation's Political, Social and Economic Context," *Canadian Business Law Journal* 61, no. 2 (2018): 205.

8 Jeffery Frankel and Andrew Rose, "An Estimate on the Effect of Common Currencies on Trade and Income," *The Quarterly Journal of Economics* 117, no. 2 (2002): 437–9.

9 See *Reference Re: Anti-Inflation Act* [1976] 2 SCR 373, 68 DLR (3rd) [*Inflation Reference* cited to SCR].

10 Ibid.

11 Ibid., 422.

12 See Robert A. Mundell, "A Theory of Optimum Currency Areas," *The American Economic Review* 51, no. 4 (1961); Ronald I. McKinnon, "Optimum Currency Areas," *The American Economic Review* 53, no. 4 (1963); Peter B. Kenen, "The Theory of Optimum Currency Areas: An Eclectic View," in *Monetary Problems of the International Economy*, ed. Robert A. Mundell and Alexander K. Swoboda (Chicago: University of Chicago Press, 1969).

13 Paul R. Masson, "Fiscal Asymmetries and the Survival of the Euro Zone," *International Economics* 129 (2012): 26–7.

14 See Maxym Chaban and Graham M. Voss, "Is Canada an Optimal Currency Area? An Inflation Targeting Perspective," *Canadian Journal of Economics* 49, no. 2 (2016).

15 Weights and Measures Act, RSC 1985, c W-6; Thomas Flanagan, "Models of Metrication," in *Game Theory and Canadian Politics* (Toronto: Toronto University Press, 1998).

16 Hugh Whalen, "Social Credit Measures in Alberta," *The Canadian Journal of Economics and Political Science* 18, no. 4 (1952): 504–13.

17 J.R. Mallory, "Disallowance and the National Interest: The Alberta Social Credit Legislation of 1937," *The Canadian Journal of Economics and Political Sciences* 14, no. 3 (1948): 350. The Credit of Alberta Regulation Act, the Bank Employees Civil Rights Act, and the Judicature Amendment Act were disallowed on 17 August 1937. Later that year, the legislature of Alberta passed the Bank Taxation Act, the Credit of Alberta Regulation Act, 1937, and the Accurate News and Information Act which were declared unconstitutional by the Supreme Court of Canada in *Reference Re Alberta Statutes – The Bank Taxation Act; The Credit of Alberta Regulation Act;* and the *Accurate News and Information Act,* [1938] SCR 100, [1938] 2 DLR 81.

18 Constitution Act, 1867, ss 91(1A), 91(4), 91(8).

19 Ibid., s 91(3).

20 Ibid., s 92(2).

21 Peter W. Hogg and Wade Wright, *Constitutional Law of Canada,* 5th ed. Supp. (Scarborough, ON: Carswell, 2007), Part II, 31.1, (a)-(b).

22 Gérard V. La Forest, *The Allocation of Taxing Power Under the Canadian Constitution,* 2nd ed. (Toronto: Canadian Tax Foundation, 1981), 1–8; Peter W. Hogg and Wade K. Wright, "Canadian Federalism, the Privy Council and the Supreme Court: Reflections on the Debate about Canadian Federalism," *University of British Columbia Law Review* 38, no. 2 (2005): 334.

23 McKinnon, "Optimal Currency Areas," 717; Mark Baimbridge and Philip B. Whyman, "The Eurozone as a Flawed Currency Area," in *Crisis in the Eurozone: Causes, Dilemmas and Solutions* (London: Palgrave MacMillan, 2015), 1–13.

24 Hogg and Wright, "Canadian Federalism," 346; J. Harvey Perry, *A Fiscal History of Canada: The Postwar Years* (Toronto: Canadian Tax Foundation, 1989): 370–3.

25 Ben Eisen, Bacchus Barua, Jason Clemens, and Steve Lafleur, "The State of Canadian Public Finances," in *Less Ottawa More Province: How Decentralization Is Key to Health Care Reform* (Vancouver, BC: Fraser Institute, 2016), 6–11, online (PDF), https://www.fraserinstitute.org/sites/default/files/LessOttawaMoreProvinceHowDecentralizationisKeytoHealthCareReform.pdf.

26 Hamish Telford, "The Federal Spending Power in Canada: Nation-Building or Nation-Destroying?" *Publius: The Journal of Federalism* 33, no. 1 (2003): 23–35.

27   Masson, "Fiscal Asymmetries and the Survival of the Euro Zone," 26–7.

28   Cf. *National Federation of Independent Business v. Sebelius*, 567 US 519 at 522–3 (2012).

29   Andrew Petter, "Federalism and the Myth of the Federal Spending Power," *Canadian Bar Review* 68, no. 3 (1989): 465–8; David W.S. Yudin, "The Federal Spending Power in Canada, Australia and the United States," *National Journal of Constitutional Law* 13 (2002): 466–72; Roderick A. Macdonald, "The Political Economy of the Federal Spending Power," *Queen's Law Journal* 34, no.1 (2008): 249, 272–3; Hoi Kong, "The Spending Power, Constitutional Interpretation and Legal Pragmatism," *Queen's Law Journal* 34, no. 1 (2008).

30   N. Gregory Mankiw, *Principles of Microeconomics*, 6th ed. (Mason OH: South-Western Cengage Learning, 2012), 218–9.

31   Constitution Act, 1867, ss 91(6), 91(7), 91(22), 91(23).

32   Donald Creighton, *The Road to Confederation: The Emergence of Canada 1863–1867*, rev. ed. (Don Mills, ON: Oxford University Press, 2012), 369.

33   Richard A. Posner, *Economic Analysis of Law*, 8th ed. (New York: Aspen Publishers, 2011), 48–9.

34   This purpose of copyright and patent is made explicit in the text of US Const., art I, § 8. On the other justifications for copyright, see David Lametti, "Coming to Terms with Copyrights," in *In the Public Interest: The Future of Canadian Copyright Law*, ed. Michael Geist (Toronto: Irwin Law, 2005), 480.

35   George Brown, *Charlottetown Conference*, 12 September 1864, cited in *R v. Comeau*, 2016 NBPC 3 at para 92, rev'd 2018 SCC 15.

36   See, e.g., Comprehensive Economic and Trade Agreement, Canada and European Union, 30 October 2016, ch. 20 (provisional application 21 September 2017).

37   Constitution Act, 1867, s 91(12).

38   Robert J. Lennox, Craig Paukert, Kim Aarestrup, Marie Auger-Méthé, Lee J. Baumgartner, Kim Birnie-Gauvin, Kristin Bøe et al., "One Hundred Pressing Questions on the Future of Global Fish Migrations Science, Conservation, and Policy," *Frontiers in Ecology and Evolution* 7, no. 286 (2019): 2, 7.

39   In the twentieth century, the extension of countries' exclusive economic zones to 200 miles offshore aimed to solve this problem, to a degree, at the international level. See United Nations Convention on the Law of the Sea, 10 December 1982, 1833 UNTS 397, 21 ILM 1261 (entered into force 16 November 1994).

40   Creighton, *Road to Confederation*, 358.

41   Ibid., 416.

42   Albert Bohémier, *La faillite en droit constitutionnel canadien* (Montreal: Les Presses de l'Université de Montréal, 1972), 23.

43   *The Federalist No. 42* (James Madison); Bohémier, *La faillite en droit constitutionnel canadien*, 19–21.

44 Thomas Telfer, *Ruin and Redemption: The Struggle for a Canadian Bankruptcy Law, 1867–1919* (Toronto: University of Toronto Press, 2014), 22; Pierre Carignan, "La compétence législative en matière de faillite et d'insolvabilité," *Canadian Bar Review* 57, no. 1 (1979): 47–73.

45 Bohémier, *La faillite en droit constitutionnel canadien*, 22, 25.

46 Ibid., 26.

47 Telfer, *Ruin and Redemption*, 4–5.

48 Constitution Act, 1867, s 91 Preamble; *R. v. Crown Zellerbach Canada Ltd.*, [1988] 1 SCR 401 at 445–7, 49 DLR (4th) 161 [*Crown Zellerbach*].

49 *Reference re Greenhouse Gas Pollution Pricing Act*, 2019 SKCA 40; *Reference re Greenhouse Gas Pollution Pricing Act*, 2020 ABCA 74; *Reference re Greenhouse Gas Pollution Pricing Act*, 2019 ONCA 544; *References re Greenhouse Gas Pollution Pricing Act*, 2021 SCC 11.

50 *Citizens Insurance Co of Canada v. Parsons*, [1881] UKPC 49 (BAILII) at 10–11, [1881] 7 AC 96 [*Parsons*].

51 Kathleen M. Sullivan and Noah Feldman, *Constitutional Law*, 18th ed. (New York: Foundation Press, 2013), 136.

52 *Parsons*.

53 Ibid., 12.

54 Hogg and Wright, *Constitutional Law*, Part II, 20.2(a).

55 Ibid., Part II, 20.3; *3510395 Canada Inc. v. Canada (Attorney General)*, 2020 FCA 103, application for leave to appeal dismissed, 2021 CanLII 15598 (SCC).

56 *General Motors of Canada Ltd. v. City National Leasing*, [1989] SCR 641 at 661–2, 58 DLR (4th) 255.

57 Malcolm Lavoie, "Understanding 'Trade as a Whole' in the Securities Reference," *University of British Columbia Law Review* 46, no. 1 (2013).

58 *Parsons; Reference re Insurance Companies*, [1916] 1 AC 588, 26 DLR 288; *Re Board of Commerce Act, 1919 and the Combines and Fair Prices Act, 1919*, 1921 CarswellNat 2, [1922] 1 AC 191; *Toronto Electric Commissioners v. Snider*, [1925] UKPC 2, [1925] AC 396; *The King v. Eastern Terminal Elevator Co*, [1925] SCR 434, 3 DLR 1; *Reference re Natural Products Marketing Act 1934* (1936), [1937] AC 377, 1 DLR 691; *Canadian Federation of Agriculture v. Attorney-General of Quebec et al.*, 1950 CarswellNat 226, [1951] AC 179 [*Margarine Reference*]; *Reference re Securities Act*, 2011 SCC 66.

59 David Vaver, *Intellectual Property Law: Copyright, Patents, Trade-Marks*, 2nd ed. (Toronto: Irwin Law, 2011), 529–30.

60 *3510395 Canada Inc. v. Canada (Attorney General)*.

61 Lavoie, "Understanding 'Trade as a Whole'"; *Reference Re Pan-Canadian Securities Regulation* 2018 SCC 48 at para 101.

62 Richard Whish, *Competition Law*, 7th ed. (Oxford: Oxford University Press, 2012), 25.

63 Ibid.

64 Lavoie, "Understanding 'Trade as a Whole," 171.

65 Ibid.

66 Ibid.

67 See Donald Creighton, *British North America at Confederation: A Study Prepared for the Royal Commission on Dominion-Provincial Relations* (Ottawa: J.O. Patenaude, 1939); William Francis O'Connor, *Report Pursuant to Resolution of the Senate to the Honourable the Speaker by the Parliamentary Counsel Relating to the Enactment of the British North America Act, 1867, any lack of consonance between its terms and judicial construction of them and cognate matters* (Ottawa: King's Printer, 1939). For a recent overview of competing views of the POGG power, see Andrew Leach and Eric M. Adams, "Seeing Double: Peace, Order, and Good Government, and the Impact of Federal Greenhouse Emissions Legislation on Provincial Jurisdiction," *Constitutional Forum* 29, no. 1 (2020).

68 Hogg and Wright, *Constitutional Law*, Part II, 17.2.

69 Ibid., Part II, 17.4.

70 *Charles Russell v. The Queen (New Brunswick)* [1882] UKPC 33, [1882] 7 AC 829; *Crown Zellerbach*.

71 Hogg, *Constitutional Law*, Part II, 17.3(a).

72 See the dissent of Justice La Forest in *Crown Zellerbach* at 438–60; See also the split decisions of the provincial courts of appeal in *Reference re Greenhouse Gas Pollution Pricing Act*, SKCA, *Reference re Greenhouse Gas Pollution Pricing Act*, ONCA, and *Reference re Greenhouse Gas Pollution Pricing Act*, ABCA. The Ontario Court of Appeal and Saskatchewan Court of Appeal held that the *Greenhouse Gas Pollution Pricing Act* was a valid exercise of federal POGG "national concern" branch in a 4–1 decision, and 3–2 decision respectively, while the Alberta Court of Appeal held that the act was wholly unconstitutional in a 4–1 decision. The federal legislation was ultimately upheld in a divided decision from the Supreme Court. *References re Greenhouse Gas Pollution Pricing Act*, SCC.

73 *References re Greenhouse Gas Pollution Pricing Act*, SCC at para 163.

74 Ibid., at para 164.

75 Ibid., at para 165.

76 Ibid., at para 164.

77 Ibid.

78 Ibid., at paras 182–4. See also *Crown Zellerbach* at 431–2.

79 *Johannesson v. Municipality of West St. Paul*, [1951] 4 DLR 609, [1952] 1 SCR 292; *Ontario Hydro v. Ontario (Labour Relations Board)*, [1993] 3 SCR 327, 107 DLR (4th) 457; *Munro v. National Capital Commission*, [1966] SCR 663; 57 DLR (2nd) 753; *Crown Zellerbach*; *References re Greenhouse Gas Pollution Pricing Act*, SCC, at para 192.

80 *Munro v. National Capital Commission*.

81 Constitution Act, 1867, ss 91(21), 91(26), 91(27).

82 Cf. U.S Const., Austl. Const.

83 Martin L. Friedland, *A Century of Criminal Justice: Perspectives on the Development of Canadian Law* (Toronto: Carswell Legal Publications, 1984), 47–52; D.B. Sterling, "The Criminal Law Power and Confederation," *University of Toronto Faculty of Law Review* 15 (1957): 4–6. On presence of moral considerations in constitutional jurisprudence regarding the criminal law power, see Eric M. Adams, "Touch of Evil: Disagreements at the Heart of the Criminal Law Power," *Supreme Court Law Review*, 2nd ed., 104 (2022).

84 A.H.F. Lefroy, *The Law of Legislative Power in Canada* (Toronto: Toronto Law Book Publishing, 1897), 549, cited in Adams, "Touch of Evil."

85 John Stuart Mill, *Considerations on Representative Government* (London, UK: Parker, Son, and Bourn, 1861), ch. XV.

Chapter Six

1 John Hart Ely, *Democracy and Distrust: A Theory of Judicial Review* (Cambridge, MA: Harvard University Press, 1980), 83–4.

2 In the United States, constitutional protections for interstate trade have been developed as a negative implication of the Interstate Commerce Clause, referred to as the "Dormant Commerce Clause." See US Const., art I, § 8, cl 3; Erwin Chemerinsky, *Constitutional Law: Principles and Policies*, 5th ed. (New York: Aspen, 2015), 443–78. The Australian Constitution contains a standalone provision protecting free trade among the states. See Commonwealth of Australia Constitution Act 1900 (UK), 63 & 64 Vict, c 12, s 92; Suri Ratnapala and Jonathan Crowe, *Australian Constitutional Law: Foundations and Theory*, 3rd ed. (Melbourne: Oxford University Press, 2012), 303–15. As discussed in this chapter, Canadian constitutional protections for internal trade take two broad forms: (1) negative implications of exclusive federal economic powers; and (2) stand-alone protections for interprovincial trade, particularly Constitution Act, 1867 (UK), 30 & 31 Vict, c 3, s 121, reprinted in RSC 1985, Appendix II, No 5.

3 Treaty on European Union, 7 February 1992, OJ C 326/13, art 3 (originally entered into force on 1 November 1993 as the Maastricht Treaty, and entered into force under its current name on 1 December 2009); Treaty on the Functioning of the European Union, 1 January 1958, OJ C 326/47, arts 4(2), 26–35, 45–66, 114–8 (originally entered into force on 1 January 1958 as the Treaty of Rome, and entered into force under its current name on 1 December 2009).

4 Donald Regan, "The Supreme Court and State Protectionism: Making Sense of the Dormant Commerce Clause," *Michigan Law Review* 84, no. 6 (1986): 1112–6; Amelia Simpson, "Grounding the High Court's Modern Section 92

Jurisprudence: The Case for Improper Purpose as the Touchstone," *Federal Law Review* 33, no. 3 (2005): 463–5.

5   Regan, "The Supreme Court and State Protectionism," 1113.

6   The "chicken-and-egg war" culminated in the Manitoba Egg Reference. *Attorney-General for Manitoba v. Manitoba Egg and Poultry Association et al.*, [1971] SCR 689, 19 DLR (3d) 169 (*Manitoba Egg Reference*). See Peter W. Hogg and Wade Wright, *Constitutional Law of Canada*, 5th ed. Supp. (Scarborough, ON: Carswell, 2007), Part II, 20.9(c).

7   Proposed amendments to the Environmental Management Act, SBC 2003, c 53, Part 2.1; Preserving Canada's Economic Prosperity Act, SA 2018, c P-21.5.

8   *Reference re Environmental Management Act (British Columbia)*, 2019 BCCA 181, affirmed on appeal, 2020 SCC 1; *Manitoba Egg Reference*.

9   Michael J. Trebilcock, "The Supreme Court and Strengthening the Conditions for Effective Competition in the Canadian Economy," *Canadian Bar Review* 80, no. 1–2 (2001): 553–4.

10   Constitution Act, 1867, s 121.

11   Andrew Smith, "The Historical Origins of Section 121 of the Constitution Act, 1867: A Study of Confederation's Political, Social and Economic Context," *Canadian Business Law Journal* 61, no. 1 (2018–2019).

12   Ibid.

13   Janet Ajzenstat, Paul Romney, Ian Gentles, and William D. Gairdner, eds, *Canada's Founding Debates*, (Toronto: University of Toronto Press, 2003), 135 per George Brown, Legislative Assembly of the Province of Canada, 8 February 1865.

14   Ibid., 127 per John McMillan, House of Assembly of New Brunswick, 31 May 1865.

15   Ibid., 134 per George Brown, Legislative Assembly of the Province of Canada, 8 February 1865.

16   Ibid., 281 per John A. MacDonald, Province of Canada Legislative Assembly of the Province of Canada, 6 February 1865; Janet Ajzenstat, "The Canadian Founding, John Locke and Parliament," in *Roads to Confederation: The Making of Canada, 1867*, ed. Jacqueline D. Krikorian, David R. Cameron, Marcel Martel, Andrew W. McDougall, and Robert C. Vipond, 2 vols (Toronto: University of Toronto Press, 2017), 1:147.

17   See the foundational jurisprudence relating to the "Dormant Commerce Clause": *Gibbons v. Ogden* 22 US (9 Wheat) 1 (1824); *Cooley v. Board of Wardens* 53 US (12 How) 299 (1851).

18   Ibid.

19   *Cooley*; *The Federalist No. 7* (Alexander Hamilton).

20   See generally George Vegh, "The Characterization of Barriers to Interprovincial Trade under the Canadian Constitution," *Osgoode Hall Law Journal* 34, no. 2 (1996).

21 Malcolm Lavoie, "R. v. Comeau and Section 121 of the Constitution Act, 1867: Freeing the Beer and Fortifying the Economic Union," *Dalhousie Law Journal* 40, no. 1 (2017); Kerri A. Froc and Michael Marin, "'The Supreme Court's Strange Brew' History, Federalism and Anti-Originalism in Comeau," *University of New Brunswick Law Journal* 70 (2019); Ian Blue, "On the Rocks? Section 121 of the Constitution Act, 1867, and the Constitutionality of the Importation of Intoxicating Liquors Act," *Advocates' Quarterly* 35, no. 3 (April 2009); Malaïka Bacon-Dussault, "L'importation interprovinciale des boissons alcoolisées à des fins personnelles: R c. Comeau et la confirmation de règles de droit de la période de la prohibition," *McGill Law Journal* 64, no. 1 (2018–19); Smith, "The Historical Origins of Section 121"; Ian Blue, "Long Overdue: A Reappraisal of Section 121 of the Constitution Act, 1867," *Dalhousie Law Journal* 33, no. 2 (2010).

22 In contrast to the division of powers on economic matters, the scope of section 121 has only been considered by the Supreme Court or the Privy Council a handful of times: *Gold Seal v. Alberta (Attorney General)* (1921), 62 SCR 424, 62 DLR 62; *Atlantic Smoke Shops Limited v. Conlon*, [1943] AC 550, [1943] 4 DLR 81(PC); *Murphy v. CPR*, [1958] SCR 626 at 634, Locke J, but see 638–43, Rand J, concurring, 15 DLR (2d) 145; *Reference re Agricultural Products Marketing*, [1978] 2 SCR 1198 at 1224, 1261, 1266–8, Laskin CJC, partially dissenting, 84 DLR (3d) 257; *R v. Comeau*, 2018 SCC 15 [*Comeau* (SCC)].

23 See, e.g., *Manitoba Egg Reference*, in which egg quotas applicable to in-province and imported eggs were found to relate in pith and substance to interprovincial trade.

24 Constitution Act, 1867, ss 91, 92.

25 See, e.g., *Manitoba Egg Reference*; *Central Canada Potash Co Ltd. et al. v. Government of Saskatchewan*, [1979] 1 SCR 42, 88 DLR (3d) 609; *Prince Edward Island Potato Marketing Board v. Willis*, [1952] 2 SCR 392, [1952] 4 DLR 146; *Canadian Industrial Gas & Oil Ltd. v. Government of Saskatchewan et al.*, [1978] 2 SCR 545, 80 DLR (3d) 449; *Burns Foods Ltd. et al. v. Attorney General for Manitoba*, [1975] SCR 494, 40 DLR (3d) 731.

26 See, e.g., *Reference re Environmental Management Act* (BC).

27 Hogg and Wright, *Constitutional Law*, Part II, 15.9(c); *General Motors of Canada Ltd. v. City National Leasing*, [1989] 1 SCR 641, 1989 CarswellOnt 125 at para 48; *Kirkbi AG v. Ritvik Holdings Inc*, 2005 SCC 65 at para 32.

28 *Bell Canada v. Quebec (Commission de la Santé et de la Sécurité du Travail)*, [1988] 1 SCR 749, 51 DLR (4th) 161; *Canadian National Railway Co. v. Courtois*, [1988] 1 SCR 868, 51 DLR (4th) 271; *Alltrans Express Ltd v. British Columbia (Workers' Compensation Board)*, [1988] 1 SCR 897, 51 DLR (4th) 253; *Commission de Transport de la Communauté Urbaine de Québec v. Canada (National Battlefields Commission)*, [1990] 2 SCR 838, 74 DLR (4th) 23; *Quebec*

(*Attorney General*) *v. Canadian Owners and Pilots Association*, 2010 SCC 39; *Rogers Communication Inc v. Châteauguay (City)*, 2016 SCC 23.

29 *Canadian Western Bank v. Alberta*, 2007 SCC 22 at paras 35–47; *Tsilhqot'in Nation v. British Columbia*, 2014 SCC 44 at paras 140–51; *Quebec* (AG) *v. Canadian Owners and Pilots Association; Rogers Communication Inc v. Châteauguay (City); Bank of Montreal v. Marcotte*, 2014 SCC 55.

30 *Quebec* (AG) *v. Canadian Owners and Pilots Association*; see also *Rogers Communication Inc v. Châteauguay (City); Toronto (City) v. Bell Telephone Co.*, 1904 CarswellOnt 809, [1905] AC 52; *Ontario (Attorney General) v. Winner*, [1954] AC 541, 1954 CarswellNB 40; *Registrar of Motor Vehicles v. Canadian American Transfer*, [1972] SCR 811, 26 DLR (3d) 112; *Campbell-Bennett v. Comstock Midwestern Ltd.*, [1954] SCR 207, [1954] 3 DLR 481.

31 Ibid. In contrast, the Supreme Court has taken a relatively permissive approach towards the secondary effects of provincial measures on areas of federal jurisdiction.

32 Regan, "The Supreme Court and State Protectionism."

33 Hogg and Wright, *Constitutional Law*, Part II, 16.1.

34 For example, Dwight Newman has suggested a strategy of adopting a comprehensive code of regulation for an interprovincial transportation project as a means of definitively ousting provincial jurisdiction. See Dwight Newman, *Pipelines and the Constitution: Canadian Dreams and Canadian Nightmares* (Ottawa: Macdonald-Laurier Institute, April 2018), online (PDF), https://macdonaldlaurier.ca/files/pdf/MLICommentary_April2018_Newman_FWeb.pdf.

35 *Attorney-General for Ontario v. Attorney-General for the Dominion of Canada*, [1896] AC 348 at 371, 1896 CarswellNat 45 (PC); *Air Canada v. Ontario (Liquor Control Board)*, [1997] 2 SCR 581 at para 57, 148 DLR (4th) 193.

36 *Reference re Environmental Management Act (BC)*.

37 Constitution Act, 1867, s 91(3).

38 Ibid., s 92(2).

39 Hogg and Wright, *Constitutional Law*, Part II, 31.1(b).

40 *Air Canada v. British Columbia*, [1989] 1 SCR 1161 at 1189, 59 DLR (4th) 161; Gérard V. La Forest, *The Allocation of Taxing Power Under the Canadian Constitution*, 2nd ed. (Toronto: Canadian Tax Foundation, 1981), 75–6.

41 Constitution Act, 1867, s 91 Preamble.

42 John Stuart Mill's definition of direct and indirect taxation has been treated as authoritative in Canadian law. See John Stuart Mill, *Principles of Political Economy: With Some of their Applications to Social Philosophy*, 2 vols (London: John W. Parker, 1848) 2: Book V, chap. 2; La Forest, *Allocation of Taxing Power*, 78.

43 La Forest, *Allocation of Taxing Power*, 92.

44 Ibid.

45 See Don Fullerton and Gilbert E. Metcalf, "Tax Incidence," in *Handbook of Public Economics*, ed. Alan J. Auerbach and Martin Feldstein, 4 vols (Amsterdam: North Holland, 2002), 4:1787–872.

46 La Forest, *Allocation of Taxing Power*, 92.

47 Ajzenstat et al., *Canada's Founding Debates*, 135 per George Brown, Legislative Assembly of the Province of Canada, 8 February 1865; A.T. Galt, *Speech on the Proposed Union of the British North American Provinces, Delivered at Sherbrooke, C.E.* (Montreal: Longmoore & Co, 1864), 10, cited in Smith, "The Historical Origins of Section 121"; Province of Canada, Legislative Assembly, *Parliamentary Debates on the Subject of the Confederation*, 8th Leg, 3rd Sess (7 February 1865) at 60 (George-Étienne Cartier).

48 Constitution Act, 1867, s 121.

49 Lavoie, "R. v. Comeau and Section 121," 200–1.

50 *R v. Comeau*, 2016 NBPC 3, at paras 61–2; Ian Blue, "Long Overdue"; Lavoie, "R. v. Comeau and Section 121," 199–200.

51 Smith, "The Historical Origins of Section 121."

52 *Comeau* (SCC), at paras 108–11.

53 *Gold Seal Ltd. v. Alberta (Attorney-General)* (1921), 62 SCR 424 at 456, Duff J, 466, Anglin J, 469–70, Migneault J; *Atlantic Smoke Shops Limited v. Conlon*, [1943] 4 DLR 81 at 567–70, [1943] AC 550; *Murphy v. CPR*, [1958] SCR 626 at 634, Locke J, but see 638–43, Rand J, concurring, 15 DLR (2d) 145.

54 I make this argument in Lavoie, "R. v. Comeau and Section 121."

55 *Comeau* (SCC), at para 114.

56 Malcolm Lavoie, "Supreme Court's 'free-the-beer' decision privileges one part of the Constitution over another," CBC *News*, 19 April 2018, online, https://perma.cc/H6P9-AAFE.

57 See also Constitution Act, 1867, section 125, exempting federal and provincial lands and properties from taxation, and section 96, which has been somewhat creatively interpreted to protect judicial independence from interference by both federal and provincial measures. See *MacMillan Bloedel Ltd. v. Simpson*, [1995] 4 SCR 725, 130 DLR (4th) 385.

58 Constitution Act, 1867, s 92A(1).

59 Ibid., s 92A(2).

60 Ibid., s 92A(4).

61 Canadian Charter of Rights and Freedoms, s 6, Part I of the Constitution Act, 1982, being Schedule B to the Canada Act 1982 (UK), 1982, c 11.

62 Ibid., s 6(2).

63 *Canadian Egg Marketing Agency v. Richardson* (1997), [1998] SCR 157, 166 DLR (4th) 1. As will be discussed in chapter 10, the holding of the majority in *Richardson* is arguably inconsistent with the majority opinion in the prior case of *Black v. Law Society of Alberta*, [1989] 1 SCR 591, 58 DLR (4th) 317.

Chapter Seven

1 Criminal appeals to the Privy Council were abolished earlier in 1933, see Criminal Code Amendment Act, SC 1932–33, c 53, s 17; see generally "Abolition of Appeals from Canadian Courts to the Privy Council," *Harvard Law Review* 64, no. 1 (1950).

2 Peter W. Hogg and Wade K. Wright, "Canadian Federalism, the Privy Council and the Supreme Court: Reflections on the Debate about Canadian Federalism," *University of British Colombia Law Review* 38, no. 2 (2005): 339; Alan Cairns, "The Judicial Committee and Its Critics," *Canadian Journal of Political Science* 4, no. 3 (1971): 312.

3 Donald Creighton, *British North America at Confederation: A Study Prepared for the Royal Commission on Dominion-Provincial Relations* (Ottawa: J.O. Patenaude, 1939); Frank R. Scott, "The Development of Canadian Federalism," in *Papers and Proceedings of the Canadian Political Science Association* (1931), 3; Frank R. Scott, "The Special Nature of Canadian Federalism" *Canadian Journal of Economics and Political Science* 13, no. 1 (1947); Frank R. Scott, "Centralization and Decentralization in Canadian Federalism," *Canadian Bar Review* 29, no. 10 (1951); Frank R. Scott, *Canada Today: A Study of Her National Interests and National Policy* (London, UK: Oxford University Press, 1938); William Francis O'Connor, *Report Pursuant to Resolution of the Senate to the Honourable the Speaker by the Parliamentary Counsel Relating to the Enactment of the British North America Act, 1867, any lack of consonance between its terms and judicial construction of them and cognate matters* (Ottawa: King's Printer, 1939).

4 See Donald Wright, "Introduction," in *The Road to Confederation: The Emergence of Canada 1863–1867*, rev. ed. Donald Creighton, (Don Mills, ON: Oxford University Press, 2012), xv, citing Paul Romney, *Getting It Wrong: How Canadians Forgot their Past and Imperilled Confederation* (Toronto: University of Toronto Press, 1999); Brian Hodgins, "Disagreements at the Commencement: Divergent Ontario Views of Federalism, 1867–1781," in *Oliver Mowat's Ontario: Papers*, ed. Donald Swainson (Toronto: Macmillan, 1972), 21; Cairns, "The Judicial Committee and Its Critics"; Robert Vipond, *Liberty and Community: Canadian Federalism and the Failure of the Constitution* (Albany, NY: SUNY Press, 1991). See also Gerald Peter Browne, *The Judicial Committee and the British North America Act: An Analysis of the Interpretative Scheme for the Distribution of Legislative Powers* (Toronto: University of Toronto Press, 1967); Hogg and Wright, "Canadian Federalism, the Privy Council and the Supreme Court."

5 Constitution Act, 1867 (UK), 30 & 31 Vict, c 3, s 91, reprinted in RSC 1985, Appendix II, No 5.

6 See chapter 3.

7   *Tennant v. Union Bank of Canada*, 1893 CarswellOnt 35, [1894] AC 31;
    Reference re Bill of Rights Act (Alberta), [1947] 4 DLR 1, [1947] 2 W.W.R. 401;
    Toronto (City) v. Bell Telephone Co., 1904 CarswellOnt 809, [1905] AC 52;
    Ontario (Attorney General) v. Winner, [1954] 4 DLR 657, [1954] 2 WLR 418.

8   See Asher Honickman, "Watertight Compartments: Getting Back to the
    Constitutional Division of Powers," *Alberta Law Review* 55, no. 1 (2017).

9   *Attorney-General v. De Keyser's Royal Hotel Limited*, [1920] AC 508 (HL), [1920]
    5 WLUK 46.

10 *Manitoba Fisheries Ltd. v. R* (1978), [1979] 1 SCR 101 at 109, 118, 88 DLR (3d)
    462 [*Manitoba Fisheries*].

11 *Smith v. R*, [1960] SCR 776, 128 CCC 145; *Canada (Attorney General) v.
    Nykorak*, [1962] SCR 331, 33 DLR (2d) 373; *Multiple Access Ltd. v. McCutcheon*,
    [1982] 2 SCR 161, 138 DLR (3d) 1; *General Motors of Canada Ltd. v. City
    National Leasing*, [1989] 1 SCR 641; 58 DLR (4th) 255.

12 *Québec (Commission du salaire minimum) v. Bell Telephone Co. of Canada Ltd.*,
    [1966] SCR 767, 59 DLR (2d) 145; *Bell Canada v. Québec (Commission de la
    santé & de la sécurité du travail)*, [1988] 1 SCR 749, 51 DLR (4th) 161.

13 See *R v. Dominion Stores Ltd*, [1980] 1 SCR 844, 106 DLR (3d) 58.

14 *Manitoba Fisheries*.

15 Ibid., 118.

16 *Reference re Secession of Quebec*, [1998] 2 SCR 217 at paras 44–8, 161 DLR (4th)
    385 [*Secession Reference*].

17 See Douglass C. North and Barry R. Weingast, "Constitutions and
    Commitment: The Evolution of Institutions Governing Public Choice in
    Seventeenth-Century England," *Journal of Economic History* 49, no. 4 (1989);
    See also A.V. Dicey, *An Introduction to the Study of the Law of the Constitution*,
    10th ed. (London: MacMillan, 1959), 110 (Dicey's first of three meanings
    of the rule of law is that "no man is punishable or can be made to lawfully
    suffer in body or goods except for a distinct breach of law established in the
    ordinary Courts of the land.").

18 Dicey, *Introduction to the Study of the Law of the Constitution*.

19 John Rawls, *A Theory of Justice*, rev. ed. (Cambridge, MA: Harvard University
    Press, 1999), 206–13; F.A. Hayek, *The Constitution of Liberty* (New York, NY:
    Routledge, 2006), 180–92; F.A. Hayek, *Law, Legislation and Liberty*, 3 vols
    (London, UK: Routledge, 2012), 2:106–10, 115–8.

20 *Secession Reference*, at para 70.

21 Ibid., at para 58.

22 Ibid.; *References re Greenhouse Gas Pollution Pricing Act*, 2021 SCC 11 at paras
    48–9 [*Greenhouse Gas Reference*].

23 Dwight Newman, "Changing Division of Powers Doctrine and the Emergent
    Principle of Subsidiarity," *Saskatchewan Law Review* 74, no. 1 (2011); *114957*

Canada Ltée (Spraytech, Société d'arrosage) v. Hudson (Town), 2001 SCC 40; *Canadian Western Bank v. Alberta*, 2007 SCC 22; *Québec (AG) v. Lacombe*, 2010 SCC 38; *Reference re Assisted Human Reproduction Act*, 2010 SCC 61; *Greenhouse Gas Reference*, at paras 48–50 (the SCC held the principle of federalism allows for broad provincial autonomy in order to develop local and regional societies, and, in turn, federal power is restricted to matters that effect the country "as a whole").

24 Robin Elliott, "References, Structural Argumentation, and the Organizing Principles of Canada's Constitution," *Canadian Bar Review* 80, no. 1–2 (2001): 134–6; *Murphy v. CPR*, [1958] SCR 626, 15 DLR (2d) 145; *Winner v. SMT (Eastern) Ltd.*, [1951] SCR 887, [1951] 4 DLR 529.

25 *Black v. Law Society of Alberta*, [1989] 1 SCR 591, 58 DLR (4th) 317 [*Black* cited to SCR].

26 Ibid., 609.

27 Ibid., 608–14.

28 *Canadian Egg Marketing Agency v. Richardson*, [1998] 3 SCR 157, 166 DLR (4th) 1 [*Richardson*]. See also Michael J. Trebilcock, "The Supreme Court and Strengthening the Conditions for Effective Competition in the Canadian Economy," *Canadian Bar Review* 80, no. 1–2 (2001): 563–4.

29 *R v. Comeau*, 2018 SCC 15 at para 62 [*Comeau* (SCC)].

30 Gérard V. La Forest, *Disallowance and Reservation of Provincial Legislation* (Ottawa: Department of Justice, 1955), 83–101.

31 Ibid.

32 Ibid.

33 Ibid.

34 Ibid., 52, 101.

35 There have been a few notable exceptions to federal respect for provincial jurisdiction, including in particular the "Canadian New Deal" legislation enacted in response to the Great Depression. See Hogg and Wright, "Canadian Federalism, the Privy Council and the Supreme Court," 340; *Re Unemployment Insurance Reference*, [1937] AC 355, [1937] 1 DLR 684 (PC); *A-G BC v. A-G Can (Price Spreads)*, [1937] AC 368, [1937] 1 DLR 688 (PC); *A-G BC v. A-G Can (Re Natural Products Marketing)*, [1937] AC 377, [1937] 1 DLR 691 (PC); *A-G BC v. A-G Can (Farmers' Creditors Arrangement)*, [1937] AC 391, [1937] 1 DLR 695 (PC); *A-G Ont v. A-G Can (Canada Standard Trade Mark)*, [1937] AC 405, [1937] 1 DLR 702 (PC).

36 After initially passing insolvency legislation in 1869 and 1875, Parliament repealed the legislation in 1880, abandoning the field of bankruptcy and insolvency for a period of almost forty years, until 1919. Thomas Telfer, *Ruin and Redemption: The Struggle for a Canadian Bankruptcy Law, 1867–1919* (Toronto: University of Toronto Press, 2014), 4–5.

37 Constitution Act, 1982, Schedule B to the Canada Act 1982 (UK), 1982, c 11, s 36.

38 Constitution Act, 1867, s 91(2A).

39 Eric M. Engen and Jonathan Gruber, "Unemployment Insurance and Precautionary Saving," *Journal of Monetary Economics* 47, no. 3 (2001).

40 Gabriel Chodorow-Reich and John Coglianese, "Unemployment Insurance and Macroeconomic Stabilization," in *Recession Ready: Fiscal Policies to Stabilize the American Economy*, ed. Heather Boushey, Ryan Nunn, and Jay Shambaugh (Washington, DC: Brookings Institution, 2019). Responding to the Great Depression in 1935, the federal government enacted the first unemployment insurance. In 1937, the legislation was struck down for being ultra vires. In response, the Rowell-Sirois Royal Commission was established and recommended that unemployment insurance fall under federal jurisdiction because the wide-spread economic responsibility was costly and "national in scope," and provinces were not in a position to finance unemployment programs. The Constitution was amended in 1940, adding unemployment to section 91. Donald V. Smiley, ed., *The Rowell-Sirois Report: An Abridgement of Book I of the Royal Commission Report on Dominion-Provincial Relations* (Toronto: McClelland & Stewart, 1967), at 188–9, 194–5.

41 The amendment was enacted in 1940. Constitution Act, 1940, 3–4 Geo VI, c 36 (UK).

42 Constitution Act, 1867, s 94(A).

43 Canadian Bill of Rights, SC 1960, c 44, ss 1–2.

44 Dwight Newman and Lorelle Binnion, "The Exclusion of Property Rights from the Charter: Correcting the Historical Record," *Alberta Law Review* 52, no. 3 (2015): 555, 558–9.

45 Ibid., 551–5.

46 See Alexander Alvaro, "Why Property Rights Were Excluded from the Canadian Charter of Rights and Freedoms," *Canadian Journal of Political Science* 24, no. 2 (1991), arguing that provinces opposed to the entrenchment of property wanted to safeguard the supremacy of democratic institutions.

47 Canadian Charter of Rights and Freedoms, Part I of the Constitution Act, 1982, being Schedule B to the Canada Act 1982 (UK), 1982, c 11, s 6.

48 Ibid., s 6(3)(a).

49 General Agreement on Tariffs and Trade, 15 April 1994, 1867 UNTS 187 arts 1, 3 (entered into force on 1 January 1995); Canada–United States–Mexico Agreement, 30 November 2018, Can TS 2020 No 5 arts 14.4, 14.5, 17.4 (entered into force on 1 July 2020); Canadian Free Trade Agreement, (entered into force on 1 July 2017) arts 102, 201.

50 Constitution Act, 1867, s 92A.

51 Larissa Katz, "Property's Sovereignty," *Theoretical Inquiries in Law* 18, no. 2 (2017): 302–3.

52 See Sean Simpson, "Nine in Ten Canadians Support Fewer Trade Restrictions Between Provinces," *Ipsos*, 29 March 2018, online, https://perma.cc/56RU-REAN.

53 Dwight Newman, *Pipelines and the Constitution: Canadian Dreams and Canadian Nightmares* (Ottawa: Macdonald-Laurier Institute, April 2018), 8–9, online (PDF), https://macdonaldlaurier.ca/files/pdf/MLICommentary_April2018_Newman_FWeb.pdf.

54 *Richardson*; *Comeau* (SCC).

55 *Greenhouse Gas Reference*, at paras 214–8.

56 *Canadian Pacific Railway Co. v. Vancouver (City)*, 2006 SCC 5. The Supreme Court decision in *Annapolis Group Inc v Halifax Regional Municipality*, 2022 SCC 36 (released as this book was going to print) could help to reinvigorate protections against de facto expropriation.

Chapter Eight

1 John Locke, *Two Treatises of Government,* ed. Peter Laslett (Cambridge, UK: Cambridge University Press, 1960).

2 Janet Ajzenstat, *The Canadian Founding: John Locke and Parliament* (Montreal: McGill-Queen's University Press, 2007), 52–3, 59–60

3 Locke, *Two Treatises*, Book II, ch. 5.

4 Thomas W. Merrill and Henry E. Smith, "What Happened to Property in Law and Economics?" *Yale Law Journal* 111, no. 2 (2001): 357, 360–6.

5 William Blackstone, *Commentaries on the Laws of England: Book II: Of the Rights of Things*, ed. Simon Stern (Oxford, UK: Oxford University Press, 2016), 5; Adam Smith, *The Wealth of Nations*, ed. Jonathan B. Wight (Petersfield, UK: Harriman House, 2007), 252–4.

6 Janet Ajzenstat, Paul Romney, Ian Gentles, and William D. Gairdner, eds, *Canada's Founding Debates* (Toronto: University of Toronto Press, 2003), 58 per Robert Pinsent, Newfoundland House of Assembly, 11 February 1869, 154–5 per Hugh Hoyles, Newfoundland House of Assembly, 11 February 1869, 174 per Charles Tupper, Nova Scotia House of Assembly, 10 April 1866, 247 per Judge John Black, Convention at Fort Gary, English and French Delegates in Council, 1 February 1870, 290 per John Sanborn, Legislative Council of the Province of Canada, 9 February 1865, 335 per George-Étienne Cartier, Legislative Assembly of the Province of Canada, 7 February 1865. See also editors' comments on 229; Ajzenstat, *The Canadian Founding*, 50 per F.B.T. Carter, Newfoundland House of Assembly, 23 February 1969.

7 Randy Barnett, *Our Republican Constitution: Securing the Liberty and Sovereignty of We the People* (New York, NY: HarperCollins, 2016): 31–51; Randy Barnett, *The Structure of Liberty: Justice and the Rule of Law* (New York, NY: Oxford University Press, 1998), 63–8.

8   Jeremy Waldron, *The Right to Private Property* (New York, NY: Oxford University Press, 1988), 390–422.

9   Ibid.

10   Richard Posner, *Economic Analysis of Law*, 8th ed. (New York: Aspen Publishers, 2011), 40–1; Frank Knight, "Some Fallacies in the Interpretation of Social Cost," *The Quarterly Journal of Economics* 38, no. 4 (1924); Garrett Hardin, "Tragedy of the Commons," *Science* 162, no. 3859 (1968).

11   Posner, *Economic Analysis of Law*.

12   Elinor Ostrom, *Governing the Commons: The Evolution of Institutions for Collective Action* (New York, NY: Cambridge University Press, 1990), 101–2; Robert C. Ellickson, "Property in Land," *Yale Law Journal* 102, no. 6 (1993): 1346–52.

13   Ibid.; Robert C. Ellickson, *Order Without Law: How Neighbors Settle Disputes* (Cambridge, MA: Harvard University Press, 1991), 177–8.

14   Friedrich A. Hayek, "The Use of Knowledge in Society," *American Economic Review* 35, no. 4 (1945); Friedrich A. Hayek, *Law, Legislation, and Liberty*, 3 vols (Chicago: University of Chicago Press, 1983), 1:85–8, 106–10; Malcolm Lavoie, "Property and Local Knowledge," *Catholic University Law Review* 70, no. 4 (2021).

15   Ostrom, *Governing the Commons*; Lavoie, "Property and Local Knowledge."

16   Lavoie, "Property and Local Knowledge."

17   Margaret J. Radin, "Property and Personhood," *Standard Law Review* 34, no. 5 (1982): 957; Kenneth H. Bobroff, "Indian Law in Property: Johnson v. M'Intosh and Beyond," *Tulsa Law Review* 37, no. 2 (2001): 537–8.

18   Gregory S. Alexander, "The Social-Obligation Norm in American Property Law," *Cornell Law Review* 94, no. 4 (2008); Gregory S. Alexander and Eduardo M. Peñalver, "Properties of Community," *Theoretical Inquiries in Law* 10, no. 1 (2009); Gregory S. Alexander, "Ownership and Obligations: The Human Flourishing Theory of Property," *Hong Kong Law Journal* 43, no. 2 (2013); David Lametti, "The (Virtue) Ethics of Private Property: A Framework & Implications," in *New Perspectives on Property Law: Obligations and Restitution*, ed. Alistair Hudson (London, UK: Cavendish Press, 2003).

19   Ibid.

20   Ibid. See also Rachael Walsh, *Property Rights and Social Justice: Progressive Property in Action* (Cambridge, UK: Cambridge University Press, 2021).

21   Arthur Ripstein, "Beyond the Harm Principle," *Philosophy and Public Affairs* 34, no. 3 (2006); Arthur Ripstein, *Force and Freedom: Kant's Legal and Political Philosophy* (Cambridge, MA: Harvard University Press, 2009), 86–106.

22   Malcolm Lavoie, "Property Law and Collective Self-Government," *McGill Law Journal* 64, no. 2 (2018); Malcolm Lavoie, "Why Restrain Alienation of Indigenous Lands?" *University of British Columbia Law Review* 49, no. 3 (2016).

23   Lavoie, "Property and Local Knowledge"; See also Gregory Alexander, "Pluralism and Property," *Fordham Law Review* 80, no. 3 (2011).

24 Robert K. Vischer, "Subsidiarity as a Principle of Governance: Beyond Devolution," *Indiana Law Review* 35, no. 103 (2001): 108–26.

25 Dwight G. Newman, "Federalism, Subsidiarity, and Carbon Taxes," *Saskatchewan Law Review* 82, no. 2 (2019): 192; John Stuart Mill, *Considerations on Representative Government* (London, UK: Parker, Son, and Bourn, 1861).

26 Mill, *Considerations on Representative Government*, 266.

27 Ibid., 268–9, 272–3.

28 Newman, "Federalism, Subsidiarity, and Carbon Taxes," 192; Ajzenstat, *The Canadian Founding*, 7.

29 Mill, *Considerations on Representative Government*, 273–4.

30 Ibid., 274–5.

31 Ajzenstat et al., *Canada's Founding Debates*, 277–84 per John A. MacDonald, Province of Canada Legislative Assembly, 6 February 1865.

32 Ibid., 296–7 per Alexandre-Antonin Taché, Legislative Council of the Province of Canada, 1865; Asher Honickman, "Watertight Compartments: Getting Back to the Constitutional Division of Powers," *Alberta Law Review* 55, no. 1 (2017): 228–9; Paul Romney, "Why Lord Watson Was Right," in Janet Ajzenstat, ed., *Canadian Constitutionalism, 1791–1991* (Ottawa: Canadian Study of Parliament Group, 1993), 187–8; Donald Creighton, *The Road to Confederation: The Emergence of Canada, 1863–67*, rev. ed. (Don Mills, ON: Oxford University Press, 2012), 77, 145, 191. See also Ajzenstat et al., *Canada's Founding Debates*, 279 per John A. MacDonald, Province of Canada Legislative Assembly, 6 February 1865.

33 Paul Romney, *Getting it Wrong: How Canadians Forgot Their Past and Imperilled Confederation* (Toronto: University of Toronto Press, 1999), 87–108.

34 The influence on modern conceptions of pluralism on Canadian constitutional law can arguably be traced to the time of Viscount Haldane's tenure on the Privy Council in the early decades of the twentieth century. See David Schneiderman, "Harold Laski, Viscount Haldane, and the Law of the Canadian Constitution in the Early Twentieth Century," *University of Toronto Law Journal*, 48 (1998).

35 John Finnis, *Natural Law and Natural Rights*, 2nd ed. (Oxford: Oxford University Press, 2011), 144–7.

36 Ibid.; Vischer, "Subsidiarity as a Principle of Governance: Beyond Devolution," 108–10; James L. Huffman, "Making Environmental Regulation More Adaptive through Decentralization: The Case for Subsidiarity," *University of Kansas Law Review* 52, no. 5 (2004): 1378–9; Aurelian Portuese, "The Principle of Subsidiarity as a Principle of Economic Efficiency," *Columbia Journal of European Law* 17, no. 2 (2011): 236–7; Lavoie, "Property and Local Knowledge"; Andreas Føllesdal, "Survey Article: Subsidiarity," *The Journal of Political Philosophy* 6, no. 2 (1998): 204–6.

37 John Sewell, "Toward City Charters in Canada," *Journal of Law and Social Policy* 34, no. 8 (2021); Kristin R. Good, "The Fallacy of the 'Creatures

of the Provinces' Doctrine: Recognizing and Protecting Municipalities' Constitutional Status," IMGF Papers on Municipal Finance and Governance no. 46 (Toronto: University of Toronto, 2019); Emmett Macfarlane, "A Constitutional Safeguard for Municipalities: Entrenching Protections for Local Democracy," (paper presented at "Constitutional Space for Cities" Massey Cities Summit, University of Toronto, Toronto, 8 April 2021).

38   See *Toronto (City) v. Ontario (Attorney General)*, 2021 SCC 34, rejecting Toronto's Charter argument in a 5–4 decision.

39   James Scott, *Seeing like a State: How Certain Schemes to Improve the Human Condition Have Failed* (New Haven: Yale University Press, 1998), 1–8.

40   Ronald Rudin, *Kouchibouguac: Removal, Resistance, and Remembrance at a Canadian National Park* (Toronto: University of Toronto Press, 2016), 28; Alan Marcus, *Out in the Cold: The Legacy of Canada's Inuit Relocation Experiment in the High Arctic* (Copenhagen: International Work Group for Indigenous Affairs, 1992).

41   These assumptions are somewhat weaker than typically adopted in rational-choice-theory analysis. See, e.g., Posner, *Economic Analysis of Law*, 3 ("The task of economics … is to explore the implications of assuming that man is a rational maximizer of his end in life, his satisfactions – what we shall call his self-interest."). See also Gary Becker, *The Economic Approach to Human Behavior* (Chicago: University of Chicago Press, 1976).

42   Richard Epstein, "Why Restrain Alienation?" *Colombia Law Review* 85, no. 5 (1985): 972.

43   Smith, *The Wealth of Nations*, Book 1, ch. 1–2.

44   Ibid.

45   David Ricardo, *On the Principles of Political Economy and Taxation*, 3rd ed. (London, UK: John Murray, 1821), 139.

46   Ibid.

47   See generally Ronald Coase, "The Problem of Social Cost," *Journal of Law and Economics*, 3 (1960).

48   Natasha Riebe, "Alberta Brewers Push for open Beer Borders Between Provinces," CBC News, 2 March 2018, online, https://www.cbc.ca/news/canada/edmonton/alberta-craft-beer-edmonton-alley-kat-1.4558545.

49   Jane Shaw, "Public Choice Theory," *The Concise Encyclopedia of Economics*, 2015, online, https://www.econlib.org/library/Enc1/PublicChoiceTheory.html.

50   Mill, *Considerations on Representative Government*, ch. XV, XVII; *The Federalist No. 41–43* (James Madison).

51   Donald H. Regan, "The Supreme Court and State Protectionism: Making Sense of the Dormant Commerce Clause," *Michigan Law Review* 84, no. 6 (May 1986): 1113–8.

52   Adam Smith, *The Theory of Moral Sentiments* (Indianapolis: Liberty Press, 1976), Part IV, section II (Smith argues we have greater sympathy are care for those closest to us and those within our own society).

53 See Emilie M. Hafner-Burton, "Trading Human Rights: How Preferential Trade Agreements Influence Government Repression," *International Organization* 59, no. 3 (2005) (preferential trade agreements create a mechanism, such as higher cost association with defection, in order to enforce commitments and coordinate market polices).

54 Mill, *Considerations on Representative Government*, ch. XVII.

55 See Jeffery Frankel and Andrew Rose, "An Estimate on the Effect of Common Currencies on Trade and Income," *The Quarterly Journal of Economics* 117, no. 2 (2002): 437–9.

56 Malcolm Lavoie, "Understanding 'Trade as a Whole' in the Securities Reference," *University of British Columbia Law Review* 46, no. 1 (2013).

57 Louis Kaplow and Steven Shavell, *Fairness versus Welfare* (Cambridge, MA: Harvard University Press, 2002), 18–19.

58 John D. Whyte, "Constitutional Aspects of Economic Development Policy," in *Division of Powers and Public Policy* (Toronto: University of Toronto Press, 1985), 45.

59 Regan, "The Supreme Court and State Protectionism," 1113.

60 Creighton, *Road to Confederation*, 369; Ajzenstat et al., *Canada's Founding Debates*, 181–2 per James Currie, Legislative Council of the Province of Canada, 7 February 1865, 182–5 per George-Étienne Cartier, Legislative Assembly of the Province of Canada, 7 February 1865, 185–190 per Thomas D'Arcy McGee, Legislative Assembly of the Province of Canada, 9 February 1865.

61 Asher Honickman and Ben Woodfinden, "Canada needs a New National Policy," *National Post*, 26 May 2020, online, https://nationalpost.com/opinion/canada-needs-a-new-national-policy.

Chapter Nine

1 Malcolm Lavoie, "Property and Local Knowledge," *Catholic University Law Review* 70, no. 4 (2021).

2 Gérard V. La Forest, "The Canadian Charter of Rights and Freedoms: An Overview," *Canadian Bar Review* 61, no. 1 (1983).

3 Ibid., 20.

4 Ibid., 20–1.

5 Ibid., 21.

6 Russell Brown, "The CP Decision's Effect on How Municipalities Can Circumvent Expropriation Laws," (Paper delivered at the Canadian Property Rights Conference, Ottawa, 15 September 2012) [unpublished]. On the diminishment of traditional rights that were not enumerated in the Charter, see Ryan Alford, *Seven Absolute Rights: Recovering the Historical Foundations of Canada's Rule of Law* (Montreal: McGill-Queen's University Press, 2020), 36–7.

7 Constitution Act, 1867 (UK), 30 & 31 Vict, c 3, s 53, reprinted in RSC 1985, Appendix II, No 5.

8 Ruth Sullivan, *Sullivan on the Construction of Statutes*, 6th ed. (Markham, ON: LexisNexis, 2014), 497–8; *Attorney-General v. De Keyser's Royal Hotel Limited*, [1920] AC 508 at 542, [1920] 5 WLUK 46 (HL) [*De Keyser's Royal Hotel*].

9 *Manitoba Fisheries Ltd v. R* (1978), [1979] 1 SCR 101, 88 DLR (3d) 462 [*Manitoba Fisheries* cited to SCR].

10 *De Keyser's Royal Hotel*, 542.

11 *R v. Tener*, [1985] 1 SCR 533, 17 DLR (4th) 1.

12 *Rock Resources v. British Columbia*, [2003] 229 DLR (4th) 115, 15 BCLR (4th) 20 (CA); *Casamiro Resource Corp v. British Columbia (AG)*, [1991] 80 DLR (4th) 1, 55 BCLR (2d) 346 (CA).

13 *Canadian Pacific Railway v. Vancouver*, 2006 SCC 5.

14 Ibid., at para 8.

15 Russell Brown, "Legal Incoherence and the Extra-Constitutional Law of Regulatory Takings: The Canadian Experience," *International Journal of Law in the Built Environment* 1, no. 3 (2009): 189–92; Russell Brown, "The Constructive Taking at the Supreme Court of Canada: Once More, Without Feeling," *University of British Colombia Law Review* 40, no. 1 (2007): 320–1.

16 Brown, "Legal Incoherence," 188–92.

17 Ibid.; Brown, "Once More, Without Feeling"; Malcolm Lavoie, "Canadian Common Law and Civil Law Approaches to Constructive Takings: A Comparative Economic Perspective," *Ottawa Law Review* 42, no. 2 (2011).

18 Brown, "Legal Incoherence"; Agreement Between the Government of Canada and the Government of the People's Republic of China for the Promotion and Reciprocal Protection of Investments, 9 September 2012, Can TS 2014 No 26, art 10 (entered into force 1 October 2014); Trans-Pacific Partnership, 4 February 2016, USTR 2010 00014, art 9.8.

19 There have been some exceptions. See, eg, *Lynch v. St John's (City)*, 2016 NLCA 35; *Sun Construction Company Limited v Conception Bay South (Town)*, 2019 NLSC 102. As this book was going to print, the Supreme Court of Canada released its decision in *Annapolis Group Inc v Halifax Regional Municipality*, 2022 SCC 26, which clarifies aspects of the CPR test and which will have important implications for this area of law going forward. The *Annapolis* decision addresses some of the concerns with the CPR test identified in this book, particularly with respect to the beneficial interest requirement.

20 La Forest, "The Canadian Charter," 20.

21 Art 952 CCQ.

22 Lavoie, "Canadian Common Law and Civil Law," 244; *Wallot c. Québec (Ville de)*, 2011 QCCA 1165; *Lynch c. Aylmer (Ville de)*, [1989] RDI 768, [1989] JQ no 32405 (CS); *Donnacona (Ville de) c. Gagni-Lambert*, [1976] RJQ 503 (CA)

[*Donnacona*]; *Aubry c. Trois-Rivieres Ouest (Ville de)*, [1978] 4 MPLR 62, 1978 CarswellQue 72 (CA); *Vincent c. Longueuil (Ville de)*, [1972] RJQ 821 (CS); *Ivanhoe Corp c. Val d'Or (Ville de)*, [1973] RJQ 904 (CS); *Montréal (Ville de) c. Benjamin*, [2004] JQ no 12943, 2004 CarswellQue 9263 (CA) [*Benjamin*]; Daniel Chénard, "La Cour d'appel du Québec et l'expropriation déguisée : le prix à payer," in *Développements récents en droit municipal*, vol. 247 (Cowansville, QC: Yvon Blais, 2006), 107–9, 125–30.

23 Lavoie, "Canadian Common Law and Civil Law," 244.

24 Ibid.; *Dupras c. Ville de Mascouche*, 2020 QCCS 2538 at para 109 [*Dupras*]; *Donnacona*, at 505; Chénard, "La Cour d'appel du Québec," 107–8.

25 *Dupras*; *Donnacona*; *Benjamin*.

26 Lavoie, "Canadian Common Law and Civil Law," 244–5.

27 Ibid.

28 See *Lucas v. South Carolina Coastal Council*, 505 US 1003 at 1014–6 (1992).

29 Lavoie, "Canadian Common Law and Civil Law," 245–52.

30 Constitution Act, 1867, s 90.

31 Janet Ajzenstat, Paul Romney, Ian Gentles, and William D. Gairdner, eds, *Canada's Founding Debates* (Toronto: University of Toronto Press, 2003), 59–60.

32 *Reference re Agricultural Products Marketing*, [1978] 2 SCR 1198 at 1290–7 per Pigeon J, 84 DLR (3d) 257 [*APM Reference*].

33 *Westbank First Nation v. British Columbia Hydro and Power Authority*, [1999] 3 SCR 134 at paras 21–8, 176 DLR (4th) 276 [*Westbank*]; *620 Connaught Ltd v. Canada (Attorney General)*, 2008 SCC 7 at paras 25–8 [*Connaught Ltd.*]; *References re Greenhouse Gas Pollution Pricing Act*, 2021 SCC 11 at para 213 [*Greenhouse Gas Reference*].

34 *Connaught Ltd.*, at paras 20–1; *Westbank*, at paras 20–9; *Greenhouse Gas Reference*, at para 215.

35 *Connaught Ltd.*, at paras 39–40.

36 Ibid., at para 48.

37 *Greenhouse Gas Reference*, at para 216.

38 *An American Dictionary of the English Language* (Springfield, MA: Merriam, 1865).

39 *Lawson v. Interior Tree Fruit and Vegetable Committee of Direction*, [1931] SCR 357, 2 DLR 193.

40 *An American Dictionary of the English Language*.

41 Samuel Johnson, *Dictionary of the English Language*, 2nd ed. (London, UK: J & P Knapton, 1755).

42 Constitution Act, 1867, ss 91(3), 92(2).

43 *Greenhouse Gas Reference*, at para 408, citing *Attorney-General for Canada v. Attorney-General for Ontario*, [1937] AC 355 (PC) at 367.

44 Gérard V. La Forest, *The Allocation of Taxing Power Under the Canadian Constitution*, 2nd ed. (Toronto: Canadian Tax Foundation, 1981), 60–70.

45   *Eurig Estate (Re)* [1998] 2 SCR 565 at para 30, 165 DLR (4th) 1, as interpreted by Peter W. Hogg, "Can the Taxing Power Be Delegated?" *The Supreme Court Law Review*, 2nd ed., 16, no. 1 (2002): 308–9.

46   *Ontario English Catholic Teachers' Assn v. Ontario (Attorney General)*, 2001 SCC 15 at para 74.

47   Hogg, "Can the Taxing Power Be Delegated?" 310.

48   Ibid. Emphasis as per original.

49   *Canada (Minister of Citizenship and Immigration) v. Vavilov*, 2019 SCC 65 at paras 30–1.

50   Sullivan, *Sullivan on the Construction of Statutes*, 497–8.

51   Dwight Newman and Lorelle Binnion, "The Exclusion of Property Rights from the Charter: Correcting the Historical Record," *Alberta Law Review* 52, no. 3 (2015): 543, citing Gregory S. Alexander, *The Global Debate over Constitutional Property: Lessons for American Takings Jurisprudence* (Chicago: University of Chicago Press, 2006), 41.

52   US Const., amend V.

53   Constitution of the Republic of South Africa, 1996, No. 108 of 1996, s 25.

54   Dwight Newman, "The Bilateral Amending Formula as a Mechanism for the Entrenchment of Property Rights," *Constitutional Forum* 21, no. 2 (2012).

55   See Rainer Knopff, "Why We Shouldn't Entrench Property Rights," *Policy Options* (July–August 2002): 49–52.

56   Ibid.

57   Canadian Bill of Rights, SC 1960, c 44.

58   *Authorson v. Canada (Attorney General)*, 2003 SCC 39.

59   In the case of Alberta, this would mean amending the existing Alberta Bill of Rights, RSA 2000, c A-14, which is modeled on the Canadian Bill of Rights.

60   Constitution Act, 1982, Schedule B to the Canada Act 1982 (UK), 1982, c 11 ss 44, 45.

61   Malcolm Lavoie, "Our Lack of Property Rights Make Canadians Uniquely Vulnerable to Digital Jail," *The Hub* (11 March 2022), online, https://thehub.ca/2022-03-11/malcolm-lavoie-our-lack-of-property-rights-make-canadians-uniquely-vulnerable-to-digital-jail/.

62   Julien Boudreault, "Flexible and Cooperative Federalism: Distinguishing the Two Approaches in the Interpretation and Application of the Division of Powers," *National Journal of Constitutional Law* 40, no. 1 (2020).

63   Ibid.; *APM Reference*.

64   Boudreault, "Flexible and Cooperative Federalism."

65   See Jean Leclair, "The Supreme Court of Canada's Understanding of Federalism: Efficiency at the Expense of Diversity," *Queen's Law Journal* 28, no. 2 (2003): 416–21.

66   Eugénie Brouillet, "The Supreme Court of Canada: The Concept of Cooperative Federalism and Its Effect on the Balance of Power," in *Courts in*

Federal Countries: Federalists or Unitarists? ed. Nicholas Theodore Aroney and John Kincaid (Toronto: University of Toronto Press, 2017), 157–8.

67 Ibid.

68 Boudreault, "Flexible and Cooperative Federalism," 19–24.

69 Ibid., 27–8.

70 Peter W. Hogg and Wade Wright, *Constitutional Law of Canada*, 5th ed. Supp. (Scarborough, ON: Carswell, 2007), Part II, 15.5(c).

71 *Ontario (Attorney General) v. OPSEU*, [1987] 2 SCR 2 at 18, 41 DLR (4th) 1.

72 *Greenhouse Gas Reference*, at paras 125–30, 197.

73 Ibid., at paras 373–8.

74 Ibid., at paras 357–8.

75 Ibid., at paras 449, 454–6.

76 Competition Act, RSC 1985, c C-34.

77 Ibid., s 36.

78 *General Motors of Canada Ltd v. City National Leasing*, [1989] 1 SCR 641, 58 DLR (4th) 255 [*General Motors* cited to SCR].

79 *Papp v. Papp*, [1970] 1 OR 331, 8 DLR (3d) 389 [ONCA]; *R v. Zelensky*, [1978] 2 SCR 940, 86 DLR (3d) 179; *Multiple Access Ltd v. McCutcheon*, [1982] 2 SCR 161, 138 DLR (3d) 1.

80 *R v. Foundation Co of Canada Ltd*, [1980] 1 SCR 695, 106 DLR (3d) 193; *Regional Municipality of Peel v. MacKenzie*, [1982] 2 SCR 9, 139 DLR (3d) 14.

81 *General Motors*, at 670–2.

82 *Kirkbi AG v. Ritvik Holdings Inc.*, 2005 SCC 65.

83 Hogg and Wright, *Constitutional Law of Canada*, Part II, 15.9(c).

84 *R v. Comeau*, 2018 SCC 15 [*Comeau* (SCC)].

85 Ibid., at para 106.

86 Ibid., at para 113.

87 All of the key "necessarily incidental" cases involved federal intrusions onto provincial jurisdiction, rather than vice versa. It may be that the Court still sees a place for a more stringent standard for federal encroachments, even if such a standard does not apply to provincial encroachments. However, there is no principled reason to limit the scope of the "necessarily incidental" standard. Scholars have generally taken the position that it applies to both federal and provincial encroachments. See Hogg and Wright, *Constitutional Law of Canada*, Part II, 15.9(c); George Vegh, "The Characterization of Barriers to Interprovincial Trade under the Canadian Constitution," *Osgoode Hall Law Journal* 34, no. 2 (1996).

88 See, generally, Impact Assessment Act, SC 2019, c 28; *Reference re Impact Assessment Act*, 2022 ABCA 165, appeal to the SCC pending.

89 Vegh, "Characterization of Barriers to Interprovincial Trade," 388. Bruce Ryder, "The Demise and Rise of the Classical Paradigm in Canadian Federalism: Promoting Autonomy for the Provinces and First Nations," *McGill Law Journal* 36, no. 2 (1991): 312–3.

91 *Greenhouse Gas Reference*, at paras 393–4, Brown J, dissenting.

92 One notable exception is the *Securities Reference*, 2011 SCC 66, in which the Court held that proposed federal securities legislation was ultra vires. In other cases, controversial legislation has been enacted based on an expansive conception of the federal criminal law power. See *Reference re Genetic Non-Discrimination Act*, 2020 SCC 17; RJR-MacDonald Inc. v. Canada (Attorney General)*, 1995 CanLII 64 (SCC), [1995] 3 SCR 199; *R v. Hydro-Québec*, 1997 CanLII 318 (SCC), [1997] 3 SCR 213; *Reference re Assisted Human Reproduction Act*, 2010 SCC 61, [2010] 3 SCR 457.

93 Impact Assessment Act; Canada, Department of Finance, *Budget 2021: A Canada-wide Early Learning and Child Care Plan*, (Ottawa: Department of Finance, 12 April 2021).

94 Hogg and Wright, *Constitutional Law of Canada*, Part II, 15.5(c).

95 Ibid.

96 *Comeau* (SCC), at para 113.

97 See, generally, Hoi Kong, "The Spending Power, Constitutional Interpretation and Legal Pragmatism," *Queen's Law Journal* 34, no. 1 (2008). The Supreme Court of Canada has so far failed to impose limits on the coercive use of the federal spending power. See *Reference Re Canada Assistance Plan (B.C.)*, [1991] 2 SCR 525 at 567; John T. Saywell, *The Lawmakers: Judicial Power and the Shaping of Canadian Federalism* (Toronto: University of Toronto Press, 2002), 277–8.

98 See *National Federation of Independent Business v. Sebelius*, 567 US 519 at 575–85 (2012).

99 La Forest, "Allocation of Taxing Power," 41–5.

100 This understanding is reflected in early division of powers case law. See St Catherine's *Milling and Lumber Co v. The Queen* (1888), 14 AC 46 (PC).

101 Constitution Act, 1982, being Schedule B to the Canada Act 1982 (UK), 1982, c 11, s 35.

102 *R v. Pamajewon*, [1996] 2 SCR 821 at 832–6, 138 DLR (4th) 204; *Delgamuukw v. British Columbia*, [1997] 3 SCR 1010 at 1114–5, 153 DLR (4th) 193; *Mitchell v. Minister of National Revenue*, 2001 SCC 33 at para 10, McLachlin CJ, 125–73, Binnie J, concurring; John Borrows, "The Durability of Terra Nullius: Tsilhqot'in Nation v British Columbia," *University of British Colombia Law Review* 48, no. 3 (2015).

103 First Nations Land Management Act, SC 1999, c 24; An Act Respecting First Nations, Inuit and Métis Children, Youth and Families, SC 2019, c 24.

104 An Act Respecting First Nations, Inuit and Métis Children, Youth and Families, SC 2019, c 24. See also *Renvoi à la Cour d'appel du Québec relatif à la Loi concernant les enfants, les jeunes et les familles des Premières Nations, des Inuits et des Métis*, 2022 QCCA 185; Jean Leclair, "Zeus, Metis and Athena. The Path towards the Constitutional Recognition of Full-Blown Indigenous

Legal Orders," 13 July 2022, ssrn, online, https://papers.ssrn.com/sol3/papers.cfm?abstract_id=4148715.

105   United Nations Declaration on the Rights of Indigenous Peoples, unga Res 61/295 (adopted 13 September 2007).

106   *Tsilhqot'in Nation v. British Columbia*, 2014 scc 44 at paras 140–51 [*Tsilhqot'in*], overturning *R v. Morris*, 2006 scc 59.

107   *Tsilhqot'in*, at para 143.

108   Kent McNeil, "Aboriginal Title and the Provinces after Tsilhqot'in Nation," *The Supreme Court Law Review* 71, no. 2 (2015).

109   Agreement Between the Inuit of the Nunavut Settlement Area and Her Majesty the Queen in Right of Canada, 25 May 1993, online (pdf), Government of Nunavut, https://perma.cc/6CX9-6L3X, art 4. Implemented by the Nunavut Act, sc 1993, c 28.

110   Nunavut Act, sc 1993, c 28, s 23.

111   See Nisga'a Final Agreement, 27 April 1999, online (pdf), https://perma.cc/3DN9-LPS2. See also Westbank First Nation Self-Government Agreement between Her Majesty the Queen in Right of Canada and Westbank First Nation, 24 May 2003, online (pdf), https://perma.cc/Q63A-9XUQ.

112   Nisga'a Final Agreement, ch. 8, paras 68–74.

113   First Nations Land Management Act; An Act Respecting First Nations, Inuit and Métis Children, Youth and Families.

114   Jean Leclair, "Federal Constitutionalism and Aboriginal Difference," *Queen's Law Journal* 31, no. 2 (2006); Richard Stacey, "The Dilemma of Indigenous Self-Government in Canada: Indigenous Rights and Canadian Federalism," *Federal Law Review* 46, no. 4 (2019).

115   I have previously written at length on the link between property in land and Indigenous collective autonomy. See Malcolm Lavoie, "Why Restrain Alienation of Indigenous Lands?" *University of British Columbia Law Review* 49, no. 3 (2016); Malcolm Lavoie, "Property Law and Collective Self-Government," *McGill Law Journal* 64, no. 2 (2018); Malcolm Lavoie, "Models of Indigenous Territorial Control in Common Law Countries," in *Research Handbook on the International Law of Indigenous Rights*, ed. Dwight Newman (Cheltenham, uk: Edward Elgar, 2022); Malcolm Lavoie, "The Implications of Property as Self-Government," *University of Toronto Law Journal* 70, no. 4 (2020). See also Joseph William Singer, "Sovereignty and Property," *Northwestern University Law Review* 86, no. 1 (1991).

6   Larissa Katz, "Exclusion and Exclusivity in Property Law," *University of Toronto Law Journal* 58, no. 3 (2008).

7   Lavoie, "Property Law and Collective Self-Government."

8   Lavoie, "Implications of Property as Self-Government"; Jamie Baxter, "Property, Information, and Institutional Design," *Journal of Aboriginal Economic Development* 8, no. 2 (2013).

119 Malcolm Lavoie, "Aboriginal Rights and the Rule of Law," *Supreme Court Law Review*, 2nd ed., 92, no. 2 (2019): 171; *Delgamuukw v. British Columbia*.

120 Lavoie, "Aboriginal Rights and the Rule of Law," 169–70; *Tsilhqot'in*, at para 74.

121 *Johnson v. M'Intosh* 21 US (8 Wheat) 543 at 584–5 (1823); The Royal Proclamation, 1763, reprinted in RSC 1985, Appendix, II, No 1.

122 Lavoie, "Why Restrain Alienation of Indigenous Lands."

123 *Tsilhqot'in*, at para 74; emphasis added.

124 Lavoie, "Aboriginal Rights and the Rule of Law," 170.

125 While there are certain complexities involved in recognizing greater Indigenous control over property systems, including the challenges involved in exercising jurisdiction over non-member or non-Indigenous landowners, there are also potential ways to address these issues. For instance, First Nations eager to attract investment will often establish advisory boards for residents who are non-members. Some of my previous work has addressed tensions that arise where Indigenous governments exercise jurisdiction over non-member property owners. See Lavoie, "Models of Indigenous Territorial Control in Common Law Countries: A Functional Comparison."

126 First Nations Land Management Act; Nisga'a Land Act, NLGSR 2000/10; Nisga'a Land Title Act, NLGSR 2010/06, s 125(2).

Chapter Ten

1 Michael J. Trebilcock, "The Supreme Court and Strengthening the Conditions for Effective Competition in the Canadian Economy," *Canadian Bar Review* 80, no. 1–2 (2001): 553–4.

2 For an overview of trucking issues requiring harmonization within Canada, see Task Force on Trucking Harmonization, "Supporting the Efficient Movement of Trucks Across Canada: Suggested Approaches by the Task Force on Trucking Harmonization," (Ottawa: Council of Ministers Responsible for Transportation and Highway Safety, 2018), online (PDF), https://comt.ca/reports/truckingharmonization-e.pdf.

3 *Total Oilfield Rentals Limited Partnership v. Canada (Attorney General)*, 2014 ABCA 250; *A-G Ont. v. Winner*, [1954] AC 541 (PC) [*Winner*]. But see *Consolidated Fastfrate Inc. v. Western Canada Council of Teamsters*, 2009 SCC 53 (holding that an interprovincial logistics firm was not an interprovincial undertaking because it contracted out the actual shipping of goods). While the *Consolidated Fastfrate* decision appears to narrow the federal power over interprovincial transportation, arguably inappropriately, the decision still recognizes federal jurisdiction over undertakings that do physically ship goods across provincial borders.

4 Motor Vehicle Transport Act, RSC 1985, c 29 (3rd Supp); Peter W. Hogg and Wade Wright, *Constitutional Law of Canada*, 5th ed. Supp. (Scarborough, ON: Carswell, 2007), § 14:13.

5 Importation of Intoxicating Liquors Act, RSC 1985, c I-3, s 3(1) [IILA]. The provision was recently amended to remove the federal prohibition on the interprovincial sale of alcohol except by a provincial government body. However, in light of the applicable provincial restrictions, this amendment certainly did not "free the beer." See Rainer Knopff, "Why Killing the IILA Didn't Free the Beer," *C2C Journal* (25 August 2020), online, https://c2cjournal.ca/2020/08/why-killing-the-iila-didnt-free-the-beer/.

6 Parliament's jurisdiction over interprovincial liquor sales has long been recognized, *R v. Nat Bell Liquors Ltd.*, [1922] 2 AC 128, 65 DLR 1; *Manitoba (AG) v. Manitoba License Holders' Association* (1901), [1902] AC 73, 12 CRAC 333; *Ontario (AG) v. Canada Temperance Federation*, [1946] AC 193, 2 DLR 1. In occupying the field and directing that only federal limits apply to such sales, Parliament would in theory render inconsistent provincial laws inoperative under the doctrine of paramountcy.

7 *Toronto v. Bell Telephone Co.*, [1905] AC 52 (PC); *Winner*; *Alberta Government Telephones v. (Canada) Canadian Radio-television and Telecommunications Commission*, [1989] 2 SCR 225, 61 DLR (4th) 193.

8 *Dominion Stores Ltd v. R*, [1980] 1 SCR 844, 106 DLR (3d) 581 [*Dominion Stores*]; *Reference re Natural Products Marketing Act 1934*, [1937] 1 DLR 691, [1937] AC 377; *R v. Eastern Terminal Elevator Co.*, [1925] SCR 43, [1925] 3 DLR 1; *Labatt Breweries v. Canada (Attorney General)*, [1980] 1 SCR 914, 110 DLR (3d) 594. But see *Caloil v. AG Can*, [1971] SCR 543, 20 DLR (3d) 472, upholding a condition on imported oil products requiring they only be sold east of the Ottawa Valley on the basis that this requirement was necessarily incidental to the federal scheme. As Katherine Swinton has argued, this case raised the prospect of a more permissive approach to necessary federal intrusions into areas of provincial jurisdiction. However, the later decision in *Dominion Stores* appeared to reverse course. Katherine E. Swinton, *The Supreme Court and Canadian Federalism: The Laskin-Dickson Years* (Toronto: Carswell, 1990), 141–2.

9 *Dominion Stores.*

10 Canada Agricultural Products Standards Act, RSC 1970, c A-8.

11 Hogg and Wright, *Constitutional Law*, Part II, 20.2(b).

12 The federal government has taken the initiative on securities regulation, first proposing a national securities regulator based on federal legislation, which was found to be unconstitutional, and later proposing national securities regulation through a cooperative federal-provincial scheme. See *Reference re Securities Act*, 2011 SCC 66; *Reference re Pan-Canadian Securities Regulation*, 2018 SCC 48.

3 Dwight Newman, *How to Create Pipelines Certainty – The Legal Options: Dwight Newman for Inside Policy* (Ottawa: Macdonald-Laurier Institute, 12 April 2018), online, https://www.macdonaldlaurier.ca/create-pipelines-certainty-legal-options-dwight-newman-inside-policy/.

4 *Campbell-Bennett v. Comstock Midwestern Ltd.*, [1954] SCR 207, 3 DLR 481.

15 Brian Topp, "A National Energy Grid Would Be a Clean Win for Canada," *Policy Options*, 18 January 2019, online, https://policyoptions.irpp.org/magazines/january-2019/a-national-energy-grid-would-be-a-clean-win-for-canada/; Pierre-Olivier Pineau, "Fragmented Markets: Canadian Electricity Sectors' Underperformance," in *Evolution of Global Electricity Markets: New Paradigms, New Challenges, New Approaches*, ed. Fereidoon Sioshansi (Waltham, MA: Elsevier Academic Press, 2013); Richard Pierce, Michael J. Trebilcock, and Evan Thomas, *Beyond Gridlock: The Case for Greater Integration of Regional Electricity Markets* (Toronto: C.D. Howe Institute, 2006); Jan Carr, *Power Sharing: Developing Inter-Provincial Electricity Trade* (Toronto: C.D. Howe Institute, 2010).

16 Topp, "A National Energy Grid Would Be a Clean Win for Canada."

17 James W. Coleman, "The Jurisdictional Anticommons," in *Getting to Yes on Linear Infrastructure Projects*, ed. James W. Coleman, Ken Coates, Steven Saddleback, Malcolm Lavoie, and Dwight Newman (Ottawa: MacDonald-Laurier Institute, January 2021), online (PDF), https://macdonaldlaurier.ca/files/pdf/20201210_Linear_Infrastructure_Projects_COLLECTION_FWeb.pdf; James W. Coleman, "Pipelines & Power-Lines: Building the Energy Transport Future," *Ohio State Law Journal* 80, no. 2 (2019): 263.

18 Malcolm Lavoie, *Assessing the Duty to Consult* (Vancouver, BC: Fraser Institute, 2019), online (PDF), https://www.fraserinstitute.org/sites/default/files/assessing-the-duty-to-consult.pdf.

19 *Ermineskin Cree Nation v. Canada (Environment and Climate Change)*, 2021 FC 758.

20 *Tsilhqot'in Nation v. British Columbia*, 2014 SCC 44 at paras 67–74.

21 Canadian Free Trade Agreement – Consolidated Version (entry into force on 1 July 2017) [CFTA].

22 Jane Cordy and Diane Bellemare, "Interprovincial Trade Barriers are a National Embarrassment: Senators Cordy, Bellemare," *SenCA Plus*, 17 January 2019, online, https://sencanada.ca/en/sencaplus/opinion/interprovincial-trade-barriers-are-a-national-embarrassment-senators-cordy-bellemare/.

23 CFTA, Part IV – "Exceptions."

24 Constitution Act, 1867 (UK), 30 & 31 Vict, c 3, s 91, reprinted in RSC 1985, Appendix II, No 5.

25 *Reference re Pan-Canadian Securities Regulation*, at para 101.

26 *Kirkbi AG v. Ritvik Holdings Inc.*, 2005 SCC 65; *General Motors of Canada Ltd. v. City National Leasing*, [1989] 1 SCR 641, 58 DLR (4th) 255; *Reference re Securities Act*, 2011 SCC 66; *Reference re Pan-Canadian Securities Regulation*.

27 *References re Greenhouse Gas Pollution Pricing Act*, 2021 SCC 11. [*Greenhouse Gas Reference*].

28 Ibid., at paras 207–11.

29 *Reference re Securities Act*, 2011 SCC 66; Malcolm Lavoie, "Understanding 'Trade as a Whole' in the Securities Reference," *University of British Columbia*

Law Review 46, no. 1 (2013). But see *Reference re Pan-Canadian Securities Regulation* (upholding a federal-provincial cooperative scheme for securities regulation).

30 *Greenhouse Gas Reference*, at paras 148–9.

31 Ibid., at paras 152–7.

32 *Reference re Securities Act*, at paras 108, 118–21.

33 Ibid., at paras 112–3.

34 Ibid., at paras 128–9. A number of scholars had anticipated that federal securities legislation would be upheld. See, e.g., Don Tse, "Establishing a Federal Securities Commission," *Saskatchewan Law Review* 58, no. 2 (1994); Robert Leckey and Eric Ward, "Taking Stock: Securities Markets and the Division of Powers," *Dalhousie Law Journal* 22, no. 2 (1999); Ian B. Lee, "Balancing and Its Alternatives: Jurisprudential Choice, Federal Securities Legislation and the Trade and Commerce Power," *Canadian Business Law Journal*, 50 (2011). But see Noura Karazivan and Jean-François Gaudreault-DesBiens, "On Polyphony and Paradoxes in the Regulation of Securities within the Canadian Federation," *Canadian Business Law Journal* 49 (2010).

35 *Greenhouse Gas Reference*, at paras 173–4, 181–7.

36 Ibid., at paras 80, 88.

37 Greenhouse Gas Pollution Pricing Act, SC 2018, c 12, s 186, Parts I and II. [GHG Pollution Pricing Act].

38 Ibid., ss 166(3), 189(2).

39 Prices in the cap-and-trade regime applicable in Quebec have remained in the range of CAD 20 in recent years. See Government of Quebec, "Québec and California Current Auction Price History," 27 May 2021, online (PDF), https://www.environnement.gouv.qc.ca/changements/carbone/ventes-encheres/historique-prix-encheres-WCI-en.pdf; California Air and Resources Board, "California Cap-and-Trade Program and Québec Cap-and-Trade System Summary Results Report: Joint Auction #27," May 2021, online (PDF), https://ww2.arb.ca.gov/sites/default/files/2021-05/nc-summary_results_report.pdf. In the provinces subject to the federal regime, the carbon price is currently set at CAD 40. See also Randall Denley, "Quebec's Exemption from Trudeau's Carbon Tax will come at Ontario's Expense," *National Post*, 17 December 2020, online, https://nationalpost.com/news/politics/randall-denley-quebecs-exemption-from-trudeaus-carbon-tax-will-come-at-ontarios-expense. Admittedly, determining the equivalency between a carbon tax regime and a cap-and-trade regime is a complex question. However, given that the federal power was characterized in terms of minimum national pricing standards, it is noteworthy that the allowable effective price varies to such an extent.

GHG Pollution Pricing Act, s 192.

Output-Based Pricing System Regulations, SOR/2019-266; *Greenhouse Gas Reference*, at para 338, Brown J, dissenting; Grant Bishop, *Living Tree or*

Invasive Species? Critical Questions for the Constitutionality of Federal Carbon Pricing (Toronto: C.D. Howe Institute, 2019), 15–20.

42 *Greenhouse Gas Reference*, at paras 337, 339, 346, Brown J, dissenting, 599, Rowe J, dissenting.

43 *Greenhouse Gas Reference*, at paras 236–40, Côté J, dissenting.

44 See, generally, *Re: Anti-Inflation Act*, [1976] 2 SCR 373 at 442–59, 68 DLR (3d) 452, Beetz J, dissenting with respect to the emergency branch but concurring with respect to the national concern branch.

45 *R v. Comeau*, 2018 SCC 15 [*Comeau* (SCC)].

46 *Gold Seal Ltd. v. Alberta (Attorney-General)* (1921), 62 SCR 424 at 456, Duff J, 466, Anglin J, 469–70, Mignault J; *Atlantic Smoke Shops Limited v. Conlon*, [1943] 4 DLR 81 at 567–70, [1943] AC 550; *Murphy v. CPR*, [1958] SCR 626 at 634, Locke J, but see 638–43, Rand J, concurring, 15 DLR (2d) 145.

47 *Atty-Gen of Ontario v. Atty-Gen of Canada*, 65 LJPC 26, [1896] AC 348; *Manitoba (AG) v. Manitoba License Holders' Ass'n*, [1902] AC 73; *Hudson's Bay Company v. Heffernan* (1917), 39 DLR 124, 29 CCC 38 (SKCA) [*Heffernan*]; *Prince Edward Island (Potato Marketing Board) v. HB Willis Inc.*, [1952] 2 SCR 392, 4 DLR 146; *Reference Re Farm Products Marketing Act*, [1957] SCR 198, 7 DLR (2d) 257; *Manitoba (Attorney General) v. Manitoba Egg & Poultry Assn.*, [1971] SCR 689, 19 DLR (3d) 169 [*Manitoba Egg*]; *Burns Foods Ltd. et al. v. Attorney General for Manitoba et al.*, [1975] SCR 494, 40 DLR (3d) 731. However, the Supreme Court has not always been consistent in its treatment of the effect of provincial legislation on interprovincial transactions. See George Vegh, "The Characterization of Barriers to Interprovincial Trade under the Canadian Constitution," *Osgoode Hall Law Journal* 34, no. 2 (1996): 502.

48 *Atty-Gen of Ontario v. Atty-Gen of Canada*; *Heffernan*.

49 IILA, c I-3, s 3(1). The provision was recently amended to remove the federal prohibition on interprovincial liquor transactions by parties other than provincial government bodies.

50 *Reference re Agricultural Products Marketing*, [1978] 2 SCR 1198, 84 DLR (3d) 257, discussing a cooperative scheme enacted following the holding in *Manitoba Egg* to the effect that comprehensive marketing schemes could not be enacted by provinces alone.

51 Liquor Control Act, RSNB 1973, c L-10, s 134(b).

52 Malcolm Lavoie, "Supreme Court's 'free-the-beer' Decision Privileges One Part of the Constitution Over Another," *CBC News*, 19 April 2018, online, https://perma.cc/H6P9-AAFE.

53 For an overview of this trend in division of powers jurisprudence, see Julien Boudreault, "Flexible and Cooperative Federalism: Distinguishing the Two Approaches in the Interpretation and Application of the Division of Powers," *National Journal of Constitutional Law* 40, no. 1 (2020). See also Kate Glover,

"Structural Cooperative Federalism," *Supreme Court Law Review*, 2nd ed., 76 (2016): 47–53.

54 *Comeau* (scc), at paras 112–4.

55 Knopff, "Why Killing the IILA Didn't Free the Beer."

56 See *Manitoba Egg*.

57 *Ontario (Attorney General) v. OPSEU*, [1987] 2 SCR 2 at 18, 41 DLR (4th) 1.

58 *Comeau* (scc), at para 124.

59 My thanks to Rainer Knopff for emphasizing this point. Knopff, "Why Killing the IILA Didn't Free the Beer."

60 Asher Honickman, "A Marriage Made in Britain: Section 121 and the Division of Powers," *Advocates for the Rule of Law*, 21 October 2016, online, http://www.ruleoflaw.ca/a-marriage-made-in-britain-section-121-and-the-division-of-powers/; Vegh, "The Characterization of Barriers," sets out a similar approach to trade barriers grounded in the division of powers.

61 63 CFTA.

62 Ibid., ch. 2.

63 *Campbell-Bennett v. Comstock Midwestern Ltd.*, [1954] SCR 207, 3 DLR 481; *Winner*; *Registrar of Motor Vehicles v. Can American Transfer*, [1972] SCR 811, 26 DLR (3d) 112; *Bell Canada v. Quebec*, [1988] 1 SCR 749, 51 DLR (4th) 161; *Quebec (Attorney General) v. Canadian Owners and Pilots Association*, 2010 SCC 39 [*COPA*]; *Rogers Communications Inc v. Châteauguay (City)*, 2016 SCC 23 [*Châteauguay*].

64 *Canadian Western Bank v. Alberta*, 2007 SCC 22 at paras 42–7.

65 *British Columbia (Attorney General) v. Lafarge Canada Inc.*, 2007 SCC 23.

66 Hogg and Wright, *Constitutional Law*, Part II, 15.8(c).

67 See, e.g., *Bank of Montreal v. Marcotte*, 2014 SCC 55 at paras 62–9.

68 *Tsilhqot'in Nation v. British Columbia*, at paras 140–51.

69 Ibid., overturning *R v. Morris*, 2006 SCC 59.

70 *COPA*.

71 *Châteauguay*.

72 *Reference re Environmental Management Act (British Columbia)*, 2019 BCCA 181 [*EMA Reference* (BCCA)], affirmed by 2020 SCC 1 (for the reasons given by the Court of Appeal) [*EMA Reference* (scc)].

73 David Robitaille, "It's Not Up to Ottawa to Dictate the Rules of the Game," *Vancouver Sun*, 16 April 2018, online, https://vancouversun.com/opinion/op-ed/david-robitaille-its-not-up-to-ottawa-to-dictate-the-rules-of-the-game.

74 Stephanie Ip and Patrick Johnston, "Kinder Morgan Halts Non-Essential Work on Trans Mountain Pipeline and Sets Drop-Dead Deadline," *Vancouver Sun*, 9 April 2018, online, https://vancouversun.com/news/local-news/kinder-morgan-to-halt-its-spending-on-trans-mountain-pipeline-due-to-b-c-opposition.

75 See *EMA Reference* (BCCA).

76 Ibid.; *EMA Reference* (SCC).

77 Moira Lavoie, "The EMA Reference and Beyond: Pipelines and the Scope of Federal Jurisdiction under 92(10)" [unpublished, on file with author].

78 Donald H. Regan, "The Supreme Court and State Protectionism: Making Sense of the Dormant Commerce Clause," *Michigan Law Review* 84, no. 6 (1986).

79 Canadian Charter of Rights and Freedoms, Part I of the Constitution Act, 1982, being Schedule B to the Canada Act 1982 (UK), 1982, c 11, s 6(2)(b).

80 Ibid., s 6(3)(a).

81 *Black v. Law Society of Alberta*, [1989] 1 SCR 591 at 608–10, 58 DLR (4th) 317.

82 *Canadian Egg Marketing Agency v. Richardson* (1997), [1998] 3 SCR 157 at para 66, 166 DLR (4th) 1 [*Richardson*].

83 Ibid., at paras 122–7, McLachlin J, dissenting.

84 Ibid., at para 123; John Laskin, "Mobility Rights under the Charter," *Supreme Court Law Review* 4 (1982): 93.

85 *Richardson*, at paras 97–102. On the range of interests that are served by mobility rights, see Ilya Somin, *Free to Move: Foot Voting, Migration, and Political Freedom* (Oxford: Oxford University Press, 2020).

86 Ibid., at paras 171–3.

87 Michael J. Trebilcock, "The Supreme Court and Strengthening the Conditions for Effective Competition in the Canadian Economy," *Canadian Bar Review* 80, no. 1–2 (2001): 564.

Index